Management for Professionals

More information about this series at http://www.springer.com/series/10101

Ulrich Weigel · Marco Ruecker

The Strategic Procurement Practice Guide

Know-how, Tools and Techniques
for Global Buyers

 Springer

Ulrich Weigel
Eschenburg, Germany

Marco Ruecker
Braunfels, Germany

ISSN 2192-8096 ISSN 2192-810X (electronic)
Management for Professionals
ISBN 978-3-319-57650-3 ISBN 978-3-319-57651-0 (eBook)
DOI 10.1007/978-3-319-57651-0

Library of Congress Control Number: 2017940241

Translation from the German language edition: Praxisguide Strategischer Einkauf by Ulrich Weigel and Marco Rücker, © Springer Fachmedien Wiesbaden GmbH 2015, All Rights Reserved.

Printed on acid-free paper

This Springer imprint is published by Springer Nature
The registered company is Springer International Publishing AG
The registered company address is: Gewerbestrasse 11, 6330 Cham, Switzerland

CoreTrust Europe

CORETRUST EUROPE

CoreTrust Europe (CTE) operates as the European arm of CoreTrust, the definitive group purchasing organisation (GPO) for companies and Private Equity firms. By leveraging the aggregated spend of the collective, CTE enhances member profitability for companies across multiple verticals by negotiating and offering contracts with best-in-class pricing for non-production supplies and services.

www.coretrusteurope.com

Preface

Science Meets Reality: A Guide for the Modern Buyer

Four years have now passed since the first edition of this book was published in German followed by a second edition in 2015. In order to consider the international environment of the procurement function, the original German edition is now updated and published in English language.

As there is nothing more constant than change, there is once again news to report from the world of Procurement. The declining price of oil and the collapsing Rouble are just two examples. For very different reasons, China, once a major player on the world procurement stage, is settling for a considerably smaller international role over the medium term, while other Asian states bound ahead. South-East Asia is currently being touted as a new business location with great potential. The Association of Southeast Asian Nations (ASEAN), with a total population bigger and considerably younger than the entire EU, is well on its way to becoming a duty-free economic zone. Leading the way here are Indonesia and Thailand; however, the Philippines, Malaysia, Vietnam, Myanmar, Brunei, Singapore, Laos, and Cambodia are also adding clout.

In creating this English language edition, consideration has now been given to recent developments in the area of information technology. The digitalisation of business processes has become an increasingly important force driving the modern corporate organisation. Particularly in the area of procurement, where intensive networking and cross-boundary collaboration is required, innovative transaction options are offering enormous potential for the execution of electronic business processes. An entirely new chapter focuses on the theme of eProcurement.

While bringing you the English edition, the authors have also experienced personal developments. Marco Ruecker and Ulrich Weigel now provide further insights into the theme of Procurement in their roles as advisors, coaches, and tutors, further enriching what is already a wealth of experience involving many industries. As a result, this book will take a more detailed look at the topic of management (even suppliers need to be managed) and the right way to deal with monopolists.

This book has been realised thanks to the friendly support of the SAM Xlation and Coretrust companies.

Eschenburg, Braunfels   Ulrich Weigel
March 2017   Marco Rücker

Preface for the First German Edition (Translated from German Original Text)

Science Meets Reality: A Guide for the Modern Buyer

There are plenty of professionally written books and articles that address the theme of procurement; however, few are penned by authors who have gained such a wealth of experience within this realm or who bear the relevant responsibility. And that is why this book will avoid muddying the waters with extensive theory or a lack of practical relevance, destined to gather dust on a shelf. Instead, we have aimed to provide the reader with 200 plus pages of strong, occasionally humorous and largely entertaining text, which should serve as a useful tool for both young professionals and experienced purchasing experts as they navigate working life.

Basic scientific knowledge will be coupled with tried-and-tested purchasing techniques, as well as professional advice drawing on positions of responsibility across five different industries. Using methods that have developed and evolved over the course of 25 years, the reader will be shown how to implement, simply and profitably, the most varied of purchasing techniques anywhere in the world, for example simple methods for determining the value of items without knowing the supplier's calculation. Answers will be provided for the following: Is it possible to manage heterogeneous supplier structures while tailoring to industry requirements? What approach should be taken for partners from the various cultures? What is needed to survive procurement crises and what proactive measures can be taken to minimise their impact? How are employees managed, including those over long distances, and is it possible to improve the standing of procurement both internally and externally?

Just a few examples of the content covered in both theory and practice in this book.

Marco Rücker has provided the scientific basis, while Ulrich Weigel has shared his wealth of experience. Drawing on countless purchasing negotiations in the USA, Western, Southern and Eastern Europe, Vietnam, Malaysia, and India, however primarily China, Japan, and Korea, assessment of the different cultures and thus behaviours has been possible. In addition to the basic purchasing information, Global Sourcing (with a focus on Asia), Supplier Management, and Purchasing

Negotiations will be discussed in detail. The individual chapters will be rounded off with a number of practical examples, thus providing guidance for both managers and employees with experience in procurement, as well as buyers just starting out in their career and looking to move from operational tasks to strategic procurement with managerial responsibilities.

This book is also ideally suited as teaching material for students of Purchasing, Logistics, and Supply Chain Management, because a successful career beckons any buyer who is able to improve quality, minimise risks, and thereby measurably lower procurement costs over the long term along the supply chain.

A big thank you for the support provided by Leica Camera AG, where both authors are currently employed: Ulrich Weigel as Vice Chief Operating Officer and Head of Purchasing and Marco Rücker as Industrial Engineer in Strategic Purchasing, responsible for process development in the supply chain, risk management, and strategy development, among other things. This book has also been realised thanks to the friendly support of the Bisnode and Pool4Tool companies.

The authors also wish to extend a special thanks to their colleagues Ms. Carolin Knebel, Mr. Wolfgang Schermuly, Mr. Frank Kraft, Mr. Jan Meyer and photographer Michael Agel, as well as Professor Sebastian Heilmann from the University of Trier, Mr. Jochen Bruns from NEXUS21 GmbH, and Mr. Peter Hermann from Sell GmbH. Intercultural experts Dr. Kim Nam Hui and Mr. Shuzo Matsushita also provided valuable input, particularly for the chapters concerning Asia.

Not forgetting StudiumPlus, an initiative from the Central Hesse Technical University, which provided Marco Rücker with the opportunity to explore, in both theory and practice, the various aspects of purchasing as part of his industrial engineering studies.

And, last but not least, thank you to Maria Troussas and Tanja Weigel and all our friends who provided advice and assistance over the past 15 months, lending support with understanding and patience.

Eschenburg, Leun   Ulrich Weigel
February 2013   Marco Rücker

Contents

Principles of Modern Purchasing

1

1.1 Introduction

In recent years, the significance of Purchasing has increased at a rate greater than in almost all other business functions. This book, amongst others, is evidence of a trend that is fairly obvious and caused by the fact that, in academic teaching as well as in practice, Purchasing has for a long time been treated as an afterthought—more so than any other area of Business Economics. In teaching, the topics of Purchasing, Materials Management and Procurement were filed subordinately somewhere under the subjects of "Production" and "Logistics". The organisational structures of companies show a similar picture. Central Purchasing departments, where they exist, have only existed in large corporations. In most businesses, employees were assigned responsibility for the material supply of their particular departments. They have also negotiated prices, monitored delivery dates and complained about poor quality. But cross-functional approaches that had long been established in such areas as Distribution, Production, or Marketing only developed in Purchasing a few years ago.

This change of thinking within businesses has not been a matter of chance. On the contrary, changing conditions have made Purchasing the focus of business transactions. Increased global competition, ever shorter product life cycles, and steadily increasing pricing pressures are only some of the factors involved. Companies wishing to perform successfully in the market are forced to "think outside the box" by organising not only their internal but also their external supply chains as efficiently and economically as possible. In this context, Purchasing is given a totally new range of tasks. Merely executing and supervising order procedures is being superseded by long-term management of complex supply chains—a change that has occurred in many, but not all, enterprises, and for this change to occur, new and innovative approaches to management are needed.

© Springer International Publishing AG 2017
U. Weigel, M. Ruecker, *The Strategic Procurement Practice Guide*, Management for Professionals, DOI 10.1007/978-3-319-57651-0_1

1.2   Purposes and Aims of Purchasing

A uniform and coherent definition of the Purchasing business function cannot be found in current Business Economics literature. For now, prevailing ideas and concepts are too diverse to give a consistent picture. Traditional concepts such as Procurement and Materials Management are gradually disappearing while keywords such as "Strategic Purchasing", "global procurement", and "Supply Chain Management" find their way into academic discourse. This is evidence of the change that has occurred in Purchasing in the last few years and that will probably continue in the near future. Yet the core task of Purchasing has remained the same. Purchasing is in charge of supply into the organisation. Its responsibility is to ensure the availability of supplies such as products, facilities, resources, and services. The classic aim of Purchasing—to secure the right products in the right quantity and quality at the right time and the right place, while considering economic principles—still holds true. But due to the increased importance of purchasing activity, additional strategic approaches have been developed. Purchasing activities need integrated and long-term planning. Suppliers must be developed to become strategic partners, and procurement markets must be developed globally. Out of these considerations, an extended field of action has evolved: Strategic Purchasing. This development often leads to a division of personnel within Purchasing according to areas of operational and strategic areas of competence. While Operational Purchasing is in charge of the routine handling of order processes, the Strategic Buyer develops the long-term framework conditions subject to the business strategy.

But this is not a complete picture of the Buyer's field of activity. Working with projects in the context of product development processes is a further extension of the Buyer's activities. Apart from the Project Manager's considerations of costs and deadlines, suppliers are more frequently being engaged in technology partnerships at an early stage of development projects, which means that Purchasing also obtains new significance in project work. Its tasks in this respect are, amongst others, to help, to coordinate, to mediate, and to actively organise the process.

In summary, there are three basic functions of Purchasing today:

- Operational Purchasing: Securing supplies
- Strategic Purchasing: Long-term planning
- Project Purchasing: Support of the product development processes and other business areas

It is clear that the Buyer's area of responsibility can be quite different, according to the respective range of functions. Depending on line of business and significance, further areas of responsibility may open up. But the basic aim of Purchasing remains the same—to secure the organisation's supply of the required factors of production.

1.2.1   Operational Purchasing

Basically, Operational Buyers assume the classical purchasing functions with regard to routine operations. As a rule, they will make recourse to the conditions established by the Strategic Buyer. Within the tasks of Operational Purchasing we have, for example, the handling of routine order processes, expediting deliveries, operational planning of procurement activities in terms of demand planning, scheduling, and the processing of returns and notices of defects. The main aim of Operational Purchasing is to secure the availability of materials at any time and also to achieve optimum stock levels. As this field of activity is closely connected with the business function of Material Management, Operational Purchasing activities are often located there. Thus, in classical Purchasing departments, necessary latitude to perform strategic tasks is realised without a need for additional personnel.

1.2.2   Strategic Purchasing

In the context of strategic considerations, activities prior to the actual order process have become increasingly important. This function is assumed by Strategic Purchasing. Strategic Buyers make decisions that are beyond the scope of day-to-day operations. In doing so, they create the framework conditions of Operational Purchasing. The first step is to define the basic strategic direction of procurement activities in terms of supplier, commodity groups, and risk strategies that support the overall business strategy. Furthermore, Strategic Buyers research potential procurement markets, negotiate framework agreements, and manage the supplier portfolio. Last but not least, they are also responsible for process improvements within the value chain, which also means questioning their own function. Ideally, this results in the continuous optimisation of the whole procurement process including its points of interface.

1.2.3   Project Purchasing

Project Purchasing is a multidisciplinary procurement function within the context of product development projects in which Purchasing is increasingly gaining significance. One of its main tasks is to co-ordinate all purchasing activities within the scope of the project. Project Purchasing therefore represents the suppliers involved, and it also represents the interests of the Purchasing department in the project team. In doing so, it makes use of the resources of Strategic Purchasing and hands over the established framework conditions once the project has been approved.

The importance of Project Purchasing becomes especially clear if one considers that roughly two-thirds of the product costs are determined in the early opening stages of development projects. For this reason, the early involvement of Purchasing at the start of the project is becoming increasingly important and should be backed by the management.

Project Buyers are also involved in the case of complex, indirect supplies with long lead times. This may be, for example, capital investments such as new plant, machinery, or workshops. That is why Project Buyers need a sound basic knowledge of technical and commercial aspects and a distinct understanding of Project Management.

Practical Tip

As shown in Fig. 1.1, the tasks and responsibilities of Strategic, Operational, and Project Purchasing are not always clearly separated. The crucial question is to which part of the product life cycle the supplied item belongs. At the beginning, Project Purchasing will have the greatest responsibility, but depending on the project these tasks may also be performed by the persons in charge of Strategic Purchasing. From the beginning, Project Purchasers monitor the whole product development process and organise the external value chain. Once production readiness and release have been achieved, the project is committed to Operational Purchasing which will safeguard the material supply with respect to cost, quality, and time. But this holds true only as long as the supplier delivers in accordance with the previously agreed framework conditions. In cases of deviation, Strategic Purchasing will again take up the responsibility as long as these have not been addressed. In practice, this means that while Strategic Buyers are still leading their commodity groups strategically and company-wide, their tasks may be dominated by more technical demands according to the industry. "Front Loading" is the key phrase here—the earlier Strategic Purchasing is involved with selected suppliers, the more efficient the results will be for the company. Ideally, this

Fig. 1.1 Purchasing-fields of action and points of interface

involvement already takes place in the early innovation stages. The result is that not only are innovations and time-to-market improvements contributed—often free of charge—by the suppliers, but also costs and suppliers are brought under professional control from the outset.

1.3   The Growing Importance of Purchasing Within the Company

When considering the reasons for the growing importance of Purchasing, one will inevitably end up at costs. No other business function can influence costs and consequently the company results to such an extent as Purchasing. This is mainly due to the fact that many companies tend to reduce their own vertical range of manufacture. In the context of the division of labour, companies increasingly tend to concentrate on their own core competences which results in higher external value creation. Thus, in German manufacturing enterprises, the proportion of material costs measured against turnover has doubled during the last 20 years. With an external material quota of often more than 50%, Purchasing is responsible for the lion's share of operating costs.

On the one hand, this shows how great the responsibility of Purchasing is. On the other hand, this fact shows that Purchasing has a direct influence on the operating results and the return on investment (ROI) of the company. The latter may be illustrated by a ROI model.

In Fig. 1.2, it is assumed that 50% of the original costs are caused by bought-in parts. If one succeeds in cutting down this pool of costs (with several methods which will be explained afterwards) by 4%, gains will increase from 10 million euros to 12.6 million euros. The operating margin will increase to 9%, from which comes an increase in ROI to 36%. This shows that a 26% gain in profitability is achieved by a material cost reduction of only 4%!

One can also see the influence of Purchasing on the return on investment with regard to inventory. By reducing stock, for example, by establishing consignment stocks, the necessary operating capital is reduced, which in turn results in a positive effect on asset turnover and also on return on investment.

In a further example calculation, several means of achieving increased profits shall be compared.

In Fig. 1.3, the effects of increasing sales are compared to the effects of labour cost reductions and material cost reductions. On the premise that costs will develop proportionally to the turnover, an increase of 5% in turnover will also mean a profit increase of 5%. With unchanged framework conditions, labour cost reductions by 5% result in a 25% profit increase; however, the greatest increase is achieved by a 5% material cost reduction. In this case, profit is increased by 50%. This leverage effect shows the direct influence of Purchasing on the performance of the company.

But the growing importance of Purchasing is caused not only by its contribution to the performance of the company; internal as well as external challenges have

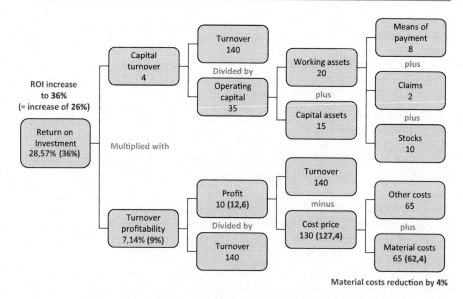

Fig. 1.2 Influence of purchasing on the return on investment (data in million euros)

	Base values in Euro	Turnover +5%	Labor costs -5%	Material costs -5%
Turnover	100.000	105.000	100.000	100.000
Material costs	50.000	52.500	50.000	47.500
Labor costs	25.000	26.250	23.750	25.000
Other costs	20.000	21.000	20.000	20.000
Profit	5.000	5.250	6.250	7.500
Change in profit		+5%	+25%	+50%

Fig. 1.3 Effects of sales increase compared to labour costs reduction and material costs reduction

enlarged the range of tasks Purchasing must fulfil. Increasing costs in the R&D sector, shorter product life cycles, and ever-advancing globalisation provide new challenges for companies to face. In this context, functioning, flexible, and efficient value chains and technology co-operation contribute immensely to the performance differentiation of the company, e.g. through shorter delivery times, higher quality levels, and cost leadership. Cross-departmental management of the internal and external added value may thus make the difference with respect to competitors.

As a consequence of these challenges, an integrated and cross-departmental management of the company's supply is absolutely necessary, and therefore the requirement for a Purchasing department that has a strong position becomes clear.

1.4   Future Challenges to Purchasing

In the future, the range of purchasing tasks will increase disproportionately. Even today, a lot of business functions such as Strategic Planning, Commercial, Risk Management, and Project Management are included in this range. It is therefore clear why Purchasing has already reached a strong position in many companies. However, the greatest challenge will be to further enhance the strategic position of Purchasing within the company. Despite its growing importance, procurement activities by other departments are still the order of the day in most companies. This so-called "maverick buying" (meaning uncoordinated purchases) in many companies quite often amounts to 20–30% of total purchasing. In this context, a lot of explanatory work is required, and one's words must be followed up with action. Specialised departments cannot command the same information and market knowledge that Purchasing should have; quite often they will react with surprise when unrealized benefits are shown to them.

To accomplish this, Buyers must have the necessary know-how at their disposal. This particularly includes a basic technical understanding of the products to be procured and of their manufacturing processes, in addition to the requirement for ample commercial knowledge. Only with such background knowledge will Buyers be able to purposely apply the variety of available purchasing techniques and be taken seriously in discussions with technical departments. This is the prerequisite for optimally combining in-house requirements with the competencies of suppliers and thus contributing to the company's goals.

Concluding technology co-operation agreements with suppliers and integrating them early in the product development process becomes increasingly important, especially in the light of shorter product life cycles and reduced vertical ranges of manufacture. For this, close and long-term partnerships must be formed and developed.

With regard to potential supply markets, Buyers must meet the challenge to open up and exploit new, interesting regions for their own companies without losing sight of the risks involved. One must never forget that an increase in external added value also means an increased dependence on this added value. Significant hazards and risks are hidden in global and highly branched supply chains. For example, the impacts of natural disasters on the other side of the world may become relevant to one's own production line as a result of global purchasing activities. The failure of merely one component may cause a standstill of the whole value chain. Purchasing has responsibility to proactively devise risk strategies in order to counter such scenarios with suitable measures.

Another challenge is presented by the personal requirements Buyers must meet to successfully occupy their increased scope of responsibilities. Apart from inter-cultural competence, technical and commercial know-how as well as negotiating skills, Buyers will need soft skills and leadership abilities. Although only a few Buyers bear leadership responsibilities in a direct sense, negotiating internal con-flict and the management of supplier partnerships call for a high degree of leader-ship competence. Suppliers must be led, motivated, encouraged, and warned in

Fig. 1.4 Challenges to the organisation of purchasing

exactly the same way as members of staff. That is why communication skills, assertiveness, and social intelligence are among the essential requirements modern Buyers must meet.

To cope with the challenges shown in Fig. 1.4, diverse, tried-and-tested approaches and management methods will be suggested. These serve to enable modern Buyers to proactively manage their scope of responsibilities and to meet the requirements of their new, strong position within the company.

The Strategy of Purchasing

2.1 Strategic Principles

The importance of Purchasing with regard to business success has been discussed in Chap. 1. In many companies, this insight is already fixed firmly at the front of one's mind. But the acknowledgement of this fact alone is not enough to achieve the strategic and integrated management of the company's supply. The next step must be to develop an approach by which such an integrated view is made possible and thus specific courses of action are opened up—Purchasing needs a strategy.

Basically, the term "strategy" refers to an operational framework which is geared to the attainment of long-term goals. The strategy forms the highest level in the planning process, answering the question: "What does the company want to achieve?" Frequently, the strategy is derived from a company vision, a formalised picture of the company in the future. So for example, the Volkswagen car company has stated its vision to become the biggest car company in the world by 2018. In this way, a vision has a normative nature; it is often compared to the Pole Star as it is setting the agenda.

From this vision, the business strategy is derived, but it will still depend on many factors. In defining the strategy, the following issues must be taken into consideration:

- What are my core competences?
- Which services do I offer?
- How do I distinguish myself from competitors?
- What are the needs of my stakeholders?
- What is the focus of the added value?
- What opportunities, potentials, and threats exist?

The main function of a strategy is to set out the requirements for future business success and to prevent business-critical situations. In most cases where a company is battling for its existence, it will be too late to develop a strategy.

© Springer International Publishing AG 2017
U. Weigel, M. Ruecker, *The Strategic Procurement Practice Guide*, Management
for Professionals, DOI 10.1007/978-3-319-57651-0_2

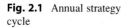

Fig. 2.1 Annual strategy
cycle

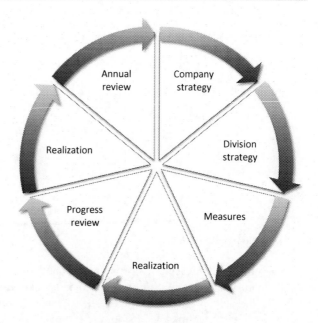

Following the overall business strategy, the next step will be to develop functional strategies such as marketing, development, and distribution strategies. At this stage, the Purchasing department also enters the strategy process by defining its purchasing strategy and aims, deriving courses of action from this strategy and implementing them. The crucial question in this context is in how far Purchasing can contribute to the attainment of the strategic goals of the company.

Strategies cover a period of 3–5 years. This does not mean that the strategy is set in stone during this period. Rather, the strategy serves as a framework for performance that needs to be reviewed regularly; on the one hand to quantify the level of implementation and on the other to adapt the basic strategic direction to changing framework conditions.

Consequently, a process of recurring reviews is established, as shown in Fig. 2.1.

2.2 Principles of the Purchasing Strategy

In planning a strategy, fundamental principles must be kept in mind to ensure that the strategic considerations will be successfully implemented rather than being accepted in name only. For this reason, strategies always cover a long-term period (of 3–5 years) although their validity during this period is not necessarily permanent. Strategies often have a high degree of uncertainty due to their predictive nature. Markets and framework conditions may sooner develop in another direction than that anticipated during the strategy development process. Therefore, purchasing strategies must be flexible and checked against changing market conditions at regular intervals and adapted accordingly.

Strategies as well as their amendments must always be documented. Only by documenting it can the basic strategic direction gain the necessary authority to prevent erratic changes of direction. Thus, strategic guidance can be implemented sustainably in routine business operations. It is therefore important to hold regular reviews of appropriate metrics, to ascertain the degree of implementation of strategic guidance.

Another principle for strategic consideration is how to adapt the level of detail of the strategy to the complexity and priority of the product to be procured. The more important the commodity group is for the company, the broader the strategic framework should be. Nevertheless, the strategy may also include extensive nonrecurring procurements such as machinery or new business facilities. And it may also be part of the strategy to have no strategy at all for commodity groups of lesser relevance.

As a rule, purchasing strategies should not be developed on the basis of conjecture and gut instinct. Goals must always be defined on the basis of hard facts and figures. For that reason, it is important to collect extensive findings from internal and external data at the outset in order to give them due consideration when strategies are developed. In this respect, internal data, resources, and organisational structures are as important as external market trends and competitive situations. The latter should be monitored systematically in order to optimally combine internal requirements with external conditions. The systematic development of a purchasing strategy is detailed in the following sections.

2.3   The Process of Developing a Strategy

The method of strategy development follows a logical thought process and can be divided into different stages as shown in Fig. 2.2. In the first stage, the initial situation is assessed by collecting and analysing internal and external information.

Fig. 2.2 The process of developing a strategy

With the help of different management methods, e.g. SWOT analysis (detailed in Sect. 2.3.1.3), core elements can be identified on which further strategic planning will be built. On the basis of these considerations, strategic targets are defined which will form the framework for the intended development of the company. In the next stage, the methods for meeting the targets shall be established, as well as determining how concrete metrics and guidelines will be developed. During the ongoing process, these methods must be checked and quantified with respect to their effectiveness and degree of implementation. The cycle of the strategy process closes with the introduction of measures which serve the correction or further development of the strategy.

2.3.1 Strategic Analysis

An analysis of the purchasing environment can serve to ascertain the relevance of Purchasing towards achieving the company's targets. What is the position of Purchasing in the business strategy and which demands does Purchasing have to meet? It can also be ascertained which internal purchasing requirements must be satisfied; for example quantities, technologies, or processes, to which the purchasing strategy must be aligned.

Monitoring external factors shows the influence the corporate environment has on the achievement of the company's goals and how far this environment is linked with internal requirements. Apart from the competitive situation and market trends, this also encompasses, amongst others, the maturity level of one's own supplier portfolio, the industry structure, and the potential of new procurement markets.

2.3.1.1 Analysis of the Internal Requirements

By analysing the internal environment, the requirements of one's own company are identified. Cross-departmental sharing of information is absolutely necessary in order to translate the identified requirements into concrete demands. Essentially, the following aspects will be considered:

Business Strategy The business strategy fundamentally determines the direction of the purchasing strategy. What position does the company want to occupy in the market in the future, and what is the role of Purchasing in this process? If, for example, the company distinguishes itself by product-related criteria such as innovation, design, or quality, the Purchasing department must align its strategy accordingly. In that case, improvements of quality and delivery performance, procurement market research, and supplier development would be in focus rather than cost-cutting. This holds true especially in the case of a growth strategy.

If the company distinguishes itself by cost leadership, price reductions and "low cost country sourcing" will have priority. Thus, in the context of strategic analysis, the share that Purchasing may contribute to the attainment of the company's goals, and the additional value that Purchasing contributes to the distinction of the company on the market, must be considered.

Increase in Value   As a rule, investors expect a lasting increase in the company's value. To ensure that increase, a cost-oriented approach may be chosen with the consequences of total cost control and the reduction of material prices. Otherwise, a growth-oriented approach may result in an increase in value of the company. In that case, an increase in turnover is sought which goes hand in hand with growing demand and higher volumes of products to be procured. In order to avoid a supply bottleneck, Purchasing must check existing capacities at an early stage and, if necessary, develop new sources of supply. No matter whether a cost-oriented approach, a growth-oriented approach or a mixture of both is chosen; in any case the Purchasing department is directly involved and must adapt its strategic considerations accordingly.

Product Roadmap   The product roadmap gives an overview of the current and future product portfolio of the company. Therefore, the roadmap shows which products the company has introduced in the market or intends to introduce at which time and in which quantities. For Purchasing, the roadmap includes important information such as product life cycles, market segments, competitive situations, planned quantities of sale, and required technologies.

Technology Planning   Closely connected to the product roadmap is technology planning. Which technologies will be required in the future, how many new developments will there be, and what is the company's own share of the innovations? Especially in view of increasing demands on time frames for development projects, there is a clear trend towards open innovation processes that require the early involvement of development partners. To enable this, Purchasing must proactively act in terms of procurement market research and supplier development in order to identify the optimum partners at an early stage.

Production Planning   On the basis of the product roadmap, a decision must be made as to how the ratio of internal to external added value should be balanced. What is the degree of the company's own added value and what preliminary work will suppliers have to contribute in the future? Will parts be bought separately or is it intended that complete modules are bought? Furthermore, in this context a general make-or-buy approach must be developed in which standardised decisions can be made as to when supply shall be kept in house or sourced externally.

Product Complexity and Product Quality   What are the company's demands regarding product quality and therefore also on the suppliers' added value? If the demands are strict they will be the decisive factor in future supplier selection exercises. Furthermore, supplier developments aimed at improving quality and a targeted supplier build-up must be initiated to meet the requirements.

Flexibility   Depending on industry and market position, companies must be able to react quickly and flexibly to shifts in the market. Competitive pressure, customer requirements, or short product life cycles determine the degree of flexibility with which Purchasing must manage its activities in order to ensure the required product availability. For example, if a high degree of delivery readiness is required, this readiness can be achieved by increasing supplier inventory or by establishing flexible logistics concepts.

2.3.1.2 Analysis of the External Environment

Just as important as the internal demands on Purchasing are the external market conditions which must be reconciled with the company's requirements. Due to the diversity and variety of the procurement markets relevant to the company, a "blanket" approach will prove to be unrewarding. For this reason, the Purchasing department will group the diverse procurement products in order to approach the relevant procurement markets for each commodity group separately. This division can be made according to different criteria such as type of material (plastics, metal), manufacturing process (metal cutting, die casting), function (mechanics, electronics), or region of purchase (Europe, Asia). A consistent classification according to one single criterion will not always be possible; in practice there will often be a mix of several classification methods.

In this way, a specific approach to the external environment, which extends to the following areas, becomes possible:

Industry Structure For Purchasing, the question of whether it is acting in a buyer or a seller market is of enormous importance. The answer will be different depending on economic situation and industry. If, for example, Purchasing acts in an oligopolistic market its bargaining power will be correspondingly weak. Another important point is the future development of supply and demand in the industry. How will procurement markets change; is there a risk of material bottlenecks or will excess capacity build up? All these factors may influence current purchasing methods.

Supplier Structure Apart from a sound knowledge of the current market situation, Purchasing must also know its own supplier structure in detail. How are the relationships of the company with its current suppliers and do their core competences meet internal requirements? Do opportunities exist that should be developed? Do suppliers compete with each other, and where does the company enjoy the status of a preferred customer? In which regions do the suppliers produce; what is the cost structure; and how great is their capacity for development? All these questions must be taken into consideration in order to devise the optimum supplier structure.

Economic Environment The review of the economic environment does not focus on individual sectors but on macroeconomic developments. This includes economic indicators, currency fluctuations, import and export provisions, or political regulations.

Areas for Further Consideration Regional characteristics may be another factor the Purchasing department has to consider. For example, are there regions that are typically suited to certain products or technologies? What influence may natural disasters have on the current purchasing strategy? How high is the risk of insolvencies or corruption?

Direct competitors must also be taken into consideration. Do they use the same materials and perhaps the same source of supply? And how greatly are Purchasing's own activities influenced by this?

2.3.1.3 SWOT Analysis

Now the collected information can be reviewed systematically with the help of a SWOT analysis in order to find the appropriate parameters for the development of a strategy. In a SWOT analysis, internal strengths and weaknesses are combined with external opportunities and threats. The collected information is entered into a four-field matrix; the particular fields may be characterised as follows:

Strengths What strengths do the existing structures have with respect to the products to be procured? Are there high volumes that strengthen one's own bargaining power; is there a high degree of technical know-how in the products to be procured; or can existing platform solutions be applied? Other Purchasing strengths may be a well-positioned supplier network or the participation in Group Purchasing Organisations (GPOs). A good company image and high brand awareness are factors that should not be underrated, especially in view of global purchasing activities.

Weaknesses Are there any actual weaknesses with regard to the products to be procured? Weaknesses may be, amongst others, limited resources, bad supplier relations, and a lack of experience with the products to be procured.

Opportunities What external opportunities might arise with regard to the products to be procured? Are there any excess capacities; do suppliers command special core competences; or is a favourable market situation beginning to emerge?

Threats What external threats and risks can be estimated? Do monopolistic procurement markets matter? Is there a share of single-source supply? Could material bottlenecks occur; or might suppliers pull out?

In this chapter, Strategic Purchasing determines the main factors in each particular quadrant and, on this basis, develops starting points for its strategic direction. It must be remembered that the main factors must always correspond to the predefined company targets.

2.3.2   Target Setting

In the next stage, Purchasing targets are defined with the aid of the collected information and the resulting overview. Essentially, purchasing targets can be divided according to two criteria: efficiency and effectivity.

Efficiency targets include the operational targets of Purchasing as shown in Fig. 2.3. From an operational point of view, the focus is on timely supply of products of the required quality at competitive prices to the company. In practice, this means: reducing costs, ensuring quality, and keeping deadlines. When setting

Fig. 2.3 Operational targets

these targets, it is important to make sure that an optimal balance should be achieved and that none of the three targets are ignored. In this context, target conflicts can arise, e.g. in cases when the quickest possible delivery irrespective of quality is desired, or in cases when high quality products are bought in without considering the cost.

Effectivity targets include the strategic targets as opposed to the operational targets of costs, quality, and time. Strategic targets aim for safety, growth, and optimisation. For the costs, this may, for example, mean the aggregation of demand; for quality, the development of suppliers; and for time, the shortening of supply chains. If the focus is broadened to include security, risk management will become relevant; by including growth, exploiting new sources of supply will be necessary; and for optimisation the design of internal processes and the training of purchasing colleagues.

When defining targets, one mistake that often occurs is the use of ambiguous and vague wording. In that case, only ostensible successes will be seen in subsequent discussions although the real target will have has been missed widely. For this reason, reference should always be made to the "SMART" rule when defining targets. Only then can measures that have been derived from these targets be evaluated in a qualified manner. The SMART rule demands that targets should be formulated:

- Specific
- Measurable
- Agreed
- Realistic
- Time-related

According to that rule, targets must be defined precisely and unambiguously; the degree of realisation must be measurable; the targets must be accepted by the Buyers; the targets must be realistic with respect to the given conditions; and they must refer to a fixed period of time.

2.3.3   Strategy Development

In the next stage, the purchasing strategy is worked out against the defined targets. From this, general codes of conduct may be formulated. These codes reflect the basic design of the purchasing activities. These rules of conduct often follow so-called guiding principles by which companies commit themselves to compliance with internationally agreed guidelines and social standards.

Such guidelines may demand, amongst other things:

- Fair and partner-like conduct in dealing with suppliers
- Compliance with ecological, social, and ethical standards
- Combating corruption

At the next stage, commodity group and supplier strategies are defined. These two aspects cannot be separated from each other. While commodity group strategies answer the question of what shall be procured, supplier strategies say how and where the products shall be procured.

2.3.3.1 Commodity Group Strategy

Once internal company requirements and external market conditions have been brought together, the Purchasing department will review the strategic importance of the individual commodity groups. To do so, the portfolio technique as shown in Fig. 2.4 and detailed in Sect. 7.4 can be used, by which the requirements of the criteria "company relevance" and "market relevance" are divided into the following four commodity groups:

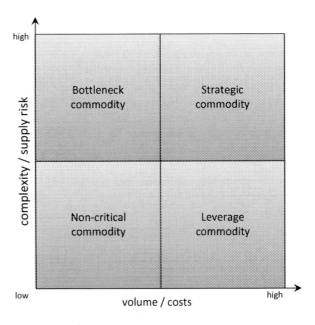

Fig. 2.4 Four different approaches are needed with respect to different commodity groups

Non-critical Commodity Groups Commodity groups classified as "non-critical" are characterised by low volumes, high availability, and low complexity. Typically, these groups encompass "C" items (identified with the help of an ABC analysis) such as screws, standard parts, and indirect material such as ancillary and operating materials or office supplies. The procedure of the ABC analysis is detailed in Sect. 7.3. With respect to non-critical commodity groups, the target must be to buy them at the best price while reducing supervision to a minimum. At the extreme, this may be achieved by outsourcing to a purchasing service provider or by automated order processes within the scope of an e-procurement system.

Bottleneck Commodity Groups While "bottleneck commodity groups" may also be characterised by low volumes, purchasing them is complicated by low availability and/or high complexity. As a rule, the procurement volumes are too low to either arouse the suppliers' interest or initiate internal measures by which the respective item might be simplified or replaced. In many cases, the only possible solution will be risk minimisation by providing high safety stocks.

Leverage Commodity Groups "Leverage" products are the Buyer's "bread-and-butter" business. They are characterised by high volumes, high availability, and low complexity. Thanks to high purchasing volumes and strong supplier competition, costs reductions can be achieved easily.

Strategic Commodity Groups These products are characterised by high volumes, low availability, high procurement risks, and high complexity. These commodities must be managed most thoroughly, e.g. by the development of strategic suppliers, by comprehensive risk management, and by incessant procurement market research.

By classifying the demands, basic strategies can be developed that allow for the management of supply, costs, and also the risks of the individual commodity groups. On this basis, the Purchasing department has to develop the best possible procurement strategy with respect to particular materials in order to satisfy all relevant demands in an optimal manner.

Practical Tip

Taking the commodity group of electronic components as an example, there now follows a description of a method for developing a commodity group strategy, which we have successfully deployed several times.

At the beginning, the current situations of the individual sub-groups such as active and passive components, systems and assemblies, assembly services and printed circuit boards need to be reviewed.

How many suppliers serve these groups, to what level of complexity, and in what volumes? What are the cost drivers? Is dual, single, or multiple sourcing predominant? How strong is our market power with respect to these suppliers or components? What are the current ratings of these suppliers? And, most importantly: What are the predictions for the respective markets, raw materials, and prices?

			turnover		subjective evaluation /forecast			
commodity	suppliers 2012	suppliers 2015	volume 2012	volume 2015	market power supplier 2012	market power supplier 2015	quality 2012	quality 2015
electronic assemblies			4.37	5.17	5.75	4.75	8.25	9
	supplier A	supplier A	1.05	1.35	9	8	9	9
	supplier B	supplier B	0.25	0.32	5	4	7	9
	supplier C	supplier C	0.75	1	3	3	8	9
	supplier D	supplier D	2.32	2.5	6	4	9	9

Fig. 2.5 Database of the commodity "Electronic assemblies"

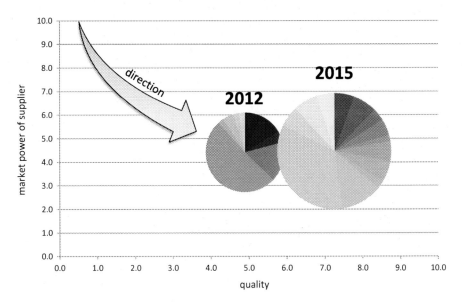

Fig. 2.6 Bubble chart of the commodity "Electronic assemblies"

The required information is collected by the Strategic Buyers, analysed, and summarised in a basic file as shown in Fig. 2.5. The criteria "market power" and "quality" are assessed subjectively. "Market power" in this respect means the combination of the external framework conditions while "quality" stands for the internal requirements of the company.

The evaluation uses a 1-to-10 scale in which 1 represents exceptionally low value and 10 exceptionally high value.

Then the supplier data is aggregated on commodity group level, and a bubble chart as shown in Fig. 2.6 is drawn up for each commodity group.

The position of the commodity group provides information on the current and the target market power and quality level. The segments of the "pie" represent the respective supplier portfolios; the relative sizes stand for the respective share of the suppliers within the commodity group. As an entrepreneur within the company, the Strategist is now called upon as a Commodity Group Manager who should be intensively involved in the "actual" and "target" positions and independently develops the strategic roadmap. In doing so, he transforms the Procurement Program Policy, the contract, and the supplier policies, which resulted from the overall business strategy, into a plan. A positive side effect is that the leap of faith invested in the Strategist responsible (a method I often used with young members of staff) will greatly boost his or her motivation—the future development of the respective commodity group will thus become his or her special concern.

The individual plans are presented by the responsible Strategists in biannual strategy workshops. These plans are then optimised by the whole team, and regular progress reports are then prepared.

2.3.3.2 Supplier Strategy

The supplier strategy is closely linked with the commodity group strategy; it aims at the sources of supply used to obtain the required procurement objects. Essentially, supplier strategies are characterised by a mix of the following approaches:

The process-oriented approach asks how suppliers can be optimally integrated in internal processes. The target may be, for example, the joint development of a logistics concept such as Kanban or Just-in-time. Kanban generally means a method of production process control that is only guided by the actual consumption of materials at the places of allocation and consumption. Further targets may be the promotion of link-ups to communication systems or early integration in development projects. Development partnerships tend to grow in number especially due to shorter product life cycles and associated time-to-market demands, and suppliers are involved more and more often during the initial stages of development projects.

The supplier-oriented approach considers the number of sources of supply available for the individual commodity groups. There are several types, which in practice will occur in hybrid forms.

Single sourcing means that there is only one supply source for the product or service. If this approach to sourcing is chosen, a high-performance supplier must be found and the relationship supported by a long-term partnership. Single sourcing is often used for highly complex procurement objects for which further suppliers are ruled out because of the item's technological peculiarity or high investments. Thanks to co-operative research and development, cost minimisation as well as differentiation may thus be exploited. On the other hand, close co-operation with the respective suppliers creates a high level of dependency. Delayed deliveries and the complete loss of the supplier can be a threat to the whole production process.

To reduce dependency and still enjoy some of the advantages of single sourcing, a re-adjustment to a dual sourcing strategy is advisable, especially with respect to critical parts. In this strategy, the procurement-specific demand is allocated to two competing suppliers. A second source of supply may be established by a targeted strategic supplier search and the associated qualification of new suppliers or by the targeted development of existing suppliers that will enable them to extend their range of products or services.

By using a multiple sourcing strategy, the procurement risk may be minimised further. However, this supplier–purchaser relationship is only geared to ad hoc demands and may lose the effects of demand aggregation.

The material-oriented approach essentially uses two approaches. Materials are classified according to different criteria resulting in concrete requirements and recommendations of action with respect to the supplier strategy. For example, complexity and availability of materials may have an impact on the number of sources of supply. So-called "system suppliers" may be established which means a departure from the procurement of single parts. Several suppliers of individual parts are subsumed under the umbrella of one system supplier that will undertake the mounting and preparation of the complete assembly group. The target is to shift labour-intensive activities to suppliers and reducing expenditure on the company's own co-ordination efforts.

The region-oriented approach goes by the geographical location of the sources of supply. Thus, a local sourcing strategy may be appropriate if local proximity is highly important. The greatest advantages of local proximity are easier co-ordination and higher flexibility. However, one must always remember that the price level may be decidedly higher than in international procurement markets. An approach that does not confine itself to local and national procurement markets is global sourcing. Global sourcing approaches aim at using the best possible sources of supply at a global level. Realising savings due to lower labour and material costs or making use of region-specific supplier know-how are two possible objectives of this approach.

The risk-oriented approach has arisen from the increasing importance of the risk aspect in Purchasing. The risks are considerable since Purchasing is responsible for the bulk of the operating costs. In the scope of the supplier strategy, the risk-oriented approach seeks to identify risks and to take them into consideration when strategies are contemplated. For example, risk management measures may aim for a reduction of dependency on suppliers, the supervision of economic and structural stability of supplier portfolios, or the evaluation of procurement markets according to risk factors such as corruption or political instability.

Practical Tip
The market rules, and so the logical consequence is the purchasing strategy is subordinate to the business strategy and must adapt to it dynamically. Strategy workshops, which are now held biannually, are tried and trusted measures to achieve this adaption. The group of participants should not be limited to Strategic Purchasing but important stakeholders (especially members of Product Management, Marketing, and Commercial) should also be involved, at least temporarily. As experience has shown, the optimum date is directly after the biannual revision of the company's product roadmap. On this basis, paired with the company's strategic targets, the purchasing strategy is

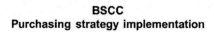

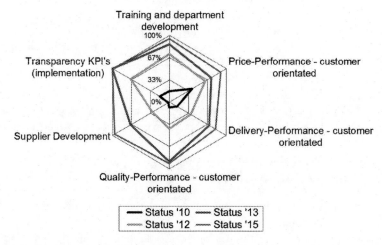

Fig. 2.7 Level of strategy implementation

Table 2.1 Level of strategy implementation by the example of "Training and Development"

		Status '10 (%)	Status '12 (%)	Status '13 (%)	Status '15 (%)
	Training and HR development	16	33	82	100
Z	Parts procurement process—define second stage	50	50	100	100
Z	Training/recruitment OEM procurement	10	30	80	100
Z	Training/recruitment production procurement process	10	30	80	100
U	Procurement of non-hardware-based services	10	20	50	100
O	Training: E-Commerce/E-Procurement	0	50	80	100
M	Installation and enhancement of Technical Purchasing		15	100	100

created and will later be revised biannually. In this process, course corrections are taken as necessary and the degree of realisation of the individual strategic measures is evaluated (see Fig. 2.7). The coloured lines show the initial situation, the rating of the respective milestones, and the target values.

Using the example of "training and department development" (Table 2.1), the percentage of realisation of the individual strategic measures is shown (for each measure there is a detailed description stating the person in charge and the finish date). These values must be updated by the team at strategy meetings; therefore, they constitute the data basis of a new coloured line showing the current status in the balanced scorecard (Fig. 2.7).

The strategy and the associated aims and measures should always be documented in writing and be released by the executive board. The Purchasing department will ensure the necessary management support and also the purchasing strategy will become binding.

As this is one of the most important processes in Strategic Purchasing, the meetings should be planned regularly and in a timely manner, and enough time should be allocated for them.

A subsequent departmental event will always boost the motivation of the team and guarantee the success and efficiency of the meetings.

> Those who only chop wood will fall behind in competition, while those who sharpen their axes preventively and regularly will succeed.

2.3.4 Tactical Implementation

To ensure the effective implementation of the purchasing strategy within the business environment, tactical decisions and measures will be derived from the strategic aspects. These decisions and measures define how the strategy shall be carried out. Cross-departmental co-ordination, the provision of resources, and the support of the board are obligatory prerequisites to ensure the efficiency of the developed action plans.

Tactical steps include the elaboration of the action plan. This plan includes the individual measures as well as the appropriate tools and methods for attaining the goal. Intensive procurement market research in a specific region, development of concrete processes, and aggregation of separate demands are examples of possible measures. The current supplier relationships also need to be reviewed. Here, the decisive question is whether and to what extent the current supplier portfolio will contribute to meeting the strategic targets. Concrete measures for supplier management result from this review, such as the search for new suppliers and their development, the development of existing suppliers, or the adjustment of the supplier portfolio by phasing out existing suppliers.

Setting interim or stage goals can be useful when determining short-term success criteria. This will make it possible to track the realisation of long-term goals and for timely corrective action to be taken in the case of a negative trend.

2.3.5 Commercial

If the strategic targets have been defined in accordance with the SMART rule (Sect. 2.3.2), the degree of their realisation can be evaluated and controlled by management. And thus, the cycle of strategic processes is complete. The emphasis of Commercial Purchasing is to quantify and assess the degree to which goals have been realised. To do so, Commercial conceives and deploys control mechanisms and aligns the parameters to the strategic targets. In this way, appropriate metrics can be defined that can ascertain whether and to what degree the implemented measures have contributed to the realisation of the goal. In practice, business indicators will often be used that show the degree of realisation in a quantified way. In this context, the development of appropriate indicators is one of the main tasks of Commercial Purchasing. With the help of business indicators, the contribution that the implemented measures have made can be shown numerically. Usually, company metrics can be transferred to appropriate procurement indicators, which can help to enable progress. Common indicators in Commercial Purchasing are:

- *Savings*: Sum of the realised P/L-effective price reductions and increases compared to the previous period.
- *Cost avoidance*: Cost avoidance realised by purchasing activities that have not arisen in the context of savings. Examples are negotiation successes for first-time purchases of materials and industrial goods or improved payment conditions.
- *Number of suppliers*: Number of suppliers that provide supplies to the company.
- *Purchasing volume*: Sum of all operating supply costs, including non-production materials and services.
- *Active parts*: Number of production materials that have been bought in addition by the Purchasing department.
- *Delivery reliability*: Reliability of the suppliers with regard to agreed delivery dates.
- *Quality of delivery*: Number of complaints to suppliers in the respective period.
- *Strategic targets*: Degree to which strategic targets have been met; often part of target agreements.

In addition to these indicators there are many others that—dependent on requirement—can be shown in a "dashboard" system and gathered automatically by regular reporting. However, in practice one principle should always be observed: No indicator without action. These indicators will only fulfil their purpose if they lead to appropriate measures being put in place that help to improve or maintain the measured results.

With respect to the strategy process, the cycle closes here. The gathered indicators shed light on the degree to which the strategic measures have been implemented. The findings from the evaluation of the indicators will inevitably lead to changes of the overall strategic concept, and, thus, the strategic process starts afresh.

Practical Tip: Tracking Critical Parts

As is often the case, this simple and down-to-earth yet very effective method has been born out of necessity and developed for the specific needs of a specific company. People working for automotive companies may have difficulties understanding the problems I will discuss here but small-series producers or manufactures know them all too well. When I took up the responsibility for Strategic Purchasing at my current employer roughly 6 years ago, on a weekly average 10 procurement parts out of c. 6500 were missing across both production facilities. As this situation mainly occurred during the start-up period of our core product, the consequences had been extreme disturbances at the start of production, sales shortfalls, and threats to the operating results. When I took the role, the Executive made it unmistakably clear that this situation had to change. So, my team and I got down to work and, supported by the Operational Purchasing departments of both production facilities, all critical parts were recorded in a centrally managed data pool that was updated weekly.

The critical parts were identified through feedback from the expediters and Production, by the dunning process of the ERP system and by divergent order confirmations and notes from the suppliers. The critical parts were recorded in the central database and divided into four groups using a traffic light system:

- *Line standstill*: Production standstill due to missing parts (status colour: Red).
- *Threat of supply shortage*: Material that is currently still available but will be missing in the following 3 weeks (status colour: Red).
- *Scarce parts*: Material that is supplied but not in sufficient quantities (status colour: Orange).
- *Under supervision*: The supplier or part in question is risky and therefore under ongoing supervision (status colour: Yellow).

By following a quality assurance method, the Strategic Buyer's main task is now to review the listed articles, suppliers, and processes in detail in order to find solutions that will remove the bottleneck as soon as possible. Based on the "8-D" ("8 Disciplines") reporting method, the obligation is to analyse the true reasons for poor performance for each of the critical parts. After that, in co-operation with the relevant operational interfaces and the suppliers, measures must be defined by which the bottleneck will be removed quickly. However, of equal importance is the definition of who shall do what and by when to prevent this bottleneck from ever happening again. In the course of weekly team meetings (including telephone conferences with both facilities), all parts are discussed and actions are defined. The database provides an opportunity to identify, with little effort, salient parts, suppliers, low performers, and processes, and trends can be extrapolated. Aside from this, the information is also useful in talks with suppliers and may even lead to the eventual phasing out of longstanding partners. The efficiency of this method is proven, as shown in Fig. 2.8, by a 50% reduction of missing parts although direct purchasing volumes have doubled in the same time.

In my opinion, all Buyers should use the tool described. The operational nature of mere delivery date monitoring is broadened to include strategic thinking and approaches. Thus, this method can contribute decisively towards boosting the long-term performance of Purchasing within the company. Then the aim of having zero missing parts during the total product life cycle is attained not only by the automotive industry.

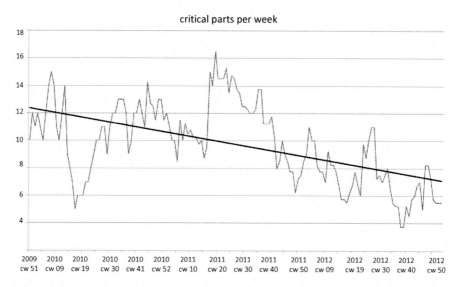

Fig. 2.8 Trend of critical parts with status colour *red* (Color figure online)

Conclusion Strategic Purchasing is highly dependent on acceptance and backing from the company management. Only with this backing will Strategic Purchasing be able to plan, implement, and control its strategy and the scope of action derived from it on a long-term basis. The business strategy, the internal requirements, as well as the external opportunities of the business environment constitute the framework for strategic considerations.

The aim is to combine these factors in an optimal manner, to select the core elements, and to tie them in to the purchasing strategy. The resulting strategic targets are supported by tactical action plans and checked at regular intervals. In this way, the degree of target achievement and the effectiveness of measures can be ascertained. Also, the validity of the targets and strategic elements can be reassessed in the light of changing conditions. Thus, a long-term and target-oriented organisation of purchasing activities is made possible, and Purchasing will directly contribute to the company successfully meeting its targets.

References

Heß, G. (2008). *Supply-Strategien in Einkauf und Beschaffung*. Wiesbaden: Gabler.
Stollenwerk, A. (2012). *Wertschöpfungsmanagement im Einkauf*. Wiesbaden: Gabler.

The Purchasing Organisation

3

3.1 Introduction to the Organisation

As shown in Chap. 2, the status of the Purchasing function is significantly influenced by the business strategy. In many companies, Purchasing is now part of the first, or at least second, level of management. Increasingly, the Chief Procurement Officer (CPO) has become a separate area of responsibility. This position in the company structure is the prerequisite for implementing the strategic approaches efficiently and company wide in order to provide a decisive contribution to the company's business success. If Purchasing is not on a par with the other business functions, it will not find the acceptance necessary for realising its targets and resisting negative influences from other business functions. The latter is especially important during the initial stages of product development, because the majority of costs tend to be set during these stages. If Purchasing lacks a strong position here it will not be able to exercise its responsibility with respect to costs and it will eventually be relegated to negotiating payment conditions.

Therefore, Purchasing must position itself strategically within the business organisation. This enables Purchasing to establish the degree to which it will contribute to hitting company targets. After Strategic Purchasing has defined its targets and the measures to realise them in the context of the strategic process, the question is then how to realise these targets. In this context, strategists then need to take a close look at the Purchasing organisation.

From a business-oriented point of view, the term "organisation" has two different meanings. On the one hand, an organisation generally is the integration of different elements in a formally structured system in which the performance of organisation members is geared to a common target. From this perspective, the Purchasing department itself can be understood to be an organisation. However, organisation usually means the structure of its members by which the attainment of diverse goals is boosted. From that perspective, the term "organisation" describes how tasks, staff, resources, and information should be subdivided and structured in order to realise goals in the most efficient way.

© Springer International Publishing AG 2017

U. Weigel, M. Ruecker, *The Strategic Procurement Practice Guide*, Management for Professionals, DOI 10.1007/978-3-319-57651-0_3

In this type of organisation, two subtypes can be identified: There is, on the one hand, the structural organisation in which the hierarchical allocation and coordination of the four above-mentioned elements is accomplished by defining structures and rules. There is also, on the other hand, the operational organisation in which the elements are ranged in workflows and processes in a spatial, chronological, and quantitative array. These two subtypes are mutually dependent and could thus not be dissociated from each other. However, a step-by-step view is advisable in order to reduce the complexity of the organisation. For this reason, different approaches to the organisation of Purchasing from a structural organisation perspective will be discussed in Sect. 3.2. Section 3.3 will show how workflows in Purchasing can be designed and what possibilities there are to make Purchasing processes more efficient.

3.2   Structural Organisation

As already mentioned in Sect. 3.1, the structural organisation is essentially the hierarchical framework of the organisation within which structures and responsibilities are defined (Fig. 3.1). To set this out, positions (the smallest organisational units) are established and related to each other in such a way that competencies and communication channels between task bearers can be designed efficiently and innovatively. The structural organisation of Purchasing is connected not only with the strategic direction of the business but also with the existing company structure. In smaller companies with only one production facility, a centrally organised purchasing is often the chosen approach. However, for corporations with production facilities all over the world a decentralisation of Purchasing can be preferable. At the extreme, particular purchasing activities may be completely outsourced to specialised external service providers. A modern approach combining centralised and decentralised purchasing is the "Lead Buyer" concept within the framework of commodity group management. The advantages and disadvantages of the four approaches mentioned above are described in the following sections.

Fig. 3.1 Role of purchasing in the corporate structure

3.2.1 Centralised Purchasing

Centralised purchasing concentrates the complete procurement processes of all necessary demands within the company. This means that a centralised department within the company is authorised to engage in purchasing activities. It is completely forbidden that particular business units or special departments purchase anything autonomously. As a rule, a centralised Purchasing department will be located at the company headquarters or at the production facility with the greatest demands. Some advantages of centralised purchasing are:

Volume Purchasing Thanks to the aggregation of company-wide demands, Purchasing is able to negotiate better purchasing conditions with suppliers. As a rule of thumb, doubling the purchasing volumes will result in a 10% reduction of costs. Furthermore, by aggregating the volume the position of Purchasing is strengthened which means that further price concessions by the supplier or the business may be given the status of preferred customer, and better conditions, better service, and better cooperation can be obtained.

Improvement in Professionalism Centralisation of Purchasing makes it possible for purchasing activities to be conducted solely by professional experts. In this way, the whole Procurement process will become more professional, especially with regard to purchasing methods such as price and value analysis, procurement market research, conduct of negotiations, and contract law.

Homogeneous Supplier Structure Conducting purchasing activities centrally will allow for a homogeneous supplier structure to be set up. In this way, one can ensure that the same items are not sourced from different suppliers or that the same conditions are secured throughout the company.

Unambiguous Responsibilities In the case of a centralised Purchasing department, there are clear and company-wide responsibilities. Therefore, compliance with processes and guidelines can be better controlled and communication will be better and quicker.

Efficient Procurement Processes Through centralised purchasing, demands that occur regularly can be processed in a standardised manner, possibly by automated procurement processes.

Uniform Control A centralised Purchasing department allows for the generation of uniform key figures pertinent to the purchasing activities for all business areas, which means that purchasing results can be shown company wide.

Centralised purchasing therefore has a number of advantages. However, the bigger a company is, the more often disadvantages will emerge that essentially can be attributed to great distances between the Purchaser and the user. These disadvantages are, amongst others.

Bureaucracy Depending on how big a company is, centralised purchasing may soon end up with excessive bureaucracy as in some cases user demands will reach the centralised Purchasing department via many other people. Therefore, handling costs might rise disproportionally and the complete procurement process might become inefficient.

Spatial Distances If the distance to the users is too great, centralised purchasing might lack necessary knowledge with respect to the operations. As a result, the centralised Purchasing department will have to be specifically informed of all changes of consumption, technical modifications, and problems. So there are disadvantages with respect to information flow and flexibility.

Target Conflicts If the accountability of procurement successes and failures has not been clearly defined, there may be conflicts between centralised Purchasing and the organisational units responsible for the result.

Poor Acceptance Centralised purchasing is often regarded as an alien element by the local organisations. This is due not only to spatial distances, but also the prevailing impression that local organisations have no say in decisions, will often result in local organisations' jeopardising the realisation of strategic targets. Therefore, central Purchasers must use their skills to communicate decisions intelligibly and transparently in order to establish them as joint decisions accepted by all.

Cultural Peculiarities Differences of culture, mentality, and language pose risks as they can easily produce misunderstandings.

Normally the field of centralised Purchasing is subdivided according to the category of procured items such as raw materials, mechanical items, optics, or industrial goods. In this case, the responsible member of the centralised Purchasing department is in charge of all procurement activities with regard to his or her respective category.

An established variation of centralised Purchasing is the functional principle. The purchasing activities are segmented in uniform process steps that are allocated to the individual members of staff. In the course of increasing process orientation, this approach tends to become less important.

3.2.2 Decentralised Purchasing

A decentralised Purchasing organisation is the opposite of centralised Purchasing, as shown in Fig. 3.2. The most extreme type has all purchasing activities conducted autonomously by the special departments in which the respective demand occurs. This type of Purchasing organisation, for which no professional Purchasers are required, is seldom in practice. Instead, Purchasing departments are established within the responsible organisational units specifically for the purpose of managing demands that occur just there. In the case of affiliated groups, the respective units

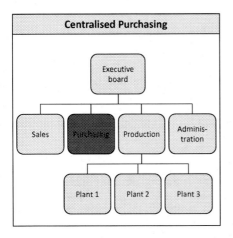 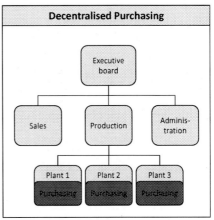

Fig. 3.2 Comparison between centralised and decentralised purchasing

may be subsidiaries or production facilities while in the context of Project Purchasing one individual Purchaser may be allocated to a Product Development team to be in charge of requirements occurring in this particular project.

The main advantage of decentralised purchasing is the optimum proximity to the users. Process times are shorter, and quick communication and decision-making are a given. Furthermore, the Purchaser has the opportunity of acquiring know-how specifically oriented towards the users. Thus, this type of Purchasing organisation realises a high degree of orientation to the needs of the internal client.

However, the main advantage of decentralised purchasing is that due to the similarity of requirements at different organisational units many redundancies occur. Owing to the division of the requirements, decentralised purchasing will have to accept less market power, less standardisation, and, eventually, different commodity group strategies.

3.2.3 The Lead Buyer Concept

The Lead Buyer concept tries to combine the advantages of centralised and decentralised organisations (summarised in Fig. 3.3) and to compensate for the disadvantages of both approaches. The Lead Buyer concept is based on a centralised purchasing organisation that will normally be located at the organisational unit with the highest demands or highest degree of commodity group-specific competence. In this approach, demands of the same kind are aggregated company wide in uniform material groups. Material group managers are made responsible for the particular material groups. These managers are strategically responsible for the demands in all organisational units. Their tasks include the total supplier and commodity group management, the development of methods and the provision of market knowledge, as well as negotiating and

Fig. 3.3 Advantages and
disadvantages of centralised
and decentralised purchasing
organisation

	advantages	disadvantages
Centralised Purchasing	• Bigger volumes • Negotiation power • Professionalising • Homogeneous supplier structure • Unambiguous responsibilities • Efficient procurement processes • Uniform control	• Bureaucracy • Spatial distances • Target conflicts • Poor acceptance • Cultural peculiarities
Decentralised Purchasing	• Spatial proximity • Short decision-making paths • Problem solving focus • High flexibility	• Low market power • Redundancy • Less standardisation • Ambigious responsibilities • Different strategies

concluding framework agreements and supply conditions. However, operational processing is conducted locally in the respective organisational units. Therefore, the order handling can be done flexibly and specifically to occurring needs. The result is a combination of centralised strategic and decentralised Operational Purchasing, in which both functions are clearly separated within the organisation. The main advantages of the Lead Buyer concept are, amongst others:

Uniform Strategy Thanks to the central management of the commodity group strategy, the strategy enjoys company-wide validity and will thus be implemented more easily and more efficiently.

Aggregation of Demand Demands are centrally aggregated into commodity groups that are managed centrally. Therefore, the economies of scale from centralised purchasing are realised while at the same time and individual requirements can still be ordered flexibly by the individual organisational units, all the while operating within the framework of agreed contracts.

Supplier Management The centralised material group management allows for the development of an efficient supplier management process. Therefore, the supplier portfolio can be purposefully formed and developed to serve company-wide demands.

3.2.4   Outsourcing of Purchasing Activities

The trend towards concentrating on core competencies does not stop at Purchasing. Nowadays, more and more particular purchasing activities will be outsourced. An example is the formation of independent companies, so-called Group Procurement Organisations, which will take over whole purchasing activities for a corporate group and also for other companies. These highly specialised purchasing companies show advantages and disadvantages similar to those of centralised purchasing. However, by aligning them as profit centres a market-regulating effect on the accounting for services is being targeted.

A second method of outsourcing purchasing activities can involve the outsourcing of extraordinarily labour-intensive process steps such as accounting control or mere order processing. In this case, the strategic competencies will remain within the company while particular operational activities will be conducted externally.

The third approach is the outsourcing of particular procurement categories. This approach is especially used for services such as travel management or facilities management in order to achieve better conditions by exploiting economies of scale.

Practical Tip

Designing and managing the Purchasing organisation strategically and operationally in a company with facilities in diverse cultural regions poses a major challenge. During my long global career as a manager responsible for Purchasing, I had to learn—sometimes the hard way—that managing from afar will never be appropriate with regard to the organisation of Purchasing and to global sourcing.

In most cases, a clear separation of Operative and Strategic Purchasing, a strategically managed centralised commodity group management, and a decentralised operational management have proven successful.

I optimised the global organisation by recruiting a small team of fully trained native speakers for a Procurement office in Asia which was directly responsible to me. The tasks of this office were of strategic as well as of operational natures and also included quality assurance measures. This Purchasing organisation is shown as an example in Fig. 3.4.

Regular mutual visits at all facilities, integration in the annual purchasing planning process as well as in strategy development, regular intercultural training, development prospects, and control with the help of target agreements have proven very successful.

However, with regard to the overall strategic and global orientation of the organisation, caution must be exercised as the most severe obstacles lurk within the company. Here, the Purchaser must act like a salesperson solving the problems by smart purchase marketing.

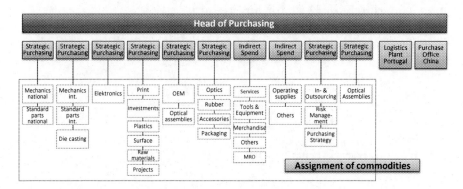

Fig. 3.4 Purchasing organisation structured by commodities

3.3   Operative Organisation

The structural organisation results in a structural framework in which the individual members of staff perform the respective subtasks assigned to them. To coordinate these subtasks efficiently with regard to space, time, and quantity, an operational organisation is necessary. By installing processes, the operational organisation structures the flow of information and resources between the individual positions by which the separate work steps are connected with each other, irrespective of the persons involved. As a rule, the operational organisation should be designed in a way that tasks arising company wide can be attended to quickly, reliably, and cost-effectively.

In Purchasing, considerations with respect to the operational organisation will focus initially on separating operational from strategic purchasing activities. Strategic purchasing activities encompass the long-term planning, development and optimisation of supplier–buyer relationships, as well as the supervision of product development processes in the context of Project Purchasing. In contrast, operational purchasing activities seek to realise the legal and physical supply of the required goods and services.

The material supply, which is the core process of Purchasing, thus includes operational as well as strategic activities. In the following, typical purchasing processes shall be discussed in consideration of strategic aspects.

3.3.1   The Purchasing Process

Traditionally, the purchasing process consists of a number of decisions that are closely interrelated. Apart from the mere operational processing of orders, in purchasing processes a great number of factors must be kept in mind. The most important aim is always to achieve optimum results with regard to materials

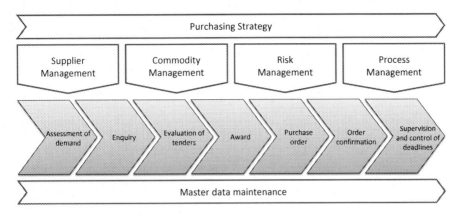

Fig. 3.5 General purchasing process

management which means the procurement of the right goods in the right quantities at the right time at the right location and at the right price.

Generally, as shown in Fig. 3.5, the purchasing process can be divided into chronological subprocesses that are managed and supported by strategic elements. The process starts with concrete requirements, which in the case of series production are triggered by Materials Management and in the case of individual requirements by the respective demand carrier. After the requirements have been checked and aggregated, potential sources of supply will be sought that are able to satisfy these demands. Based on a comparison of the advantages and disadvantages of the identified options, the procurement process ends in a legally binding order.

Subsequently, the timely physical availability of the ordered goods and services must be supervised and safeguarded.

3.3.1.1 Assessment of Demand
The demand means the input factors necessary for production and manufacture. In the case of mass production, the purchasing process starts with demands that are triggered by Materials Management that—in accordance with a plan—determines the requirements. Several methods can be used in order to estimate concrete demands.

Deterministic assessment of demand is the method mostly used in the context of mass production. In this case, as a rule, sales and production plans are available in which the quantities that will be needed in the future are listed. At the beginning, there is the primary demand based on the planned sales volume of the final product. From this demand, the secondary requirements are derived. These requirements result from the breakup of the underlying parts list and encompass the single parts needed for manufacturing the final products. In this respect, only bought-in parts are pertinent to Purchasing. From the dependent and, when necessary, expansion demands, the gross requirements are calculated. By checking these requirements against inventories, safety stocks, and orders already placed, the same requirements are transformed into the concrete net demands that will have to be satisfied in the further course of the purchasing process.

In contrast, stochastic assessment of demands is used with regard to materials that cannot be planned according to a secondary requirement. These materials, such as indirect materials and auxiliary materials, are not specified in part lists because they are not constitutive parts of the final product. Therefore, statistical methods are used to predict future demands of these materials as accurately as possible.

It is much more difficult to plan individual requirements such as investments or services. With regard to such requirements, Purchasing must be duly and completely informed about emerging demands, and technically useful information must also be provided. If the latter is not possible, invitations for innovation may be sent to suppliers in order to specify the requirements more concretely.

3.3.1.2 Enquiry

During the next subprocess, the Purchaser has to invite suppliers to submit binding tenders for the identified demands. Prior to this subprocess, intense procurement market research will be undertaken in order to identify potential suppliers for the enquiry. Care must be taken to ensure that the enquiry will be worded and specified precisely. The more precise the enquiry is, the fewer the queries and clarifications requested, and the more precisely the supplier can calculate the proposal. For this reason, invitations to tender should include the following points:

- Precise and specified description of the demand
- Exact quantities, possibly individual scale quantities
- Intended dates of delivery
- Deadline for the submission of a tender
- General terms and conditions of purchase

In production purchasing, the process of enquiring is often simplified or completely skipped because the framework and the conditions of delivery have been fixed in advance by Strategic Purchasing, and the ordering procedure follows immediately. Therefore, production purchasing offers an opportunity for a shortened, operationally standardised purchasing process.

3.3.1.3 Evaluation of Tenders

Prior to a more thorough evaluation of the tenders, the tenders are examined in order to ascertain the conformity of tender with regard especially to quality, quantity, dates of delivery, and conditions of delivery. If these data conform, the tender will enter the subprocess of a more thorough evaluation. If however deviances occur that could not be eliminated by conferring with the tendering party, these deviances must be indicated and factored into the evaluation of the total costs.

The subsequent tender evaluation serves to ensure that the order will be placed according to objective, comprehensive, and, most importantly, audit-proof criteria. The individual tenders are compared by reference to defined criteria that can make differences transparent and then choosing the best offer. However, this does not mean that the sourcing decision is based entirely on the pricing aspect. Dependent on complexity and relevance, further aspects must be taken into consideration during the decision-making process. A well-established approach for this is the value benefit analysis. Here, the requirements are defined according to criteria and weighted with regard to their relevance. The criteria are then assessed and added according to the degree of fulfilment. An evaluation indicator is formed for each tender, and the decision can be made on this basis. A handy example application of this process will be given in Sect. 4.3.3. Factors to be included in this form of analysis are, amongst others:

- Purchase price
- Time of delivery
- Level of quality
- Capacity
- Service
- Location
- Reliability
- Supply risks

3.3.1.4 Award

The scope of the commissioning subprocess depends on the relevance and importance of the respective requirements. As far as small demands are concerned, the supplier that has submitted the best offer will be commissioned following the evaluation of the tenders, if the offer is compliant with the requirements. However, with requirements of relatively high value the evaluation of the tenders will be followed by award negotiations in order to optimise the individual evaluation criteria such as price, delivery time, or quality. A detailed description of purchasing negotiations will be given below in Chap. 8.

3.3.1.5 Purchase Order

Ordering is the last step of the award procedure and represents the legally binding declaration of intent to accept, and to pay for, the respective commodities or services according to the agreed framework conditions. Normally, orders are passed in writing, registered in an inventory control system, and then sent to the supplier. Although there are no formal requirements to orders, they should include the following data in order to ensure proper processing:

- An in-house order number to which the supplier can refer at delivery
- An unambiguous description of the supply, e.g. a part number
- Quantity of the ordered item
- Price per unit as well as total price
- Delivery date and delivery period
- Reference to guaranteed properties and quality requirements such as drawings, test requirements, and acceptance specifications

– The agreed payment and delivery conditions including the place of delivery
– Reference to special agreements such as general terms and conditions of purchasing or quality assurance agreements

3.3.1.6 Order Confirmation

After the supplier has checked the order, he will normally send an order confirmation by which he agrees to the order and accepts it. In cases where the order has been preceded by an identical offer, the order confirmation may be waived from a legal point of view: in such cases, the order represents the acceptance of the offer.

In practice, order confirmations are checked, and reminders are sent in the case of overdue order confirmations. This is done for two reasons in cases of material supply: On the one hand, the supplier confirms that the order has been received and will be executed. And on the other hand, differences concerning order-specific conditions can be identified and corrected prior to the delivery of the product or service in question. It is therefore important that careful attention is paid to the confirmation's exact conformity to the order or, as the case may be, the offer. In cases where deviances are identified, the order confirmation does not constitute a purchase contract but is regarded as a new offer. If these deviances cannot be accepted, e.g. in the case of a later delivery date, the order confirmation must be rejected immediately in writing. The last statement issued by the concerned parties is then regarded as legally binding.

3.3.1.7 Supervision and Control of Deadlines

In order to safeguard the company's supply delivery, deadlines are supervised and controlled in the next process step. There are many external and in-house disruptive factors which may delay delivery so in many cases it will not be sufficient just to wait and trust in timely deliveries. In this respect, expediting deliveries aims to avoid delivery delays before they occur. In many cases, this is effected by reminders that are sent to the supplier prior to the date of delivery. The supplier is thus reminded of the timely delivery, delivery delays can be identified earlier, and the scope of counteracting measures will be wider.

Furthermore, measures safeguarding deadlines are taken within the frame of the supplier management, e.g. by choosing suppliers adhering to schedules or by disciplinary measures taken in the course of supplier development.

Deadline control will act when pending deliveries are overdue or are about to fall behind. When a delivery becomes overdue, the reminder mechanism is triggered, and the supplier is set a final deadline. If the supplier does not comply with this final deadline, he can be given formal notice of default and from that time on liquidated damages may be imposed on him.

However, in practice overdue delays are not always caused by the suppliers. Often short-term requirements of the in-house users or technical modifications of the supplies will result in deadline constraints. Therefore, many deadline control measures aim to reduce the periods of delay to the minimum in order to keep the damage to one's own company as low as possible.

3.3.2   Roles in the Decision-Making Process

In order to design and optimise purchasing processes, one has to know which persons in which departments are involved in decision-making processes and what their roles in these processes are. Purchasing cannot usually decide on its own which supplier shall be chosen or which product bought. Depending on the company structure and the volumes required, the true decision-makers will be found at higher hierarchy levels, and they will exercise massive influence over the environment of the Purchaser. An example is that suppliers may be chosen as a consequence of political decisions although with regard to rational criteria another supplier should have been selected.

Furthermore, within the scope of development and investment projects, so-called purchasing committees are often being formed. These committees consist of a group of persons who are jointly involved in the decision-making process with regard to the purchase. Through the use of such committees, cross-departmental know-how is used in order to optimise decision-making.

From the marketing-oriented view, a model has been established that includes, amongst others, the following typical roles[1]:

Users apply the products or systems to be procured. In many cases, they will command long-standing experience and comprehensive professional knowledge. The more complex the demand in question is, the more necessary it becomes to involve this group of persons in the decision-making process.

Purchasers are responsible for the purchasing process. They obtain the offers, and they are the reference persons when it comes to trading issues. Furthermore, they are the persons bearing formal responsibility and authority.

Influencers have no formal role in the decision-making process but exert significant influence. As a rule, this role is taken on by persons who command comprehensive experience in a particular field and attend to the decision-making process in an advisory capacity.

Decision-makers are the persons who ultimately bear the responsibility for the decision. Depending on the importance of the decision, this role will be taken on by the executive board, the management, or Purchasing.

From the supplier's view, a distinction can be drawn between supporters and opponents with regard to these four groups. The supporters, as a rule, are convinced by the supplier and its product and will help him to conclude the deal. The opponents, on the other side, are rather sceptical and prefer another supplier or another solution. The attributes of the supporters and opponents will be especially pronounced when it comes to preferred suppliers. Due to long-term experience and personal preferences, other departments will make stringent efforts to exert their influence on the purchasing process. Sellers know that and will therefore try to specifically address or avoid those groups.

---

[1] Cf. Fritz and von der Oelsnitz (2006, p. 83).

3.3.3 Process Optimisation

Process optimisation is concerned with the review and optimisation of company processes in order to cut process costs, to streamline and rationalise processes, and to improve their quality. In Purchasing, strategic planning and control processes as well as operational supply processes are included and evaluated. By doing this, flaws in existing processes can be identified and necessary modifications can be made. Consequently, processes will become more efficient, and the day-to-day workload of Purchasers can be reduced, for traditionally, Purchasers incessantly and elaborately strive to strengthen their negotiating position in order to reach their annual cost reduction targets. So year in and year out they hurry from one price negotiation to the next and waste precious time and capacities that in the long term are needed for more important strategic tasks. Standardising and automating of accessory processes in production purchasing offers an opportunity for creating the freedom necessary to perform these tasks. The potential of framework agreements, of Long-Term Agreements (LTAs) based on learning curve effects, of price adjustment clauses, of automated procurement of C parts (see ABC analysis in Sect. 7.3), and also of the terms and conditions of purchase has to be exploited systematically. For this reason, in the following sections some suggestions are given on how operational purchasing process can be rationalised in order to create the necessary freedom for performing strategic tasks.

3.3.3.1 Quantity Contracts

Quantity contracts are agreements in which the guaranteed purchase of a fixed quantity of goods or services within a fixed period is stipulated. In contrast to single orders and delivery schedules, quantity contracts do not include specific delivery dates but only the total volume of the deliveries and the commercial conditions of contract. The exact quantities of delivery and the exact delivery dates are fixed in so-called call-off orders based on the respective quantity contract. Normally, quantity contracts are agreed in order to regulate the collaboration of supplier and client. Often, such contracts result in a win-win situation: Due to greater volumes, clients can realise considerably better prices while lead times can be reduced significantly as the supplier can stock the necessary raw material. Consequently, the flexibility and responsiveness of the complete supply chain will increase massively. Furthermore, call-off orders can easily be standardised and automated and will in the end require only a fraction of the original ordering efforts. Suppliers on their part enjoy guaranteed sales potentials and can optimally organise their production lots. Apart from this win-win situation, this contract form also results in a significant reduction of the necessary commercial capacities of both parties. So scour your purchasing portfolio regularly for articles that are suitable for quantity contracts!

3.3.3.2 Consignment Stores

The term is derived from consignment marketing in which an importer processes the sale of an exporter's products on a commission basis. Consignation stores, however, are storage areas often near or directly at the client that the suppliers are provided with cost free. In these warehouses, the ordered products are stocked; the supplier remains the owner of the products until they are removed by the client. The products are only invoiced after their physical removal from the consignment store. Apart from the high availability and the concomitant minimisation of supply risks, consignment stores offer the further advantage of standardising and facilitating the storing, accounting, and billing processes. However, a prerequisite is that the merchandise management systems of both the client and the supplier have a common interface and are suitably cross-linked. Due to significantly higher capital commitment, this storage model is not very popular with suppliers. However, consignment stores can bring a win-win situation as there are some advantages for suppliers too. Manufacturing and shipment in optimum lot sizes, the reduction of necessary storage space, diminished planning risks, and first and foremost heightened customer loyalty are good arguments to convince suppliers of the consignment store model.

3.3.3.3 Special Price Agreements

Further optimisation of purchasing processes can be achieved by special price agreements. The automation of price adjustment clauses will take some pressure off the purchasing activity. Through such clauses, both the supplier and the client reserve the right to adjust the price of the product or service according to changing production costs. Generally, the production costs will be broken down into a fixed, unchanging price component, a variable material costs component, and a variable labour costs component. When changes occur in the variable pools of costs, the price will be recalculated in accordance with the formula shown in Fig. 3.6.

This clause is especially used in long-term supply agreements including volatile price components in order to minimise necessary price negotiations during the contract period. In this respect, it is necessary to know and fix the volatile price components in terms of value and their proportion of the total price at the inception of the agreement. After corridors in both directions (which naturally should be from Purchasing's point of view upwards be as large and downwards as small as possible) have been defined, price negotiations will further only become necessary in cases when the corridor is exceed or undercut. This fair method, which is also called a bull/bear clause, will bring steadiness in the course of business as experience has shown.

$$P_1 = P_0 * \left(a + b * \frac{M_1}{M_0} + c * \frac{L_1}{L_0} \right)$$

a	= unchanging price component	M_0	= material costs based on reference date
b	= variable material costs component	M_1	= material costs based on effective date
c	= variable labour costs component	L_0	= labour costs based on reference date
		L_1	= labour costs based on effective date

Fig. 3.6 Calculation clause for automation of price adjustment

Another approach to automating purchasing prices is based on the management concept of the learning curve. According to this concept, the inflation-adjusted unit costs of a product will fall constantly if the cumulated output quantity rises. Economies of scale arising from increased exercise gain, process safety, improvements in efficiency, and rationalisation will have a favourable impact on the production costs of a commodity or service. Therefore, it makes sense to negotiate gradually decreasing prices when it comes to contracts concerning higher volumes. As they are bound to quantities or periods of time, prices will fall and compel the supplier to realise continuous improvements. This method also automatically generates projectable savings in the following years.

3.3.3.4 General Terms and Conditions of Purchase

An instrument that is often underestimated even by Purchasing itself are the General Terms and Conditions of Purchase as a counter to the suppliers' General Terms and Conditions of Trade (GTCT). The General Terms and Conditions of Purchase set most preconditions and situations under which a purchase is made. These terms and conditions may include anything that could also be part of the contract, e.g. liability for defects, the reservation of proprietary rights, or the place of jurisdiction. With the aid of this instrument, general legal regulations (e.g. liability exclusions) can be amended or modified.

However, the implementation of General Terms and Conditions of Purchase is not easy and therefore unpopular with Purchasers. A mere reference to them in the text of the order will often not be sufficient since suppliers will normally confirm orders on the basis of their GTCT. To avoid such a stand-off, it is advisable to establish clarity in advance during the enquiry stage by linking the acceptance of the bid to the acceptance of the General Terms and Conditions of Purchase. If the supplier has difficulties with accepting them, a readiness to negotiate may be signalled and some points may be adapted in a deviant, supplier-specific agreement. At the utmost, the legal regulations (in Germany, from the HGB—*Handelsgesetzbuch*, a "commercial code" containing the core of the commercial law in Germany—and BGB—*Bundesgesetzbuch*, a "civil code", like a constitution) can be agreed as a reasonable compromise especially when, as in Germany, these regulations are much more customer friendly than the GTCT defined by the supplier. In the end, the agreed standard will greatly reduce the efforts of future contract negotiations.

3.3.4   Project Purchasing

In many companies, Purchasing nowadays can no longer be considered a separate entity since more and more often cross-departmental cooperation in projects is required in order to perform innovative, complex, and extensive tasks. A project in this sense is a temporary, one-time task that is unique, complex, or innovative and commands a limited amount of resources. As a rule, the target parameters of projects will form a "magic triangle" composed of factual (quantity, product, quality),

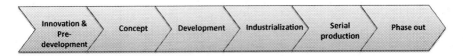

Fig. 3.7 Common product development process

scheduling (milestones, finish date), and cost targets (budget, resources, costs). These three parameters are competing with each other. When, for example, dates are rescheduled, this will necessarily have repercussions on the available budget either in the form of direct costs or by demand for human resources.

A process-driven, cross-functional management of purchasing activities becomes especially important during the product development process, which the Strategic Purchaser will decisively influence as a project member. The general course of action of a product development process is shown in Fig. 3.7.

The necessity for a process-driven, cross-functional management of purchasing activities already arises during the early innovation stage of a project when technical solutions are only vaguely discernible and specialised suppliers must be involved. In this respect, it is necessary to implement a finding and involvement process initiated by Purchasing into the company-wide innovation process in order to identify the optimum technology partners.

For projects at the predevelopment stage, established project instruments such as value analysis, target costing, or design-to-cost are indicated and should be initiated by the Project Purchaser. One must not forget that the bulk of the material costs that will occur later are already determined during this stage.

Furthermore, Project Purchasing is responsible for the supply of the requirements throughout the project. This includes, amongst others, concluding development contracts and allocating functional models and prototypes. In the course of industrialising, Project Purchasers will design the external added value and qualify the suppliers of subsequent series production. This can be done in close coordination with the Strategic Purchaser provided their tasks are not performed by the same person.

As the start of series production comes closer, the more the Project Purchaser will focus on forward cover and risk management in order to safeguard a frictionless start-up. A practice-approved method for achieving this aim is the Readiness Rollup, as detailed in Chap. 6.

After the successful start-up and the beginning of series production, the Project Purchaser will normally confer the material supply to Operational Purchasing and will now use free capacities for new projects.

Practical Tip

Through my work in quite different branches with companies of different structures and sizes, I have gained a lot of experience in centralised and decentralised procurement organisations. I have also become acquainted with mixed forms such as the Lead Buyer function and its respective advantages and disadvantages. In any case and regardless of the type of organisation, commodity group management has proven a must because of its predominant advantages. From my point of view, there is no "best" form of organisation—the trick is to dynamically adapt the structural and operational organisation of Purchasing to the specific demands of the company and the market. Thinking in departmental categories is inadequate; the main emphasis must be on the company-wide process. That does not mean that Strategic Purchasing would become less important but just the opposite: Strategic Purchasing reaches increasingly higher ranks in the company hierarchy up to the managing board. And this trend will go on.

Reference

Fritz, W., & Von der Oelsnitz, D. (2006). *Marketing: Elemente marktorientierter Unternehmensführung*. Stuttgart: Kohlhammer.

Supplier Management

4

4.1 Introduction to the Supplier Management

Supplier management is becoming ever more important in the context of steadily increasing global competition. Ever shorter product life cycles, the reduction of in-house production, as well as the concentration on companies' core competences tend to result in a growing number of suppliers, increased volumes to be procured, and growing technological dependencies on suppliers. Classical procurement relations between supplier and client have turned into much more complex types of co-operation. Total cost estimates and risk management are becoming increasingly important in Purchasing, especially when considering the increasing globalisation of supply chains.

Due to the direct influence of a suppliers' performance on the competitiveness of the company, the interest in innovative long-term partnerships is growing. At this point, supplier management is called for to make use of its tools aiming at a general design of the supplier–buyer relationship. It encompasses all proactive measures for the design, management, and development of the company's current and future supplier relations in all areas.

In this respect, the following core questions must be asked:

- How can the supplier portfolio be managed and formed on a strategic level?
- How should the best suppliers be chosen?
- How efficient is the performance of current suppliers?
- How can we be sure to buy from the best suppliers?
- What measures can be taken when flaws have been identified?

By striving for better cooperation with suppliers and their sub-suppliers, supplier management aims to develop, procure, and produce products or services better,

© Springer International Publishing AG 2017   45
U. Weigel, M. Ruecker, *The Strategic Procurement Practice Guide*, Management
for Professionals, DOI 10.1007/978-3-319-57651-0_4

Fig. 4.1 Supplier
management cycle

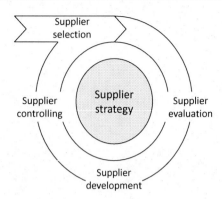

quicker, and at lower cost. The operational targets of supplier management primarily focus on better performance from the suppliers as well as on reducing procurement costs. In particular, these targets involve the following process steps: selection, evaluation, development, and control of suppliers (shown in Fig. 4.1). The strategic targets of supplier management address the middle-term and long-term optimisation of the company's supplier portfolio. This includes the creation of procurement and supplier strategies as well as the evaluation and enhancement of suppliers' contributions to added value.

4.2   Supplier Strategy

How can the supplier portfolio be managed and formed at a strategic level? Supplier strategies try to answer this question. The supplier strategy is part of the purchasing strategy and determines the general direction for long-term action plans in the context of supplier policy. The supplier strategy answers the question from whom and, particularly, in what way products and services should be bought.

Essentially, supplier strategies can be seen from five different perspectives detailed in Chap. 2:

- Process-oriented view: How and to what extent are suppliers integrated in in-house processes?
- Supplier-oriented view: How many suppliers are needed for the respective commodity groups?
- Material-oriented view: How large should the proportion of external added value be?
- Region-oriented view: In which regions are products or services bought?
- Risk-oriented view: What risks are taken and how can these risks be minimised?

Normally, a targeted mix of these different approaches will best serve the aim of devising an efficient supplier strategy.

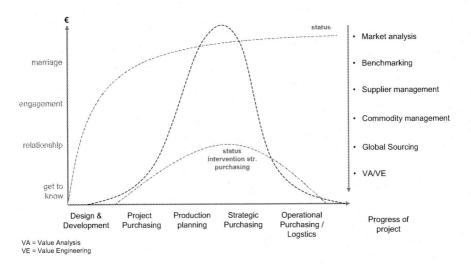

Fig. 4.2 Supplier love story along the product lifecycle

Practical Tip

Figure 4.2 illustrates a problem that is often seen in technology-driven companies, but can also be found in the marketing and logistics sectors: Shrewd salesmen use opportunities such as trade fairs for building up direct contacts to developers. Roughly 20% of suppliers purposefully try to bypass Purchasing by communicating directly to the end users.

Such suppliers promise best quality, newest technologies, and due delivery; very often they will also offer partial development services. For developers, who are always pressed for time, such offers come at exactly the right time and thus a bond of affection is created (see abscissa in Fig. 4.2).

As the project progresses, the affection will turn to true and loyal love without any rivals (competitors) that will soon end in an engagement and often in premature pregnancy. The marriage must be made quickly because project closure is just around the corner; quite often the partner (supplier) will like to be perpetuated in the marriage contract, e.g. as the mandatory supplier of construction drawings including financial consequences if the other partner is "playing around". Now, the whole thing must be rubber-stamped and thus the minister (the purchaser) must be called in. He will only have the opportunity to utter some admonitory words that nobody will listen to at this stage. At best, he will receive a meagre collection (3% cash discount as his negotiation range and if he is lucky cost-free deliveries).

I have often come across such situations, and if they occur a warning example must be made. By the way, the late involvement of the purchasers is also an essential breeding ground of monopolists. If strategists are to have the opportunity of using the tools of strategic purchasing efficiently, they must be involved from the beginning; to quote the German poet Friedrich Schiller: "Whoe'er would form eternal bonds/Should weigh if heart to heart responds. /Folly is short—repentance long".

Cost avoidance is the main challenge, especially in view of ever-shorter product life cycles. After the horse has bolted, the only helpful measures can be to calculate the damage to the company, to make it public, and to have a word with the management board and all participants about efficient avoidance measures for the future. Ideally, a cross-departmental workflow description will be established mandating that Strategic Purchasing must be involved from the beginning. This procedure will certainly conjure up a thunderstorm but it will prove helpful. Thunderstorms clear the air.

4.3 Supplier Selection

Selecting the supplier is the first step of supplier management. The core question that must be answered in the context of supplier selection is where and especially how the right partners for the company can be found. As shown in Fig. 4.3, in-depth procurement market research, pre-selection, and analysis of suppliers must precede supplier selection properly if the supplier that bests suits the company is to be found.

4.3.1 Supplier Identification

The selection of potential new suppliers starts with a supplier identification process that can be designed individually according to the respective procurement

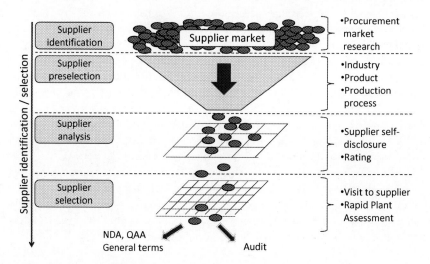

Fig. 4.3 Progress of supplier selection

objective. The task is to identify potential suppliers that can satisfy a concrete demand or would be able to do so. At first, the appropriate procurement markets must be identified, located, and selected.

In order to do so, a general requirement profile is defined that will be taken into consideration during the supplier search and pre-selection. This profile contains general requirements such as industry, size, product portfolio, dependency on competitors, or technological know-how. At this stage, supplier management is closely linked to procurement market research since information on the respective procurement markets and their suppliers must be obtained. Information can be gained by primary procurement market research (direct contacts to potential suppliers, visiting fairs or production facilities, and so on) or by secondary market research (research in catalogues, trade magazines, or the internet). A detailed description of procurement market research will be given in Sect. 7.1. On the basis of the predefined criteria, a pre-selection follows during which the potential suppliers can be identified and analysed in detail.

4.3.2 Supplier Analysis

Supplier analysis encompasses the identification, editing, processing, and represen-tation of information regarding the preselected suppliers. First, the information is compiled and ordered. The aim of supplier analysis is to gather concrete informa-tion on the capability of the potential suppliers in order to guarantee that only the best suppliers will be admitted. To find the necessary information, several tools can be used:

Supplier Self-Assessment With the help of a catalogue of criteria, several data are requested directly from the supplier. These data may refer to areas such as organisation, production, financial resources, quality assurance, logistics, service, and communication. The subjectivity of self-assessments is a problem as suppliers under certain circumstances will always be tempted to present themselves as better than they really are. Often, the supplier's lists of customer references can serve as an indicator of the supplier's proficiency levels; furthermore, these lists can be checked easily.

Company Reports Such reports compiled by agencies or credit insurers offer the opportunity of obtaining objective insights into the structure of the potential supplier. Apart from general company data, company reports as a rule contain information on responsible persons and capital structure as well as a risk assessment that allows for estimating the economic stability of the supplier. Hence, the company report is a complement to supplier self-assessment and at the same time a tool to verify the information given by the supplier.

Certification Certifications give suppliers the possibility of demonstrating the capability of their processes. One of the most important standards for realising a

QA system for all industries is the ISO 9000 series. In the ISO 9001 standard, a process model that goes beyond the company is given including the requirements of leadership responsibility, resources management, product realisation, as well as measurability, analysis, and amelioration.

Criteria for Exclusion With the help of criteria for exclusion, which are determined cross-departmentally, suppliers that do not fulfil certain minimum requirements can be filtered out. These criteria are company-specific and vary depending on the procurement objective.

4.3.3   Supplier Selection

Within the scope of the tender phase concrete selection, criteria such as quality, capacity, effectiveness, and price can be fixed and weighted cross-departmentally. In order to draw up an objective and above all reproducible shortlist, the use of pertinent selection methods such as the ABC analysis (see Sect. 7.3) or a cost-benefit analysis will be advised. The latter is a quantitative decision-making instrument, with the help of which an issue can be analysed and evaluated according to a scoring system. As shown in the following field, example criteria describing the requirement profile are established and weighted according to their different relevancies. Subsequently, points within a previously fixed scale are awarded that show the estimated degree of fulfilment with regard to each criterion. By summing up the score numbers in due consideration of their weights, a rating can be established that will serve as a basis for the ongoing decision-making process.

Before the supplier selection procedure is concluded, general contractual aspects such as purchasing, quality assurance, and non-disclosure agreements should be safeguarded in order to fix the general framework conditions. Ideally, this has already been done during the tender phase.

The supplier selection procedure ends in a joint decision-making process of all involved functions that in most cases will include commissioning first samples. As a result, the supplier is included in the list of released suppliers, and a separate parts release process is beginning.

Practical Tip
In the project shown in Fig. 4.4, the task was to identify suppliers for optomechanical components that in a break from tradition should have been capable of supplying not single parts but complete components and sub-assemblies while satisfying the highest demands in quality, look, and feel. The respective companies should be found in the Low Cost Country (LCC) areas of Asia (in which context one must not forget that "low" cost does not automatically mean "best" cost). Due to the expected know-how in combination with low wage structures, we chose Asia as the most favourable procurement region for this project. Furthermore, the supplier should not be too big; they should bring sufficient development potential as future system suppliers, and they should be independent. At first, in concert with our procurement

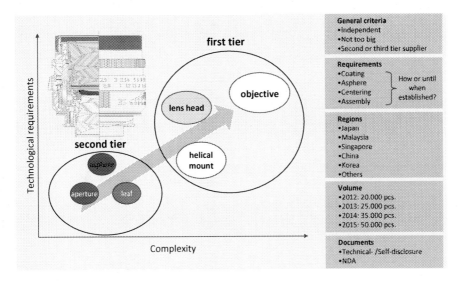

Fig. 4.4 Strategic supplier search for objective components

office in Shanghai, we identified seven suppliers in Japan (which certainly is not a low cost country but has production facilities in such countries), Malaysia, China, and South Korea from whom we wanted to request a proposal. Then we spent several weeks on developing a 12-page, internationally comprehensible catalogue of questions in co-operation with our Development and Quality Assurance departments. Every potential supplier had to answer more than 50 questions concerning all areas of their companies in detail. As far as Japan was concerned, "old-school" Japan experts warned: "No Japanese company will fill in this question-naire; for things like that you have to know the right people there and I do. I'll gladly invite you to Japan and will pay the hotel bill" (I can see what you are thinking!). We stuck to our line because Japanese companies are increasingly adapting to global business conventions—not the other way round. We duly received all our questionnaires completely filled in including the one sent to the Japanese supplier.

With the help of a cost-benefit analysis, we then filtered out four potential suppliers. To do so, we had previously defined and weighted 12 criteria (see Fig. 4.5) that we evaluated on the basis of the returning questionnaires and the subjective estimations of the members of our team. Although supplier F had the third highest scores in the ranking, we decided against them as the competitive context posed to high a risk.

Therefore, we shortlisted suppliers A, B, C, and D, and now *Gemba* was asked for. This Japanese term means: "the scene of the event". On a supplier visit, we could assure ourselves of the capabilities of the potential suppliers and started to build personal relationships with their decision-makers, which in Asia is at least as important.

In the end, the ranking of our pre-selection proved true. We chose two suppliers that after several months of intense supplier development supplied components in series.

weighting	1	1	3	1	1	5	3	3	1	10	9	8	
competence / supplier	mechanics production / assembly	mechanics, electronics production / assembly	mechanics production / assembly	mechanics, electronics production / assembly	mechanics, electronics production / assembly	mechanics, optics production / assembly	mechanics production / assembly	mechanics production / assembly	mechanics production / assembly				
supplier A	2	9	8	7	8	8	5	8	2	7	8	3	297
supplier B	1	3	8	8	8	6	2	2	2	5	5	10	263
supplier C	2	4	7	8	7	6	3	4	3	5	7	3	233
supplier D	2	5	8	6	6	6	5	5	3	9	5	10	321
supplier E	3	5	5	5	5	6	6	6	2	5	7	2	230
supplier F	10	9	7	9	9	8	10	10	8	1	9	3	281
supplier G	2	4	5	5	6	5	6	6	2	5	7	3	232

key: competence   10 = very good
      competitive situation   10 = without risk
      quality level   10 = very high
      price level   10 = very low

Fig. 4.5 Supplier selection based on cost-benefit analysis

4.4   Supplier Evaluation

Supplier evaluation is the systematic and comprehensive assessment of the performance of suppliers with respect to defined criteria. The pertinent evaluation criteria
as well as the methods to be applied must be fixed in advance. From these, a
classification of suppliers and possible consequences and measures are established
so that the evaluation can be treated as the basis of supplier development. The
evaluation then leads to supplier controlling by which permanent supervision and
control of the supplier's performance in the business relationship is targeted. In this
context, it is important to identify flaws and unused potential as soon as possible
and to initiate appropriate countermeasures. Apart from well-founded argumentation aids for the sake of negotiations, the evaluation provides an analysis of
strengths and weaknesses from which concrete measures for improvement can be
derived in order to optimise the supplier–buyer relationship. The execution of a
systematic evaluation is prescribed in ISO 9001:

> The organisation shall evaluate and select suppliers based on their ability to supply products
> in accordance with the organization's requirements. Criteria for selection, evaluation, and
> re-evaluation shall be established. Records of the results of evaluation and any necessary
> actions arising from the evaluation shall be maintained.[1]

To properly take risk into account in the framework of supplier management, it is
advisable to integrate a risk index in addition to the purely performance-oriented
criteria in the evaluation.

---

[1]DIN EN ISO 9001 (2008).

This can be done through a combination of subjective risk ratings and objective assessments of the actual procurement risk. In this way, an integrated view of the supplier's performance and its long-term stability is achieved.

Practical Tip

The supplier evaluation is conducted biannually and analysed by the Purchasing and Quality Assurance departments. Apart from measurable data ("hard facts"), subjective estimations ("soft facts") have some influence in the objective evaluation scheme. In conformity with the current purchasing strategy, the evaluation consists of eight main criteria and up to five sub-criteria in each case (see Fig. 4.6). Depending on their relevancy, the criteria are weighted differently. The evaluators can allot 1–100 points per sub-criterion, with 1 point representing "extremely bad" and 100 points representing "excellence". The scoring follows a predefined procedural instruction thanks to which the evaluation results can be compared with each other. In this process, the Purchasing department evaluates five of the eight main criteria, in detail:

1 Delivery Performance	25%	
delivery reliability	100%	82
Result		82

2 Price Performance	20%	
pricing compared with competitors	80%	75
price transperancy (calculation)	10%	60
acknowledgment of conditions of purchase	10%	1
Result		66

3 Supplier Developm.	7%	
innovation	25%	75
cooperation / know-how contribution	25%	100
strategic importance	20%	75
readiness to growth	20%	100
flexibility	10%	75
Result		86

4 Communication	3%	
internationality	20%	100
reachability	25%	100
response behavior	25%	75
data transfer	30%	100
Result		94

5 Quality Performance	25%	
lots without complaints	45%	70
lots with limited approval	35%	95
main failure on parts yes/no?	20%	100
Result		85

6 Complaints	6%	
error repititions	40%	100
information flow / 8D-Report	30%	100
actions on complaints / countermeasures	30%	75
Result		93

7 Quality Teamwork	4%	
quality agreement	20%	50
compliance to agreements	40%	100
flexibility to problem situations	40%	50
Result		70

8 Risk Performance	10%	
risk score	60%	85
supply source	20%	100
risk class	20%	75
Result		86

Fig. 4.6 Criteria for supplier evaluation

- *Delivery performance*: The delivery performance is evaluated by means of a points system subject to the days of delay. The database is produced regularly by the goods planning and control system.
- *Price performance*: Price levels, price transparency, and conditions compared to those of competitors.
- *Supplier development*: Evaluation of the innovational strength, willingness to co-operate, and development potential of the supplier.
- *Communication*: Evaluation of general communication with the supplier.
- *Risk performance*: Objective rating of the company by an external service provider plus subjective risk assessment by the members of Purchasing.

The three other criteria are evaluated by the Quality Assurance department. These criteria are:

- *Quality performance*: The rate of complaints is evaluated by means of a points system. The rate of complaints is also regularly produced by the goods planning and control system allotting a score value.
- *Complaints*: Complaints handling by the supplier and occurrence of repetitive errors.
- *Quality teamwork*: Evaluation of the co-operation with the supplier from the view of Quality Assurance and flexibility with regard to problems.

At the end of the evaluation, these eight main criteria result in a supplier rating index and a radar diagram (Fig. 4.7) showing the strengths and weaknesses of the supplier. From this, a classification of the suppliers is derived which will serve as the basis of the subsequent supplier development. The supplier classification and the measures resulting from it subdivide according to the following model:

- *A suppliers* = 95–100 points: Are declared preferred suppliers and awarded a certificate stating the evaluation results in recognition of their services.
- *B suppliers* = 80–94 points: These suppliers receive a written document in recognition of their services stating the evaluation results but also the identified improvement potentials.
- *C suppliers* = 50–79 points: These suppliers are informed of the evaluation results and the identified flaws. They are asked to present, within a given time frame, a list of measures by which the evaluation results can be improved in the medium term.
- *D suppliers* = 0–49 points: These suppliers are informed of the evaluation results and invited to a personal meeting. In this meeting, the flaws will be discussed and approaches for improvement will be developed jointly. If the flaws cannot be eliminated in the short term, the supplier may be phased out.

As a systematic evaluation of all suppliers is too laborious and unrewarding, the supplier portfolio will normally be prioritised in advance. The regular evaluation will be restricted to strong-selling, single source, bottleneck, and risk suppliers.

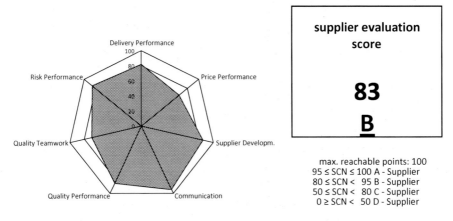

Fig. 4.7 Supplier evaluation result showing strengths and weaknesses

4.5   Supplier Development

Essentially, supplier development is composed of two elements: supplier management and supplier integration. Supplier management aims at optimising the performance structure of the supplier portfolio and adapting it to changing framework conditions. Supplier integration encompasses the improvement of the co-operation and integration of the suppliers into one's own company. The general aim is for better, quicker, and cheaper procurement and production of products and services through targeted co-operation with suppliers and sub-suppliers as early as possible. The core questions in this context are:

- How can competitive advantages be achieved?
- What are the supplier's core competencies?
- What potential is still unused?

In order to influence the supplier–buyer relationship, several instruments can be used:

Supplier Management With the aid of supplier management, Strategic Purchasing tries to establish a trustworthy, cooperative relationship with its suppliers. In this way, cooperation shall be encouraged, performance potential increased, and procurement risks minimised. The importance and appreciation of the company in the view of its business partners are always strongly influenced by the way the cooperation works. The better the relations are between both parties, the easier it is to master difficult supply situations. Positive modes of behaviour include, amongst others, mutual fairness, openness, trust, discretion, and reliability.

Supplier Education Supplier education aims at safeguarding and improving the supplier's performance with regard to the requirements. If the supplier's performance falls short, the education may be in terms of sanctions that will incite the supplier to identify and remove the flaws and performance weaknesses. Also, supplier education serves to further improve the suppliers' performance and motivate them to render above-average services. This can be achieved by special signs of recognition e.g. the awarding of a supplier prize.

Supplier Encouragement Supplier encouragement has the aim of improving the supplier's performance level and developing previously unexploited potential. This can be done by sharing know-how, providing production facilities, procuring primary materials, delegating members of one's own staff, or by analysing areas of weakness in the supplier's performance capabilities. Suppliers having exceptionally good capabilities, e.g. with regard to quality, are especially qualified for encouragement measures. It would be worthwhile to help them eliminate their shortcomings.

Supplier Substitution However, at a certain point, one has to realise that despite all efforts any further cooperation will be of no use for either party. This situation has arisen when the requirements cannot be achieved over a longer period and no future improvement is to be expected. For this reason, an average of 7.5% of suppliers are substituted each year.

Supplier substitution can be regarded as an indirect subcategory of supplier development. For substituting a supplier, systematic planning is necessary in order to guarantee the future security of supply. One must take into consideration that depending on the scope of supplies and their complexities, finding and developing other procurement sources may take a long time.

Practical Tip: How to Deal with Monopolists
All purchasers hate it—to be forced to accept price dictates and other requests of suppliers enjoying a unique selling position. In most cases, one will have no other possibility than to put on a brave front. However, monopolists are only the symptoms of a disease originating from the internal breeding grounds of maverick buying and late involvement of the Purchasing department. Apart from sustained prevention by raising the awareness of all pertinent internal points of interface, monopolists must be taken on day by day.

At first, one must differentiate between ostensible, in the medium-term substitutable, and indispensable monopolists (see Fig. 4.8). In this context, one must find out, by targeted measures such as global procurement market research or the development of current suppliers, whether in theory competition can be created or whether there is a true monopoly situation.

If the latter has been proven true, it is vital to screen the monopolist thoroughly and to procure diverse information purposefully in order to make useful that gained knowledge of the supplier for negotiations with the aid of practical methods of analysis. It is true that those who can go without a deal have negotiation power, but

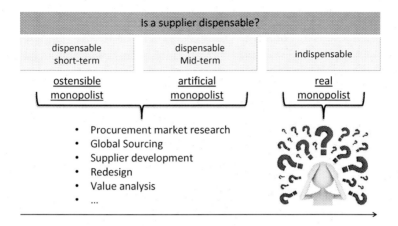

Fig. 4.8 Monopolists are often symptoms of Maverick-buying and late involvement

it is also true that knowledge is power. Furthermore, this knowledge will strengthen one's own position and self-confidence.

For that reason, the information gathering must not be limited to the company and its current situation and strategy but must rather also include the procurement objective and its cost drivers—which must be understood down to the last screw or to the last procedural detail—as well as the negotiation partner as a person. Investigative talents are needed to discover on whom the negotiation partner is reliant and what competences he or she has within the organisation. What are his/her aims; what does he/she already know about his/her client; and what especially is he/she interested in? In order to review company credit information, annual accounts, and credit rating, amongst others the use of public sources of information such as (in Germany) the *Bundesanzeiger* (similar to the Federal Register in the USA, or Companies House in the UK) as well as of fees-charging credit agencies such as Creditsafe or Bisnode is advised. Furthermore, internal data sources should definitely be used. Regular supplier evaluation as well as the detailed quality statistics will always provide starting points for criticism. In Germany, information on the supplier's pricing can be found in industry-specific publications and cost indices. Therefore, it is easy to derive a cost breakdown in order to calculate the product or service. With the aid of competitors' offers, one might even succeed in generating a price comparison. The knowledge obtained regarding unjustifiable pricing should be visualised and used during the negotiations. The high initial request is presented in a conciliatory manner to create moral pressure and the chance of eventually backing down without loss of face.

In support of this, offers and commercial samples may be obtained from potential competitors even if these are (yet) unable to supply for various reasons. The targeted dissemination of such information in the run-up to negotiations scattered by alleged "leaks" in one's own company can help to initiate a revision of the monopolist's opinion that allows for some concessions.

Making use of contacts is also very helpful in such situations. It won't do any harm to ally with like-minded purchasers who also suffer from the respective supplier's monopoly position in order to exchange and compare information and maybe even to develop a concerted course of action.

On the basis of the information gathered, an individual negotiation strategy now has to be developed, which is suitable for the specific type of monopolist. If and to what amount "dirty tricks" might be used is something which each participant has to decide for him/herself. To arouse pity or to deploy especially attractive persons as negotiators for pushing one's interests may prove successful but is not to everyone's taste.

Concluding a strategic partnership with the monopolist may also be a solution. But how can a monopolist be turned into a strategic partner?

This was the question I had to consider in the following situation: In a phase characterised by a booming economy, our company experienced extreme growth (sales doubling within 16 months) and capacity bottlenecks. The main supplier of a commodity group (and, of all things, the one with the highest growth) was not only a technological monopolist, he also belonged to the same enterprise group that we were a part of. For historical reasons, our growth forecasts were regarded with great suspicion because past expectations had failed to materialise. Despite repeated promises, investments that were absolutely necessary to cover our current and future demands were not made. Above all, there existed and still exist many interrelations between colleagues as that company once had originated from our own—a situation that does not make things easier for the purchaser! Therefore, the development of competitors was subverted by many areas in our company, and the supplier was always very well informed of the plans of Strategic Purchasing. So what could be done?

The old saying applied: "If you can't beat them, join them." This proved true and resulted in a strategy agreement between our company and that supplier. The main contents of that agreement were:

Monopolist Ltd.
Palace Avenue
9999 Marketless

in the following called "Monopolist".

Purchase commitment for a sales volume of an average of at least €420,000.00 per month, i.e. approx. €2.5 m per 6-month period; contractual penalty in the case of non-compliance.

Supply commitment of Monopolist for the supply of a sales volume conforming to the order of at least €480,000.00 per month (on average per 6-month period); contractual penalty in the case of non-compliance.

The sales guarantees are based on the current valid prices being agreed between the parties. Price changes will be based on a bull/bear clause. (Basis variable "Labour" (Ø 56%) and "Material" (Ø 29.4%). Should the aforementioned variables with respect to the preceding year change by more than 5% for "Labour" and/or more than 6% for "Material", prices will be adapted according to the share of the variables in the calculation.

The "Monopolist" accepts the client's Terms and Conditions of Purchase and its Quality Assurance Agreement.

The Parties agree to immediately form a joint purchasing pool, the main targets of which are volume aggregation and price optimisation. Apart from the Parties, the purchasing pool also includes the client's production facility in Timbuktu. The savings resulting from the volume aggregation will be shared according to the win–win principle. Biannually, strategic meetings will be conducted in order to discuss, amongst others, the following points:

- Redefinition of the mutual sales commitments
- Current state of agreed supplier development
- "hot" parts, i.e. parts that are critical with respect to price, quality, and/or volume.

With the agreement coming into effect, the distrust on both sides notably diminished. Both parties fulfilled their commitments, and already at the first purchasing pool meeting, a savings potential of €25,000 in the client's raw material procurement was identified and shared fairly according to profit and loss efficiency. But unfortunately that is not always the way things go. In cases where the methods do not promise success, the relationship with the supplier must be managed carefully. In such cases, purchasers turn into sellers and use their methods. Regular telephone calls at the representative's birthday, gifts at special occasions, and invitations to special events may help to build up the necessary sympathy.

And if all this does not help my message to monopolists (especially at the end of unsatisfactory negotiations) is always:

Purchasers are not vindictive but their memory is good.

4.6 Supplier Controlling

Apart from supplier selection, the results of the supplier evaluation are also used for supervising and controlling the suppliers over the course of time. In this context, the evaluation indices play an important role by allowing for a swift and clear performance assessment at regular intervals. In many cases, reliability and quality indices are applied, e.g.:

- Due date reliability
- Volumes reliability
- Proportion of incomplete deliveries
- Quota of complaints
- Costs of rework

- Proportion of deficient products
- Proportional frequency of misdirected deliveries
- Proportional frequency of incorrect deliveries

By regularly ascertaining these indices, supplier failures can be identified early in the trend path and the necessary countermeasures can be initiated.

Furthermore, the evaluation indices can easily be applied as actual figures in supplier development. To do so, target figures are fixed jointly with the supplier, and the supplier commits himself to reach them within a fixed time period (see Fig. 4.9). It is decisive for the successful implementation of this system that consequences, and also incentives, are given that take effect according to the respective degree of target accomplishment. By providing the basis for decision-making with regard to the application of incentive and sanction mechanisms, supplier controlling has a managing function too.

Supplier controlling also has the task of gathering and allocating information in order to aid future decisions on supplier selection as well as building up a supplier information system. Therefore, comprehensive information is provided for all future supplier evaluations and analyses.

4.7   Conclusion

Even at the supplier selection stage, my advice is to be primarily mindful of fit (willingness and conformity with the strategy) and only secondarily of skills and suitability. The latter has to be developed later with the aid of a development

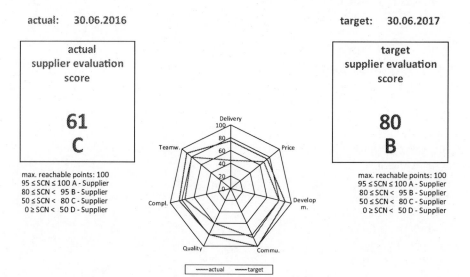

Fig. 4.9 Agreement for supplier development

agreement and regular evaluations. Greatest efforts should be invested in the supplier search stage. By all means, evaluations should be conducted regularly (biannually) and, at first, rigorously. This means that weaknesses are identified not only at the supplier but also in one's own house (which will often prove to be the more severe ones). One should not underestimate the fact that especially the top management of suppliers take evaluations very seriously and will probe the causes of any identified deviances. Therefore, it is important that the evaluators remain steadfast and single-minded. An additionally rewarding by-product is that nearly all evaluations will provide purchasers with ammunition for the "foundation" negotiation method and will furthermore be useful for complex enlargement. In my view, the Strategic Purchaser can be regarded internally as the supplier's advocate and externally as his legal guardian. Supplier management requires educational skills quite similar to those parents must command. And, as with children, there are not only "good" and "difficult" suppliers—the spectrum ranges from easy children (self-developing suppliers with good performance) to orphans (eluding Purchasing through maverick buying) and changelings (suppliers mandated by the executive board or the client). To minimise the risks for one's own company and to make the best possible and most effective contribution to its benefits, it is necessary to individually address, assess, and control the different types of "children" (see Practical Tip in Sect. 4.5).

Reference

DIN EN ISO 9001. (2008). *Qualitätsmanagementsysteme—Anforderungen (ISO 9001:2008)*. Berlin: Beuth.

Global Sourcing

5

5.1 Principles of Global Purchasing

Identifying and developing new procurement markets belongs to the core functions of Strategic Purchasers. In this context, "global sourcing" is one of the important catchphrases of our time. Generally, this term designates an internationally geared purchasing strategy and, subsequently, a globally optimised supply of products and services. Against the background of increased global interconnectedness of the economy and intensified competition, companies often have no choice but to look for the best partners for the satisfaction of their demands globally as in most cases the best suppliers will not be found on one's own doorstep. Domestic markets often are no longer competitive due to higher wage levels, especially in the area of labour-intensive and standardised products. But even high-tech products of high quality can nowadays be procured in foreign markets at reasonable prices. As material costs represent a considerable share of a company's total costs, globally oriented purchasing activities form an essential leverage for optimising the cost structure.

Companies can no longer focus on the domestic markets exclusively, not only for cost reasons but also from a technological point of view. In some industries, regional core competencies have formed over time. For example, Asiatic procurement markets command a tremendous advantage in knowledge in the electronics and computer industries as compared to the German market. There will be no alternative to developing foreign procurement markets in order to buy innovative products in this field, or even to engage in a development partnership.

A systematic and global design of the Purchasing function can thus be regarded as a major competitive advantage of one's own company.

The question of whether global sourcing should have significant importance in purchasing is a pointless one. As the opportunities are still greater than the risks, the essential question would rather be how and where purchasers should procure globally. From my own experience, I know that even today one realises savings with regard to the total cost of ownership (TCO); for example, in the tooling sector

© Springer International Publishing AG 2017
U. Weigel, M. Ruecker, *The Strategic Procurement Practice Guide*, Management for Professionals, DOI 10.1007/978-3-319-57651-0_5

savings of 60% are not uncommon, not to mention the incredibly short delivery times—especially for Europeans. Therefore, it can make sense sometimes to globally procure standard moulds for prototypes, and the development of a second source is also made easier. Direct savings even for components with high-quality requirements are daily fare. But exchange rate advantages and opportunities lying in a combination of local added value and rare or quoted raw materials may also create enormous competitive advantages. Another reason may be access to technologies that cannot yet or no longer (a consequence of global sourcing) be procured locally. The basis for the optimal exploitation of this potential creates the strategic foundations.

5.1.1   Aims of Global Sourcing

The fundamental purpose of purchasing—to safeguard the supply of necessary products and services at favourable total costs—is not changed by an international orientation of purchasing activities. What are changed are the framework conditions in which this target shall be fulfilled. In this respect, the following targets transcend the original purpose of purchasing.[1]

Global Competition On the one hand, global sourcing pursues the goal of generating cost savings by exploiting global competition potential, which can have a positive influence on the acquisition price due to lower factor costs such as wages, energy, or control costs in foreign markets. On the other hand, through global price benchmarking a higher degree of market transparency is realised, which will enable the enforcement of price reductions for domestic suppliers too. In this respect, global sourcing can also indirectly contribute to cost reduction.

Capable Suppliers The best suppliers will not always be found on one's own doorstep. An analysis of foreign procurement markets covers a greater number of providers, and new suppliers can be identified that may act at a higher level than domestic ones. Therefore, global sourcing aims at finding and making use of the best suppliers worldwide.

Innovative Technologies Today, the technological competence and level of innovation of suppliers can depend on their regional location. There are regions in which innovative technologies are further developed than in the domestic market. Some technologies do not yet exist or no longer exist at the local level. Therefore, another aim of global sourcing is to provide access to required technologies and innovations.

---

[1]Cf. Arnolds et al. (2010, p. 375 ff.).

Providing a Basis for One's Own Production Facilities If the establishment of a production facility in a foreign market is planned in the context of an internationally oriented business strategy, the prior identification and involvement of suitable suppliers can be beneficial. In this way, a supplier network can be created that will later supply the production facility.

Market Research Procurement market research conducted in the context of developing new procurement markets is cognate to sales market research, so synergy effects will occur. The collected data on markets, suppliers, moral concepts, and cultural peculiarities can offer starting points for developing new sales markets. Thus, the exploration of new sales markets can be regarded as a further objective of global sourcing.

Exchange Rate Risks Foreign currencies are always exposed to a risk of fluctuations that may bear positively or negatively on business results. If a company sells its products in different currency areas, it may aim at procuring in these areas too. Therefore, exchange rate fluctuations occurring in sales could be passed on to the suppliers.

Making Use of Government Subsidies In some countries, e.g. Mexico, corporations from the aviation and aerospace industries receive financial subsidies for the establishment of competence centres. Therefore, these potential suppliers can offer their services well below the market price level. Another example is subsidies for the production of steel in the Ukraine. Subject to a noteworthy proportion of added value, one can realise unbeatable prices for steel components there.

5.1.2 Strategies and Manifestations

The objectives of Purchasing, as derived from the strategy, are the basis for systematically identifying and developing global procurement markets. Strategic key motives in this context are:

- Long-term improvements of the cost structure
- Increasing product innovation
- Lacking alternatives in the home country or in-house manufacturing

Decisive factors will be established in the purchasing strategy through the choice of suitable commodity groups, procurement markets, and suppliers, which will define the international orientation of Purchasing. The range of parts suitable for global sourcing is selected as part of the commodity group strategy that has been described in Sect. 3.1. Often, labour-intensive as well as globally standardised products—the demands of which are highly predictable—are the most promising candidates. However, the higher the complexity and procurement risk of a product is, the more thoroughly the need for scrutiny of the adequacy of global sourcing. In this context, one must also take into consideration what influence the selected parts have on the function of the final product and how critical these parts are with respect to know-how.

Simultaneously, the range of countries from which the items could be procured are evaluated. In the case of simple and standardised products, the focus will be on low-wage countries, and the aim will be to realise cost advantages. But one must not forget that it is not the net purchase price but rather the total costs which have to be considered. However, regional technological competences will determine the selection of the procurement country when it comes to high-quality, complex, or innovative products. Over the years, particular regions have experienced technological specialisation and thus secured competitive advantages over other regions. In this context, the types and numbers of suppliers must be determined as part of the supplier strategy. Entering a new procurement market is often a very risky affair so it is advisable to first develop potential suppliers in a dual or multiple sourcing strategy and then to establish a long-term partnership later in the context of supplier management.

Depending on the objectives pursued, several approaches for implementing a global purchasing strategy have been developed. For example, the concept of low-cost country sourcing aims at buying a high share of the external added value in low-cost countries in order to realise the highest possible cost savings. Low-cost countries in this sense are offered extremely low wage levels compared to the domestic procurement market.

The concept of best-cost country sourcing goes a step further as here the total costs are considered. Apart from the price and wage levels, material and transport costs as well as quality and risk aspects are assessed.

Another manifestation of global sourcing is "offshoring" which means that business functions or processes are relocated to another region. This can be done by relocation inside the corporation or by shifting these activities to independent external companies in foreign countries.

Practical Tip: Globally Oriented Purchasing Strategy
The foundations for company-specific optimum concerns must already be laid during the strategy development stage. The current results and forecasts of procurement market research will help to position the commodity group globally at the right place or, more concretely, to answer the question of which parts of a commodity group should be strategically procured at what place with regard to risk and TCO. Subsequently, the parts must be differentiated according to their volume and complexity in order to place the right parts at right supplier. Flanked by supplier development, the demands on the global partner increase continuously; in ideal cases, they will develop from a parts supplier to a system supplier. This effect in turn assists in the objective of reducing the number of suppliers. The goal has been achieved when such a global cost leader will have become a preferred supplier that is also involved in the development of new products early at the innovation stage and participates in designing them cost-efficiently.

To orient the purchasing organisation on global requirements strategically and operationally and where local native speakers are available, to have them lead is also a significant challenge. To cope with these challenges, Strategic Purchasing must be able to manage, and even to lead, on a global level while it must also become more technical. The latter can be achieved by training staff who only have experience only in commercial aspects or by complementing the purchasing teams with technicians or engineers. Furthermore, the members of the team have to be trained interculturally, e.g. by learning the language of the foreign partners. In my case, the knowledge of Chinese and Italian that I had acquired painfully many years ago in evening schools proved very useful as a "door opener" both in the "Middle Kingdom" and in "Bella Italia"—so I can only warmly recommend learning the language of the partner. It is imperative that all the measures mentioned should be part of a globally oriented purchasing strategy.

5.1.3   New Risks at the International Level

Internationally oriented purchasing activities offer companies enormous chances for optimising their supply of products and services. However, there are also a number of risks that have to be taken into account—risks that on the domestic level up to now have hardly been important or have been quite unknown. Issues such as language barriers, import duties, and exchange rate fluctuations have a major influence on the framework conditions of the decision-making process. Due to the spatial distances and the cultural, legal, and political diversity in procurement markets, the purchasing process becomes much more complex than before. However, through comprehensive procurement market research the following risks can largely be identified and controlled:

Cultural Risks These risks occur when there are greater differences between the procurement and the domestic markets on a cultural level. These risks include all factors such as language, mentality, or legal understanding that may hamper communication and understanding between supplier and client.

Political Risks The political framework conditions of the procurement country may eventually pose risks, especially when largely unpredictable occurrences occur that are influenced by the respective rulers, and may restrict trade activities. These risks encompass statutes and regulations such as import and export controls, fluctuating rates of duty, as well as safety regulations or environmental standards. On the other hand, events such as strikes, social unrest, or wars will massively put the security of supply in jeopardy.

Economic Risks These are risks caused by macroeconomic processes. Especially important in this respect are cyclical fluctuations, fiscal exchange rate fluctuations, fluctuations of raw material prices, and high public debts.

Risk of Natural Disasters From a macroeconomic point of view, the impacts of natural disasters are increasingly exceeding the risks mentioned above. The statistical surveys of damages from disasters such as earthquakes, floods, or storms show a clear upward trend. Especially in densely populated areas, such events may have massive repercussions that may be felt all over the world due to globally interconnected supply chains.

To handle these generally region-specific risks in a professional manner, information from business and rating agencies should be used. In country risk reports, these agencies inform about the attractiveness of the respective countries with regard to investments and on the risks with regard to credit allocations. In these reports, information, amongst others, on the economic and political stability of countries that could be used for developing new procurement markets is compiled. Apart from such country-specific risks in general, there are also supplier-specific risks that could be subdivided into risks caused by their performance and by their rules of conduct.[2]

Performance risks Encompass all aspects that might lead to unfavourable results due to the supplier's performance, especially price, quality, and deadline risks.

Conduct risks As result from the supplier's behaviour, especially in the international field, one will often have difficulties to assess the conduct of suppliers in advance as normally the amount of reliable information and experience will be insufficient. For example, prior to the commissioning, promises and undertakings might be given which will afterwards prove to be unrealistic.

In order to scrutinise both risk areas, further information on potential suppliers should be gathered. Several methods (detailed in Chap. 4) such as obtaining supplier self-assessments or reviewing company reports are suitable for this purpose.

Practical Tip: Natural Disasters—Approaches to Crisis Management
Global purchasing involves a lot of risks one should always be aware of. Inconstant quality, corruption, bureaucracy, exchange rate risks, different cultures, different mentalities and customs, impending environmental disasters in ever-increasing numbers, and patent and industrial property right infringements are just some examples of risks modern purchasers must cope with.

As an example, the natural and nuclear catastrophe in Fukushima directly affected my procurement volume, which encompassed 28 suppliers at that time. It is inconceivable to imagine what such a catastrophe would have meant for our supply chain in a country other than Japan. But thanks to their outstanding fighting spirit, the Japanese suppliers managed to compensate for the consequences in amazingly short time. In the following I would like to give a short description of our line of action in that situation and what we have learned from it:

Initiated by the executive board, a crisis management group consisting of representatives of the Sales, Marketing, Logistics, and Purchasing departments

---

[2]Cf. Arnolds et al. (2010, p. 372 ff.).

convened daily. The main task that had to be tackled first consisted of assessing the supplier shortfalls and their repercussions on production. At first, roughly 500 active orders for more than 280 individual articles seemed to be affected. As difficult as the situation was, we had to stay calm and show authority. After intense discussion with our 28 suppliers, the number of affected orders could be reduced to "only" 39 for 10 different articles of which luckily we had some stocks. At the same time, the internal and external information flow was perfectly aligned. While the marketing communication exuded authority and composure, the Sales department looked for possibilities for compensating the looming revenue loss with the help of best-case and worst-case scenarios. Production readjusted its planning while Purchasing invested all its energy into developing new solutions. With joint forces—the affected suppliers were especially helpful—we succeeded in working out a great number of partly unusual measures. By substitutions, by modifications of old revision states, and by dismantling non-sellers in order to retrieve urgently necessary components, we were able to more than compensate for the lost revenues that had occurred in the first weeks following the disaster.

5.2   China as an Example of Global Sourcing

Wisdom may be learnt in three ways: By reflection, which is the noblest way; by imitation, which is the easiest way; and by experience, which is the bitterest way (Confucius, 551–479 BCE).

In the last 30 years, no other country has experienced such high economic growth as the People's Republic of China. Thanks to low labour and production costs, massive labour potential, and easy access to important raw materials, China has achieved average growth rates of 10% and has taken the economic world by storm. China has thus become a political and economic world power, and its development strategy is ranked among the most successful in the world, for China not only produces goods cheaper but in ever-increasing cases better too. Thus, the economic upstart still attracts 70–80% of all foreign investments in Asia. As Japan increasingly shows signs of cyclical weakness, its neighbours in Asia look ever more to China.

In the context of global sourcing, one will sooner or later inevitably come across China. The times when only textiles and toys were produced there are long over; China is nowadays becoming the home country of ever more highly innovative products. Due to rising education levels, China in some areas has reached considerable know-how advantages over Germany, especially in the electronics industry. At the same time, procuring in China poses considerable challenges to Purchasing since the Chinese market is more short-lived and dynamic than any other. Additional problems are the widespread lack of transparency in the Chinese procurement markets and a different understanding of quality. In the following, China as an extreme example is chosen for demonstrating the opportunities and risks of global sourcing and the design of efficient approaches with respect to it. It will soon become clear that global sourcing can be a rather time-consuming process that will need a systematic strategy. The approach described below will initially confine itself to China but runs like a thread through global procurement in other regions of the world too. Apart from cultural peculiarities, the methods and approaches for developing new procurement markets are the same anywhere.

5.2.1   Incentives and Problems with Regard to Sourcing in China

Thanks to its massive dimensions, the Chinese market offers a number of opportunities for international companies. Even small market niches reach extremely high volumes thanks to strong growth forces. A group of people equivalent in number to Germany's entire population would be a mere marginal target group in China. So China has become an important pillar of global competition as a sales market as well as a production location.

Generally, China offers the following opportunities for global purchasing:

- An increasingly developed and multifaceted supplier base; in some fields also a highly developed concentration of complementary suppliers
- A low-cost, well-trained labour force potentially bringing advantages for production but also for research and development
- Cost-saving production facilities and equipment
- Numerous incentives by the central government as well as by regional authorities

However, despite all these positive developments there are also a lot of risks in the "Middle Kingdom". Low wage levels especially often come with a lack of quality awareness. The European approach to quality is only slowly gaining ground in China and in many cases still does not meet European standards even in state-of-the-art facilities. Furthermore, Chinese companies are very interested in their clients' know-how and want to use it for developing their own products. Not without good reason China is often seen as a nation in which imitation is a well-grounded tradition.

Personal relationships have a clear bearing on business with the Chinese. Therefore, it is vital to take cultural peculiarities into consideration to avoid unpleasant surprises.

As the market is still rather confusing, there is no sure formula for entering the Chinese market. In any case, the following risks should always be noted and understood clearly:

- Cultural differences and different norms in business life
- Lack of transparency in the Chinese supplier market
- Enforcement of international copyright, patent, and property rights
- Supplier development targeted at implementing Western business processes; compliance with Western quality standards

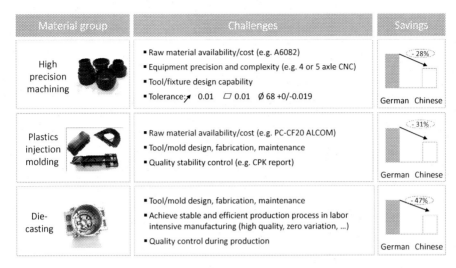

Material group	Challenges	Savings
High precision machining	• Raw material availability/cost (e.g. A6082) • Equipment precision and complexity (e.g. 4 or 5 axle CNC) • Tool/fixture design capability • Tolerance: 0.01 0.01 $\varnothing$ 68 +0/-0.019	-28% German Chinese
Plastics injection molding	• Raw material availability/cost (e.g. PC-CF20 ALCOM) • Tool/mold design, fabrication, maintenance • Quality stability control (e.g. CPK report)	-31% German Chinese
Die-casting	• Tool/mold design, fabrication, maintenance • Achieve stable and efficient production process in labor intensive manufacturing (high quality, zero variation, ...) • Quality control during production	-47% German Chinese

Fig. 5.1 Substantial cost savings achieved for different materials 1/2

Material group	Challenges	Savings
Special wires	• Extremely thin wires used for interior applications • High requirements for durability (bending) and insulation (salt water spray test, pin hole after aging, ...) • Security relevant, broken wires can inflame other interior parts	-27% German Chinese
Micro motor	• Application requires small motor • Stall torque of at least 3 Nm, most suppliers can only achieve 2.5 Nm • High quality planetary gear to achieve low noise level of 35 dBA	-25% German Chinese
Thermostat	• Part used in automotive interior • High requirements on lifetime, small tolerances for switching temperature and sealing (dust, salt water spray test) • Security relevant	-31% German Chinese

Fig. 5.2 Substantial cost savings achieved for different materials 2/2

- Complex supplier incentives going beyond regions and functions
- Management risks with regard to extended supply chains

Figures 5.1 and 5.2 illustrate the opportunities from sourcing in China (with due respect to the risks) as these figures show how high the substantial savings may be when the production of particular parts is moved to China.

This statement points out the potential of extending one's purchasing activities to the whole world. Provided the right approach is taken, global sourcing may even be used for high-quality bought-in parts. How such an approach can be designed will be shown in the following pages.

5.2.2   Sourcing in China: Development Stages

To realise successful and enduring purchasing in Chinese markets is a long-term procedure that requires a systematic, structured course of action. Those who only want to make a "fast buck" and engage in global sourcing only perfunctorily will inevitably fail. The activities concerning sourcing in China may be subdivided into four stages respective to the maturity levels of cooperation with Chinese suppliers:

Stage 1: Testing
- Establishment of a Procurement office in China
- Pilot schemes
- Development of internal and external processes
- Generate results
- Growing amount of purchases

Stage 2: Early Engagement
- Expansion by multiple-sourcing waves
- Understanding the dynamics in the Chinese supplier market
- Fine-tuning of the processes
- Extension of competences (e.g. supplier qualification and development)
- Tackling the question of industrial property rights

Stage 3: Full Integration
- Integration of Procurement in China within the company's worldwide procurement activities
- Involving the Chinese suppliers in the design stage
- Involving Chinese R&D in the design stage
- Integration of China in the extended worldwide supply chain

Stage 4: China as a Centre
- Understanding China as a vital supply base
- Shifting some Procurement functions to China
- Making Chinese suppliers integral parts of the company's product development system

Practical Tip: Establishing a Procurement Office in China
Even for medium-sized enterprises, the establishment of a Procurement office can be worthwhile. This will of course depend on the quality of the local staff. I was lucky enough to recruit a highly qualified Chinese assistant who had previously worked for a German consulting firm. Thanks to her local knowledge and global experience, I succeeded in establishing an affordable office in the best location from a strategic view (Shanghai) in a simple and uncomplicated way and without

involving external consultants. This office was initially staffed with one further employee who as the technical point of interface conducted the quality assurance measures at the local suppliers. In the long run, the office should be extended by recruiting "low-cost employees" as we plan to offer our experience with sourcing in China as a service to other companies, with the highest quality standards.

The following ten points should be considered when deciding on one's own office and the suitable course of action to establish it:

1. Identification of commodity groups and A parts with high wage proportions
2. Surveying procurement opportunities for the respective commodity groups by market tests and subsequent visits to the suppliers
3. Selection of parts that have sufficient residual terms or will be replaced by similar products
4. Selection of a strategically suitable location geographically close to the most important potential suppliers
5. Clarification of legal and fiscal questions (parent company, process of company foundation, capital stock, taxes, etc.)
6. Selection of the optimum legal form for purchasing in China (if the company also intends to sell in China or even to produce on its own there, this should also be taken into consideration when it comes to selecting the adequate legal form)
7. Development of a detailed business plan extending to several years (potential, cost, investment demands, etc.)
8. Definition of the important processes/interfaces between the headquarters and the Procurement office in China (business, technical, and quality processes)
9. Establishment and administration of a network in order to optimise the cooperation across geographical and departmental borders
10. Recruiting the right staff and especially the right leading manager (who should, by the way, be paid according to European standards); the team should command sourcing experience as well as company-specific technical knowledge

An essential key to success in China is guiding the local staff. The region-specific differences with Western Europe must of course be considered in every country and start, as everywhere, with the wages. In China, a graduate's starting salary will be roughly 3000 RMB per month, but after 2 years he or she will expect 5000–10,000 RMB on average. As a rule, there are 20 days annual leave, and 13 months salaries are paid. Furthermore, there is a variable share option corresponding to roughly 30% of the fixed salary. Salaries should be reviewed twice per year and—provided adequate performance—represent 5–10% p.a. The first labour contract should be limited to 3 years and include a probationary period of 6 months; subsequently an unlimited contract should follow. Due to above-average labour turnover, it is advisable to provide contractual penalties for quitting. These penalties may include training and education costs, flights and accommodation costs that have occurred with respect to these, as well as the variable proportion of the salary. It is also advisable to include a non-competition clause with a contractual penalty of 1 year's salary. When strategy and guidance are working well, one will normally not face situations where this regulation will apply.

Conclusion From my own experience, I would always advise to either engage with full commitment in a local Procurement office or to renounce the idea completely. Our Purchasing office, for that matter, paid off. After only 2 years, savings and, most importantly, avoided costs (as compared to tooling costs and prices of the previous supply sources) of 942,000 EUR p.a. stood out against annual costs of only 188,000 EUR.

5.2.3   Implementation

Starting with a global purchasing strategy, the full support of top management as well as the deployment of interdisciplinary teams for preparation and implementation are essential factors for successful purchasing activities in China. In order to safeguard the structured use of the different purchasing instruments, a methodical course of action must be chosen. In the following sections, a logical course shall be detailed.

5.2.3.1 Identification of Suitable Products

Within the framework of a demand analysis, a structured examination takes place, identifying the range of purchased items for materials that are suitable for sourcing in China. Especially at the beginning, the focus should be on products of high value volumes in order to justify the associated staff and financial input through potential cost savings. Provided that suitable market knowledge is available, it will often be possible to estimate the possible savings in advance.

In order to conduct an effective feasibility study on the eligible materials, the risks must be made clear. Parts of high complexity require an especially high level of supplier development and are therefore unsuitable for the initial stage of sourcing activities in China. But even with regard to supposedly easy objects, a certain time span between the requirement and the production release must be planned.

For that reason, products that have longer lifespans are to be preferred. To identify suitable objects, an evaluation form (see an example in Fig. 5.3) can be used.

5.2.3.2 Feasibility Studies and Market Tests

Once the suitable objects for purchasing in China have been selected, the next stage will be to review the supplier market as well as the procurement possibilities. The following steps should be taken in chronological order to identify suppliers with good performance and high savings potential.

1. *Identify local suppliers*: The worldwide identification of suppliers is facilitated by many supplier directories in the Internet; the difficulty is to filter out the few suppliers meeting the technical requirements.

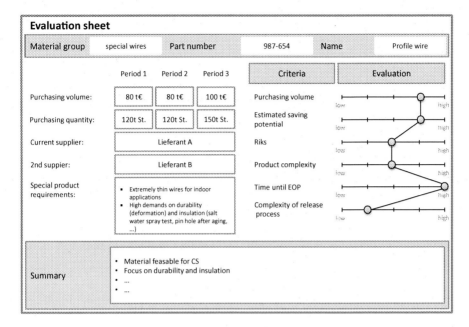

Fig. 5.3 Evaluation of a specific material

2. *Checking the supplier's background*: Apart from its technical capacities, the background of the supplier should also be checked e.g. by credit agency reports, reference customers, or visits to the supplier.
3. *Making the requirements understood and safeguarding mutual understanding*: All documents necessary for the interaction with the supplier (e.g. bid forms, terms and conditions of business, drawings, specifications, and standards) should always be available in impeccable, easily understandable English. It is absolutely imperative that all participants are open and willing to engage with suppliers with a different culture.
4. *Sending and tracking enquiries*: Chinese corporations act in a domestic market that grows by a high two-digit percentage annually. In order to attract the interest of potential Chinese suppliers, attractive volumes or a brand name that fires their imagination will be necessary. As Chinese suppliers are overwhelmed every day by enquiries from Europe and the USA, one must find a way to stand out from the crowd. A good way to start is providing the documents in Mandarin Chinese, followed up by telephone calls by a member of staff who is a native speaker of Chinese.
5. *Assessing the plausibility of the data and discussing them with the suppliers*: As soon as the first offers have been received, an intense negotiation process starts. Normally, the first offers from China will not be very different from the European price level. From a Western perspective, China is seen as a low-cost country, while China thinks that selling to Europe at the European price level is most appropriate.

6. *Selection of suppliers according to price and other criteria*: To choose the optimum supplier, the benefit analysis (described in Sect. 4.3.3) may be used for weighting and evaluating the degree to which several, previously defined criteria have been fulfilled with the help of a points system.

7. *Calculation of possible savings*: To calculate possible savings, one must always review the total costs. Apart from the offer prices, additional costs such as delivery costs and import taxes must also be taken into account.

After a price level has been found that is acceptable for both parties, the top management should visit China. The Chinese suppliers want to meet their clients in person. Establishing trusted and resilient personal relationships will be important in order to overcome future obstacles.

Practical Tip: Supplier Search in Another Way
The search for the optimum supplier can be conducted as described above. But there is also the typical Chinese way. Blessed are they who cultivate their partners and business contacts regularly!

The background: During my time in the aviation industry, I met an A supplier from a tiny neighbouring country in Western Europe. As a monopolist, he supplied high-technology material specified by the airlines. This semi-finished product is still an essential component of the structures of the supplied systems. But the general manager of the supplier exploited his monopoly and the powerlessness of his clients to such an extent that during the previous 4 years price increases of 28% in total had been dictated without any justifiable cost changes. All my predecessors, external consultants, and several managing directors had, after a first-class lunch or dinner, come home from their journeys with new price increases.

I did not want to end that way, so my team and I prepared a globally usable enquiry with sample patterns and sent it to a Chinese friend asking: "Chunwen, I need your help."

At first, neither he nor his team had a clue about this labour-intensive material. But he knew what had to be done. His network that was distributed across China went for a search of potential suppliers. He visited all of those that seemed interested enough. Within 3 weeks, I had received the data of these companies and offers of six suppliers. Subsequently, I visited those suppliers, and at the end of my journey two of these suppliers were commissioned with providing samples. One of these suppliers then played the role of our secondary source representing a price advantage of 25%. The former monopolist was warned of the fact via consciously and deliberately placed information, and the gratuitous price advances had come to an end.

5.2.3.3 Supplier Evaluation
The aim of supplier evaluation is to identify and assess possible problems occurring in structures and processes. In that context, one's attention should focus on production processes, quality standards, and upstream supply chains, the maturity level of which can be ascertained by the following general course of action:

- Assessing the strong points, weaknesses, and risks: Process analysis and Process Failure Mode Effects Analysis (PFMEA)
- Evaluating processes: Comparing the actual processes to the common and optimal courses of action in Western companies; determining the level of supplier support
- Giving priority to certain findings: Which questions are vital with regard to product quality and supply reliability?
- Defining projects: Specifying the projects for each issue/group of issues (targets, deadlines, function of the parties involved, etc.)

The Readiness Rollup, which will be introduced in Chap. 6, may be used in order to assess whether the existing structures will meet the requirements or which changes will have to be implemented.

5.2.3.4 Supplier Development

The aim of supplier development is to realise the required quality and logistics targets with regard to the start of series production and subsequently of optimising costs and performance. In this context, the Chinese supplier should be supported and actively encouraged. In so doing, a number of demanding tasks must be implemented and managed. For example, comprehensive technical knowledge is a prerequisite for solving emerging problems. Implementation and management can happen on several levels:

- Technical planning: Adaption of material specifications, identifying alternative raw materials, advice with respect to tool design
- Purchasing: Evaluation of sub-suppliers, volume aggregation
- Production: Support with respect to process optimisation and selection of equipment
- Quality: Implementation of quality reports; support with regard to the introduction of a quality assurance system
- Logistics: Development of a packaging concept; development of new logistic processes

If a company wants to operate in China for a longer time, there will be no other way than establishing a local Purchasing office. Somebody must see to it locally that the Chinese supplier will meet the required quality standards. In the first months after the production launch, they will have to be on-site almost daily; later on, weekly visits may suffice.

Practical Tip

I should never have imagined it possible that one day I would teach 20 Chinese colleagues the fundamentals of Quality Assurance. But let me tell you the events in sequence. As the person in charge of the supply chain at that time, I was also responsible for ensuring that the deliveries for a major order by a German coffee roaster met all quality and scheduling standards. Some years ago, the product in question had still been manufactured in Germany, but then the production had been discontinued due to unprofitability. Thanks to the cost advantages in China, the management costs became lucrative again, and so this deal was closed. The article, a mobile folding table, was technically and optically demanding and naturally had to fulfil the strict incoming goods inspection criteria of a client who was known for hard sanctions in cases of non-fulfilment of quality requirements and deadlines. Prior to the production launch, I personally explained to the Chinese staff on-site the technical and quality requirements and how their fulfilment should be tested. With regard to the deadline, we had already been behind schedule. And then, immediately after my return to Germany and late at night, I received bad news from my long-term Chinese business friend Alvey: "We have a problem. The mould for the big plastic part is broken and it is not possible to repair it."

That was a real catastrophe, for tools of that size have an average delivery time of 4–6 weeks. But that does not necessary apply when one has friends in China. During our call, we decided that a new tool should be built promptly. Believe it or not, after only 4 days the new injection mould delivered flawless parts. The deficit was quickly made up, and the delivery to the German centre of distribution was carried out at the last possible moment. I had the foresight to be present at the incoming goods inspection. And here, once again selling talents were required, for here, as always, human beings decided on the interpretation of the strict AQL sampling guidelines (with the help of charts this method, which was devised by the US Army during the Second World War, determines up to which number of defective products a charge can be accepted and from which number on it will be rejected).

This example clearly shows how much the occupational profile of Strategic Purchasers has developed from a mere Procurement operator to an all-rounder who must also command technical know-how.

5.2.4   In-house Resistance

There are a number of hurdles that must be overcome in order to purchase successfully in China (and all other procurement regions as well). The first and decisive one is to be found within the company itself—the overcoming of internal resistance. The end users have to be convinced of the validity of the Chinese offers, and one will need some ingenuity to achieve this. Typical problems arising from internal resistance are:

- *Recognising potential*: No clear terms of reference and no clear targets with respect to the question of whether procuring in China is suitable
- *Supplier sourcing*: Unrealistic expectations: "The Chinese supplier should perform as well as the expiring one"
- *Supplier qualification*: No resources available

- *Sample qualification*: Non-availability of resources, poor communication, and long qualification processes
- *New orders*: Other departments do not go along; old contracts are renewed; stocks are built up

Practical Tip: How to Overcome Internal Resistance

For years studies have shown that in-house resistance is the highest hurdle when it comes to global sourcing. This situation is further complicated by the fact that in most cases resulting conflicts will not be waged openly by the "opponents" but rather behind one's back. How can this situation be handled?

When the decision for sourcing globally has been made, one must not start half-heartedly for there have been good reasons for the decision. These reasons alone provide the best arguments at first. In the next step, the persons involved in the process have to be convinced by meeting demanding quality and delivery reliability targets. The savings and cost avoidances especially will always be welcome though hardly anyone, including CEOs, likes to know that these gains have been realised by procuring in low-cost countries. From my experience, it has proven successful to estimate the potential staff costs per year, which means workplaces, thereby demonstrating that the majority of jobs will be secured by such a proceeding. This is a language work councils and less well-informed employees of the company—which quite naturally will be opponents to sourcing globally—understand very well. Therefore, it is advisable to purposefully keep those people sufficiently informed. Even more effective, however, is to involve them as far as possible in the decision-making or even let them take part on a journey to the international partner. From then on, everything will go swimmingly, and the project will have become a joint one.

5.3 Compliance

The term "compliance" in this context means compliance with laws and regulations and the adherence to self-imposed ethical standards. The right conduct with regard to compliance is becoming ever more important, especially in the entrepreneurial context; in cases of misconduct, the persons involved may face severe penalties or even imprisonment, and the company may hit the headlines and suffer massive damage to its image. For that reason, rules of compliance regarding corruption, child labour, discrimination, and occupational health and safety are often determined company wide.

In this context, purchasers are especially at risk because they are responsible for the biggest part of the operating expenses which will inevitably arouse the desire of suppliers. The danger is further complicated in the context of internationally oriented purchasing activities since regulations concerning, for example, data privacy, corruption, or the proper proceedings with regard to criminal offences in other parts of the world may differ from the regulations from country to country. Cultivating personal relationships is an important part of successful deals, especially in Asiatic cultures. Therefore, gifts, invitations to expensive dinners, or favours to relatives are in no way exceptional there. However, from the view of the Western business world such conduct may quickly convey the impression of corruption. Against this background, purchasers must be prepared to handle such situations. And they must be given clear guidelines; otherwise they will have to decide on their own what conduct is ethical and justifiable and which is not.

Practical Tip

When it comes to global sourcing, many a "compliance guardian" will have difficulties. Normally, overall guidelines and clearly defined limits will provide certainty; however, they cannot be assumed to be globally valid conditions. While some purchasers who want a good dinner will no longer feel free in their decisions, others will still be able to decide independently after having enjoyed much more substantial amenities. In Germany for example it will be objectionable to invite a supplier to dinner. However, rejecting such an invitation in France, Italy, or Spain will damage the business relationship and therefore one's own company. Where then should the line be drawn?

The solution would possibly be a globally applicable compliance rule that would have to be worked out with the help of an internationally experienced purchaser. However, I have not yet come upon such a regulation, let alone a globally applicable one. In China, trust will be gained and the last Yuan earned only after it looks as if a bomb has hit the scene of a bibulous dinner. In this context, it is certainly no disadvantage that Europeans are genetically predisposed for tolerating higher quantities of alcohol than their Chinese business partners. While all this from my point of view has nothing to do with corruption, one critical point should always be taken into account: the stage at which the deal is made. At the pre-contract stage, an invitation to a VIP lounge would be quite questionable in Germany. On the other hand, at the end of a successful deal I do not see any problems with such an invitation. However, I have also had to confront some other "offers" in my business life—from a surfboard to several VIP lounge invitations at high-class football matches in Germany and abroad, to cost-free holiday trips with my family to Crete, to a surprise gift in the form of a slinky woman unknown to me who came to my room during my visit to a supplier in Greece. These are only some examples of "opportunities" offered to purchasers. More than 20 years ago I adopted a very simple rule for incidents of this kind that I observe down to the present day:

> Behave in a way that you can break up with a supplier at any time!

By the way, with the incident mentioned above, the Greek aluminium supplier had delivered his last gram (the previous sales volume had been roughly 4 m DM/year). For another commandment says: Do not lead us into temptation.

5.4   Protection of Know-How

Apart from compliance, the protection of know-how is becoming a major issue in the context of global sourcing. Prior to the transfer of knowledge, some fundamental rules should be observed:

- The notation that documents have to be treated as confidential should always be applied to them.
- Complete plans should never be handed over.
- Local purchases should be distributed between several suppliers.
- Take care when engaging translators or translation agencies.
- Non-disclosure agreements should be concluded.
- The personnel should be trained and sensitised.
- Trademark and industrial property rights should always be registered in the country in which the product is procured, even if there is no intention to sell those products there.
- If a comprehensive know-how transfer becomes necessary, exclusivity and licensing fees should be arranged if possible.

To enforce industrial property rights successfully, one must command comprehensive knowledge of the local conditions. Experience shows that trademark pirates and fakers are brought down regularly.

Practical Tip
More than 10 years ago, I regularly visited the largest consumer goods fair in Hong Kong (which today is held in Guangzhou). One day my mobile phone rang suddenly. Our sales manager had an urgent request: "We need a waste bin similar to our Veneto (trade name changed) for our client X. The product should have the same dimensions as the original but it should be made of plastics and not of stainless steel." That request, by the way, represents a common mistake in global sourcing and is also good example of how "detailed" specifications used to be in those days in global procurement in this industry—a major source of mistakes. But consumer oriented as my training had been, the task appealed to me and in good spirits I started the search for a suitable supplier that would be able to supply the requested article. One hour later, I could not believe my eyes—an exhibitor from Thailand presented exactly the model I was searching for. And he offered it in several sizes and made of plastic just as our customer had requested it. Apart from the material, it was an exact copy of our top waste bin. I approached the exhibitor and asked for the price and whether the article would also be exported to Germany. No, unfortunately, export to Germany would be impossible because of legal problems. "Your problem is standing right before you", I explained and disclosed my identity as the procurement manager of the German brand manufacturer whose property the Thai company had copied.

An old saying is: "If you cannot beat them, join them". Due to our half-hearted protection policy with regard to products and know-how (the second cardinal error), we had no legal leverage. And so after the usual price haggling we soon came to an agreement. We quickly forgot our wounded pride of having been copied in view of unnecessary investments, the low price, and the quick availability of the products.—This also is global sourcing!

5.5   Cultural Peculiarities

Cultural barriers are a major hurdle when it comes to procurement in international markets. Only when the different cultures get closer will intense cooperation with foreign partners become possible. How the conventions and manners of other cultures are interpreted will always depend on one's own culture. Their correct understanding is more important than attempts to imitate them. Some cultural differences are represented in Figs. 5.4 and 5.5.

Practical Tip: Dealings with Asian Cultures
Of course, there are many Asian cultures that cannot be equated with each other. Although I could tell some stories of my experiences with business partners from India that unfortunately have not been so positive, I shall in the following confine myself to Japan, South Korea, and China.

In Japan, discipline and above all punctuality are considered very important. Business people with no Japan-specific experience will need to get used to the extremely long lines of authority (nemawashi) of the Japanese decision-making process. But once the decisions have been made, one can relax since they will be fastidiously implemented.

Spontaneity is frowned upon, especially in meetings. The Japanese like to be informed of the arguments in advance, so it is better to present them clearly and

Criteria	China	Germany	USA	Japan
Communication	• Shy and quiet • Humble • Think and may not speak • Wait until asked to speak	• Thoughtful • Politely directive • Think before speaking • Speak up as needed	• Out going • Aggressive • Speak while thinking • Speak up	• Understated, Modest, Harmonious • Think and do not speak • Wait until asked to speak • Shy because of English language skills • Fluent if spoken in Japanese • Internal coordination before commitments • Bad news subsequently in a personal conversation
Attitude towards authority	• Submission	• Question an probe	• Challenge • Push back	• Submission • Internal decisions higher priority than authority

Fig. 5.4 Local cultures and values 1/2

Criteria	China	Germany	USA	Japan
Decision execution	• More or less as agreed insofar as it has been understood	• Do as planned	• Do as it takes	• Do as said • Decisions only after internal consultation
Attitude towards change	• Only if unavoidable	• Change as planned	• Change whenever needed • Immediately after approval	• Continuous improvement • If there is already such a case in the past, then change • If not, continue as before
Creativity	• Not always by rules	• Think logically	• Think out of box	• Flexible • Copy and innovate • New ideas only if adopted in consensus
Legal form	• Code of law	• Code of law	• Code of law & jurisdiction	• Code of law

Fig. 5.5 Local cultures and values 2/2

understandably in advance and in writing. One should refrain from giving personal feedback, even a positive one, since the individual may not stand out from his group. The talks are followed by comprehensive minutes and records.

These are only some aspects of established opinion with which my team and I became acquainted during training programmes and in the field regarding to the Japanese business world. Nevertheless, I have made several mistakes over the years. I will never forget that one day I invited a top manager of a renowned Japanese corporation to an outing in my car. I asked him to take the seat beside me; his assistants had to squash into the back seats of my two-door car. Only later I learned that the appropriate place of the highest-ranking officer of the Japanese delegation would have been the seat behind the driver while the lowest-ranking assistant should have taken the seat beside the driver.

In my view, however, the times in which one has to strictly adapt to culture-specific manners are drawing to an end. Nowadays, Japanese business partners understand European business practices and will normally excuse if some of the age-old rules are being violated involuntarily.

Despite some similarities—e.g. that no one should stand out from a group either positively nor negatively—China has its own specific peculiarities. Chinese schoolchildren learn the 36 stratagems (Chinese: Pinyin: *sanshiliu ji*), a compilation attributed to the Chinese general Tan Daoji († 436).

But what does this have to do with global sourcing? The answer is easy enough: These stratagems are still used even if in modified form. I experienced the use of some of them in the field. To give some examples:

Stratagem No. 4 *Wait at leisure while the enemy labours*

In the first years of my visits to China, the journey took more than 24 h until I had finally arrived—though not as an enemy—at the local supplier. In these cases, the host had a clear advantage, and I needed good stamina in order to keep my objectives in view (in which I did not always succeeded) and to avoid gradually dozing off.

Stratagem No. 10 *Hide a knife behind a smile*

By painful experience, I had to learn that a smile in Asia does not mean the same as in Europe.

Stratagem No. 16 *In order to capture, one must let loose*

A nice stratagem that can be applied very usefully to negotiations—at first, do not show special interest in the things you really want to press home!

Stratagem No. 28 *Remove the ladder when the enemy has climbed onto the roof*

Ironically, I got to know this strategy during my time at a ladder manufacturer. At first, I was lured (figuratively speaking) on to the roof by good prices and promises concerning quality, but when the time buffer dwindled there was no way back or, for that matter, down the ladder. I had realised the gap between promise and reality too late and had to bear the consequences as in other cases too.

Stratagem No. 29 *Deck the tree with false blossoms*

Here I am immediately reminded of the fact that the facilities we visited before commissioning and even during audits were sometimes not those in which the products were manufactured. Not until I deployed native speakers who made spot checks to ascertain if the facility was really used for production and who worked there, and not until this trick was explicitly forbidden in a contract and charged with high penalties was this problem solved.

Nevertheless, the bottom line is that despite the cultural differences one need not be afraid of sourcing in China. The opportunities are greater than the risks as well for the company as on the personal level. It is still a unique opportunity to look beyond the end of one's European nose.

5.6   Future Prospects

With regard to the future, the following trends become apparent: The number of environmental disasters will increase and especially in regions that are interesting for procurement activities. Suppliers should be integrated much earlier in product development processes and that is also true of global partners that have to be developed. In the next 3–5 years, procurement volumes will double and will then represent up to a quarter of a portfolio on average. China will in the same period remain a profitable procurement source in the best-cost sector, but the country is changing and that not only with regard to its industrial strategies. The Middle Kingdom wants to lose its image as the world's cheap production site and puts its emphasis on alternative energies and materials, security and environmental technologies, and high technologies such as large-capacity aircraft construction. However, experts expect that in 3–5 years from now, the social and political tensions will increase which means that at that time China would become less important as a procurement region.

Apart from exceptions on the local level, India even now does not fulfil the expectations that foresaw developments by which this emergent country would have become a major global procurement source. After recent adjustments, Vietnam is again evaluated more positively. Thailand showed great power of resistance during the flood disaster; its importance as a procurement region will further increase. Experts such as Prof. Dr. Heilmann of Trier University see positive developments in Bangladesh, Indonesia, and foremost in Malaysia; all these countries currently make an essential contribution to the diversification away from China.

However, global sourcing is not automatically confined to Asia, let alone China. Just before one's doorstep one can find free capacities with a very favourable price–performance ratio and much lower risks, e.g. on the Iberian Peninsula.

Reference

Arnolds, H., et al. (2010). *Materialwirtschaft und Einkauf*. Wiesbaden: Gabler.

Risk Management with Regard to Purchasing

6

6.1 Principles of the Risk Management

Mid-sized enterprises face enormous challenges when they want to stand their ground in the dynamic business environment and the fiercely contested international competition. The progressively increasing globalisation, growing complexity, and rapid developments in the field of information technologies offer enormous chances but also entail new risks incessantly. Furthermore, a devastating earthquake in Japan, a volcanic eruption in Iceland, and a once-in-a-century flood in Thailand massively influenced the global business world in the year of 2011. According to the assessment of the Swiss Re reinsurance company, 2011 with all its earthquakes, floods, and storms has at yet produced the costliest damages in history. The macro-economic total damage has been estimated at 350 billion US dollars, which represents an increase by 58% compared to 226 billion US dollars in 2010. But the long-term planning of companies is also hampered by the increasing dynamics of the whole business environment, which is marked by volatile markets and framework conditions. A growing number of company bankruptcies is a logical consequence of such developments. For all these reasons, risk management has increasingly found its way into the companies in the last years. On the one hand, legal requirements imperatively call for an integrated approach to risk management, and on the other hand companies that want to operate successfully in the long run are forced to identify risks in the business environment as soon as possible in order to implement appropriate countermeasures.

Purchasing has a special and important role in this context. Due to ever shorter product life cycles, growing price pressure, increasing buyer power, and the constantly increasing globalisation, the classical order processing has been replaced by a business function that manages the external added value. An additional important point is that e.g. in Germany during the last 20 years the share of the material costs in manufacturing companies measured against the turnover has nearly doubled. Outsourcing, a specialisation in the core competencies of the companies, and the reduction of the in-house production depths are only some of

© Springer International Publishing AG 2017
U. Weigel, M. Ruecker, *The Strategic Procurement Practice Guide*, Management for Professionals, DOI 10.1007/978-3-319-57651-0_6

the reasons for the increasing materials usage. With materials ratios of often 50% and more, added value networks have enormous hazard potentials. Unplanned incidents, triggered by supply bottlenecks or the collapse of a supplier in complex supply chains, can quickly produce a knock-on effect and thus massively compromise the business success of one's home company. Therefore, a comprehensive, integrated risk management becomes a concrete task of Strategic Purchasing, and the question must be asked which forms such a risk management will take in the corporate practice. Which kinds of risks the purchasing department has to account for and which impacts has the risk management on the purchasing strategy?

Due to the closely interconnected partnership with suppliers regarding strategy, corporate policy, and technology, one also has to ascertain which risks the bankruptcy or its inability to deliver on time might involve and how these risks may be avoided by pre-emptive measures.

Due to its novelty, topicality, and increasing relevance, the risk management as part of the tasks of Purchasing shall be discussed in detail in this chapter. At first, the conceptual basics shall be considered and defined in order to enable a better classification and to avoid different interpretations. After the legal framework conditions have been outlined and the economic importance of the risk management has been clarified, the principles and peculiarities of the risk management in the purchasing department will be discussed.

6.1.1 Definition of the Risk Concept

Down to the present day, a generally accepted definition of the risk concept has not evolved in business studies. Often, risks related to causes are distinguished from risks related to effects; these two understandings of the risk concept complement one another. Related to its causes a risk is defined as business decision made on the basis of incomplete information regarding the future. The achievement of the targets can be compromised by unforeseeable developments or events. The possibility of such (negative) deviations from the targets forms the core of the second, effects-related risk definition.[1] From these two parts, a consensus emerges related to the possibility of negative deviations from a reference parameter. Thus, risk can be understood as the possible occurrence of an event that will have a negative influence on the realisation of targets that have been defined on the basis of imperfect expectations.[2]

Risk management in this context means a method of business management which aims at reducing risks. The target is not to avoid risks completely but to control and manage them effectively. Risk management therefore includes all measures that are used to identify and evaluate potential risks as well as all measures used for controlling already identified risks with the help of suitable

---

[1]Siebermann and Vahrenkamp (2007, p. 14).
[2]Cf. Brünger (2011, p. 16).

strategies and methods. In summary, the main tasks of the risk management consist of the timely identification of risks, the in-depth understanding of the consequences if these risks are taken, the limitation of risks that might compromise the success, and the efficient handling of risks.[3]

6.1.2 Legal and Financial Framework Conditions

The risk management issue has for a long time been neglected by the legislation but is increasingly gaining in importance in current discussion. The legal requirements concerning risk management are confined to only a few laws. In Germany, the legal basis is the 1998 Corporate Sector Supervision and Transparency Act (KonTraG), which can be regarded as an addition to the German Companies Act. In this, the governing body of a company is required to take measures appropriate for the early identification of developments that might endanger the continued existence of the company, especially by establishing a controlling system. Furthermore, the risk management system of stock companies is required to safeguard the early identification of risks concerning the survival of the company. These duties of care analogously also apply to the management of companies with other legal forms (e.g. limited companies). The KonTraG aims to ensure that risks that affect the survival of the company can be detected and averted at an early stage. However, there are no concrete guidelines as to how this controlling should be implemented.

Apart from legal requirements, risk management systems are increasingly affected by financial framework conditions, e.g. by the Basel II agreement on equity capital developed by the Basel Committee on Banking Supervision (BCBS) by which the safety and solidity of the international financial system shall be stabilised. The essential point of the Basel framework agreement requires that banks must have a certain amount of equity capital which depends on the relative risks measured with the help of diverse complex methods.

These risks are composed of credit, market, and for the first time also of operational risks. In order to optimally devise the equity capital demands, banks make use of rating procedures for evaluating the credit-worthiness of their clients. If a company has an operative risk management system, this is regarded as a collateral by the lending bank and consequently has a positive influence on the company's credit-worthiness,[4] with direct repercussions on the borrowing costs of the company.

Since 2013, the Basel III reform package has gradually come into effect, a package formed in reaction to the weaknesses of the hitherto existing bank control system that had been revealed by the global financial and economic crisis of 2007. Basel III includes, amongst others, an enhancement of the core capital quota of banks. Resulting from that, further improvements concerning the quality of risk

---

[3]Grundmann (2008, p. 10).

[4]Cf. Fiege (2006, p. 71).

management systems are being expected; however, another consequence will be that these requirements will be passed on to individuals and companies.

6.1.3   The Economic Importance of Risks

According to a study of the Fraunhofer-Institut, 86% of the companies that were surveyed in 2010 believed that the importance of risk management in their companies has increased.[5] Apart from the legal requirements, this growing interest in risk management is mainly caused by economic aspects. This development is triggered by constant alterations of the economic, technical, political, legal, or social framework conditions. Further aspects are the growing expectations of holders, employees, and the public as well as increasing requirements with regard to the efficiency of the companies.

Risk management can be a decisive competitive factor especially for export-oriented companies. Fluctuations in the raw materials and currency market can considerably compromise the calculations of companies. Furthermore, natural disasters tend to occur more often globally. In the context of changed economic structures, the impacts of natural disasters are no longer confined to the areas that are directly affected by them. The repercussions of natural disasters are felt worldwide due to global financial interdependencies and supply chains. Thus, the once-in-a-century flood in Thailand that lasted several weeks during the autumn of 2011 caused worldwide supply bottlenecks and even loss of production in the electronic and automotive industries (see Chap. 5) as purchasers in the whole world were affected by delivery shortages of important Asian suppliers.

Thus, companies often have no other choice than to take risk management very seriously. Furthermore, effective risk management systems offer the opportunity for realising true result improvements provided that the decisions which risks should be taken and how the existing risks should be limited and controlled are consciously made.

6.1.4   Risk Management in Purchasing

In the classical sense, the purchasing sector includes all strategic and operative activities concerning the supply of raw materials, products, or equipment (see the detailed description in Chap. 1).

The tendency of orienting the purchasing function strategically on the one hand is based on the increased procurement volumes the Purchasing is responsible for. Due to these volumes, the results of the companies depend to an ever-growing degree on the competence of the purchasing sector. Furthermore, the purchasing is also strategically influenced by increasing complexities of the procurement fields

---

[5]Schatz et al. (2010, p. 33).

that are caused by outsourcing, concentration on core competencies, or the reduction of in-house production depths. Especially by concentrating on their strengths, many companies make themselves highly dependent on their suppliers. If these suppliers drop out all of a sudden, cost-intensive supply bottlenecks are only the tip of the iceberg as additional unplanned investments must be made for the subsequent identification and qualification of new partners. Furthermore, scheduling delays may compromise or even endanger planned projects and the market launch of new products.

In Purchasing, risk management has to tackle those points where the fundamental targets of the procurement may be put at risk.[6] Purchasing risks in this context are dependent on many factors such as the company itself, the products to be procured, the procurement markets, or the country from which the respective product is procured. Purchasing risks, for that matter, are to be regarded as an aspect of the cross-company risk management.

Classical procurement risks such as shortfalls, poor quality, or price fluctuations in the context of globalised markets gain in complexity as risks often tend to occur at interfaces between the home company and the supplier.

Concrete measures concerning purchasing that are taken by the risk management are, amongst others, the systematic selection, development, and supervision of suppliers as well as the devising of courses of action with respect to possible risk situations.

6.2   The Risk Management Process

A key success factor of risk management is the risk policy that is defined by the top management within the scope of the company strategy. Apart from the formal elements of the risk management system, the risk policy as the definition of framework conditions plays a key part. This policy is the manifestation of the company's readiness to take risks. As risks can be seen differently from different points of view, an integrated risk policy approach in tune with the normative elements of the company management is the basis for organising the risk management. Behaviour guidelines that shall instruct all employees of the company to handle risks in the same way are part of this approach. The function of such guidelines is to encourage a lasting process of establishing risk consciousness as well as the development of a risk culture. This lasting process becomes accessible by the risk management controlling circuit for the management of standard risks that includes the essential process steps of the risk management: the identification, evaluation, management, and control of risks.

---

[6]Cf. Gabath (2011, p. 15).

6.2.1   Identifying Purchasing Risks

The identification of risks is the starting point of the risk management process and is often regarded as its most important stage. Only a risk that has been identified can be included and managed in this process. To commit the task of risk identification centrally to a risk manager organisationally assigned to the controlling is a measure that has proven successful. On the basis of previously defined risk areas, this risk manager regularly conducts interviews with the respective division managers who also act as persons responsible for risks that have been identified in their respective areas.

Therefore, the Head of Purchasing bears the overall responsibility for the risk management within his purchasing division. The main interest in this context must be to design and use the risk management system in a way that meets the requirements. Only by the lasting and consistent support of the head of each division will the risk management process gain the necessary dynamics and stability. The interviews on the risks can be conducted with the help of checklists.

To identify risks, FMEA analyses by which weaknesses in systems or organisations are detected can also be conducted. This method is often used in the quality assurance division because by this method apart from the weakness also its causes and repercussions can be identified and assessed.

In the next step, the compiled risk catalogue should be extensively scrutinised during workshops. By the critical examination of the compiled risks, the participants can identify relevant threat potentials and select particular risks. These risks can normally be assigned to five risk groups:

Supplier risks comprise all risks resulting from failures of the delivery performance of the supplier, e.g. risks that arise if:

- Material supplies fail in the short run due to the bankruptcy of the supplier or material bottlenecks
- Deviances concerning date of delivery, quality, or volume occur
- Companies are highly dependent on the supplier

Product risks comprise all risks concerning quality and technology. These risks occur if:

- Materials are not delivered in the required quality or volumes
- Technologies are developed jointly with suppliers (know-how protection)
- Technologies are bought in (black-box situation)

Logistic risks comprise all risks concerning the transport as well as risks arising from failures of the supply chain. Risks of this group occur if:

- Supply chains are global, complex, and branched.
- Long replacement times compromise the predictability.
- Shipments get lost or damaged during transport.
- Demand volumes have been fixed unfavourably.

Market and country risks comprise the risks in the procurement markets. These risks occur if:

- Substitution possibilities are missing due to an oligopolistic or monopolistic competitive situation
- Economic, political, social, legal, or ecological changes occur in countries in which the material is procured
- Resource bottlenecks or gambling on the stock exchange (e.g. with regard to rare earths) cause high price volatility or product bottlenecks
- Currency fluctuations result in higher costs

Process risks are risks connected to processes or persons. This includes occurring if:

- Duties have been delimited ambiguously
- Middle-term schedules are not met
- Targets and duties of the divisions have not been optimally concerted
- Master data have not been fed in correctly
- Maverick buying (procurement activities bypassing the purchasing) occurs
- Compliance guidelines have not been defined and communicated explicitly

Subsequently, these five risks groups can be filed in a central, software-based risk management system in order to be introduced in the cross-departmental business planning.

6.2.2   Evaluation of the Purchasing Risks

To initiate appropriate control measures, risks must be quantified. In order to do so, the purchasing risks are evaluated with regard to their detriments and occurrence probabilities. Detriments are evaluated according to a real figure in the form of a possible deviation from the operative result in Euros. Normally, the limits are based on the equity capital and should be adjusted by the administrative management yearly.

As exemplarily shown in Fig. 6.1, risks with an effect from 0 to 150,000 EUR can be assigned a detriment value of "1", while risks resulting in deviances form 4 MM to 40 MM EUR can be assigned the detriment value of "4".

The evaluation of risks with regard to their occurrence probability can be effected with the aid of relative categories. The evaluation scale is subdivided into four evaluation degrees:

- Low = Occurrence of the risk highly improbable
- Middle = Occurrence of the risk improbable
- High = Occurrence of the risk probable
- Very high = Occurrence of the risk highly probable

relevance base 10.000	deviation of operational result				characteristic
	in %		in T€		
	from	to	from	to	
1	0	1,5%	0	150	Insignificant risks that wont cause discrepancies from the operating result.
2	1,5%	10%	150	1.000	Medium-term risks that cause perceptible deviations from the operating result.
3	10%	40%	1.000	4.000	Significant risks that have a significant impact on the operating result or have a long-term impact.
4	40%	400%	4.000	40.000	Serious risks which lead to major deviations from the operating result and / or have a long-term impact.
	400%	-	40.000	-	Critical risks that could jeopardize the company's continued existence.

Fig. 6.1 Evaluation of purchasing risks

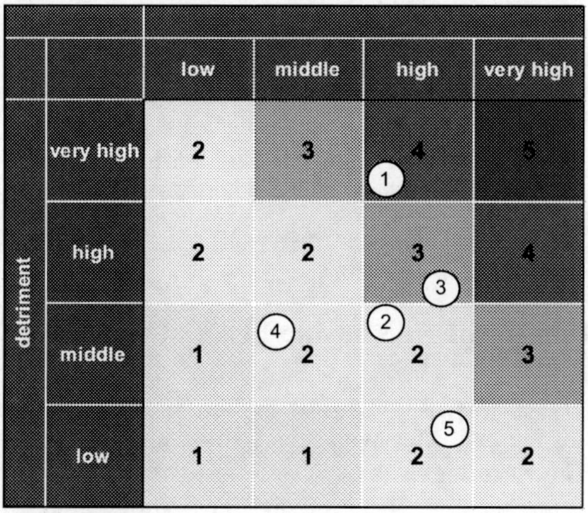

Fig. 6.2 Risk matrix as a result of the evaluation

Apart from future expectations, experiences from the past can also be included in the evaluation. Therefore, it is advised to record the results in a risk matrix (as indicated in Fig. 6.2).

The resulting relevancy enables a simplifying aggregation of many risk aspects and is thus suitable for reducing complexities. The relevancy subsequently serves as a filter to distinguish important from irrelevant risks. This in turn is the prerequisite for the selection of action alternatives concerning the risk policy, the next step in the process.

6.2.3 Controlling the Purchasing Risks

After the risk evaluation, the organisation task of risk management starts with the subprocess of risk control. Risk control has the function of defining strategies suitable for the risks that have been identified and evaluated and deriving measures to confront these risks. The foremost target of risk control is to reduce the purchasing risks. The strategies for controlling the risks essentially consist of four aspects:

Risk Avoidance This happens when companies refrain from certain activities due to risks that are considered too high. This cause-related instrument is the most unmitigated form of risk response. The occurrence of the risk is completely prevented by reducing the occurrence probability to zero. However, with this decision the company concurrently forgoes the opportunities that are connected to the risks. This happens, e.g., if the business relations to a supplier are discontinued or a procurement market due to political instability is completely avoided.

Risk Reduction With regard to their causes, the occurrence probabilities of risky events are reduced to an acceptable level but not completely eliminated. However, risk reduction can also be achieved with regard to their effects by reducing the extent of damages. The cause-related risk reduction first and foremost aims at improving the level of information of the decision-maker as well as the pre-emptive mastering of potential threats. This can be achieved by early warning signs that will help to timely identify risks and confront their causes, e.g. by developing a second source of supply early in the case of a supplier with high risk potential or by establishing training programmes to counteract risks due to poor qualification of workers.

Transfer of Risks By transferring risks, the risks endure but are transferred to a third party by the use of preventive measures. To take out insurance is the most often used control instrument in this context[7] and enjoys highest priority in cases of existence-threatening risks. Examples in this context are indemnity or business interruption insurances. Risk transfer measures may also include the transfer of risks to the supplier, e.g. by supply or quality assurance agreements, by supplier managed inventories (SMI) in the form of a consignment warehouse, or by outsourcing of particular business tasks.

Risk Acceptance Risks with a low damage amount and low occurrence probability may be accepted and taken by the companies. In this case, measures are advised that will limit the economic consequences of the risk events. Furthermore, possible financial strains should be provided for by setting aside reserves.

---

[7]Cf. Wolke (2008, p. 85).

To control the identified and evaluated risk group in the purchasing division, a mix of all these strategies is used as not all risks can be handled with one and the same approach. Therefore, in the next step the existing as well as new measures and ideas for handling risks are compiled in order to confront the identified risks. The compiled measures and risks are then transformed into concrete measures, and for each measure a start and a finish date is fixed and the person responsible named.

The implementation and adequacy of the measures is tracked in the next process step, risk control.

6.2.4   Risk Control

Due to changes that will occur over time, one cannot assume that the measures concerning the risk policy that have been selected originally will still be the best solution under changed premises. Risk control has the task of tracking the development of the risks constantly and of assessing whether the implemented measures and instruments do still conform to the defined targets. Furthermore, risk control must check whether new risks have arisen and whether an adjustment of the mix of measures has become necessary due to a changed interplay of single risks. At this point, there are strong connections to risk identification, a clear indication of the cyclical nature of the risk management process.[8]

Documentation is the basis of risk control. This can be achieved with the help of a risk management system (RMS). The RMS thus is the interface between the risk management in the purchasing division and in the company as a whole. All identified and evaluated risks and the respective measures are recorded in the RMS and updated regularly. Thus, all risks that are supervised can always be looked at. The relevant tasks are structured by diverse organisation levels (risk management, risk categories, risks, measures), and concrete responsibilities and deadlines are assigned to them. Through an integrated escalation and de-escalation mechanism, the next higher responsibility level will be informed by the RMS on deviances in the implementation of measures.

Risk control determines the organisational framework of the risk management, supplemented by risk communication. The following points must be taken care of in this context:

• All members of the company staff shall be prompted to handle risks responsibly as the RMS becomes more effective if not only the governing board but also the staff participate in it permanently. To realise this target, the communication within the company, even over hierarchical levels, must run smoothly. By a lasting and permanent process targeted at promoting risk awareness, risks can be identified and systematically attended to.

---

[8]Meierbeck (2010, p. 37).

- The risk management process must be subdivided into responsibilities and tasks. Furthermore, in-house guidelines must be established to let employees below the company management level know what they have to do concretely if they come across risks that put the company in jeopardy.
- Control cycles must be defined in a uniform way. The intervals in which risks shall be discussed will depend on the type and importance of the respective risks. There must also be a communication channel to inform on unexpected risks.
- From a defined threshold value, a risk reporting system comes into effect. The reporting channels, the dates, and persons responsible for them must be determined.

6.3   Special Safeguarding Against Supplier Risks

All 5 minutes a company changes its legal form.
All 4 minutes a company becomes insolvent.
All 2 minutes a company discontinues its business activities.
Every minute changes in the executive board of a company happen.
All 10 seconds negative information concerning a company is disclosed.
And these figures solely apply to Europe![9]

Especially high risks emerge from the area of supplier relations. By an increased concentration on selected strategic partners, strong dependencies may arise that may cause severe repercussions on the company's production in the case of one of these suppliers' insolvency. According to the default report of the Moody's rating agency (shown as an example in Fig. 6.3), one has to expect that within 3 years 4.65% of the suppliers will fail due to insolvency.[10] But the report also shows that the average insolvency-caused failure rate can be dramatically reduced from 4.65% to 1.19% if a company confines itself to suppliers with a positive investment grade ranking.

Especially in the case of a highly prevailing single-source strategy, the failure of a single supplier may result in painful losses of production. In order to prevent poor supply of their own customers, the purchasing company will often be forced to implement costly measures such as working capital credits or higher prices. The situation is aggravated by the fact that the failure of the supplier may result in the loss of technological or patented know-how. The company's own development performance may be massively compromised by the necessity to provide this know-how again. Furthermore, it may be possible that claims from warranty or guarantee cases can no longer be passed on which will result in further costs.

---

[9]aon-credit.de.
[10]Cf. Gabath (2011, p. 26).

Rating class	Freequency	3 year default rate
AAA	3,52%	0,00%
Aa	15,64%	0,00%
A	26,23%	1,16%
Baa	22,98%	2,31%
Ba	10,84%	5,91%
B	15,27%	20,62%
Caa-C	5,52%	53,39%
Investment Grade	68,37%	1,19%
Speculative Grade	31,63%	19,15%
All	100,00%	4,65%

$\frac{1}{4}$

Fig. 6.3 Moody's default report 2006

Against this background, the first tasks of the supplier risk management are developing a well-balanced supplier portfolio and reducing the dependency on particular suppliers.[11]

6.3.1   Analysis of the Supplier Portfolio

To review the supplier risks more thoroughly, it is advised to begin by analysing the supplier portfolio with respect to the respective competitive situation and to the existing dependencies and to group the suppliers according to two criteria.

Sourcing Strategy Answers which sourcing strategy is applied to the respective supplier. The classification criteria are whether the supplier is currently a single source, which means the only one from whom certain bought-in parts are procured, or whether the needed demand is currently divided between several suppliers in consequence of a multiple-source strategy. Single-source suppliers may e.g. supply tools-related parts for which it makes no economic sense to commission a second source of supply. Another example are highly complex technologies where a single-source strategy is necessary due to enormous development costs. Thus, the complete supplier portfolio is distinguished in two categories: single or multiple sources.

Dependency The direct dependency on the respective suppliers can be assessed by calculating the time for a reorganisation of the supply. With respect to the

---

[11]Gabath (2011, p. 24).

Dependence				
		low (3 month)	**middle** (6 month)	**high** (12 month)	**total**

Single Source	Dependence			
	low (3 month)	**middle** (6 month)	**high** (12 month)	**total**
no	140	56	3	199
yes	19	15	40	74
total	159	71	43	273

Fig. 6.4 Risks inside the supplier portfolio

components procured from the supplier, it is evaluated what amount of time will be needed to procure those components from another source if the original supplier should fail.

In this context, alternative suppliers as well as in-house manufacturing are put into consideration. The classification may e.g. follow the following scheme:

- 1 = Reorganisation possible in the short term, period <3 months
- 2 = Reorganisation possible in the medium term, period 3–6 months
- 3 = Reorganisation possible in the long term, period >12 months

This classification is then condensed in a matrix (Fig. 6.4).

The risks are especially high with regard to single-source suppliers that cannot be replaced in the short run. In order to illustrate the shattering power of the dependency, the evaluation may be transferred to a product of strategic importance. This will show how long a product will not be available if the supplier should fail and will aid to raise the risk awareness within the home organisation.

6.3.2   Reactive Risk Management

Reactive risk management has always been an implicit part of the corporate management. But often reactive measures were only taken when the company already faced severe difficulties. Trade and industry mainly focused on fulfilling legal requirements or stipulations of the insurance companies.[12]

In the course of supplier insolvency or a looming crisis, it may be sensible (especially if the dependency on the respective supplier is high) to find a joint solution in which the supplier can maintain operation and consequently the supply of the products. Depending on the respective case, several activities can be suitable, e.g. the provision of materials, the reduction of payment targets, advance payments, or personnel or other support for performing the demanded tasks.

---

[12]The Risk Management Network (2011).

However, one must always keep in mind that the supplier may become insolvent despite all those measures. Possible repayment debts must then be contrasted with the insolvency estate and will thus often be lost.

Collaterally always measures must be taken to reduce the dependency on single suppliers. These measures may e.g. include enquiring competitors but also sub-suppliers that may possibly be able to perform particular production steps. An important factor is also to retain particular rights previously in supply contracts. Thus, tool contracts should stipulate precisely and unambiguously that the ownership of the tools shall remain with the client and not be transferred to the supplier. The ownership must be marked accordingly. As the respective claims, e.g. the claim for return of the tools, must be made against the insolvency administrator, complete and up-to-date lists should exist as to which documents, machines, tools, etc., belonging to the client are currently in possession of the supplier. These lists will help accelerating the return and thus facilitate the near-term substitution of the failed supplier by another one.

To purposefully manage detriments that have occurred, it is advised, as shown in Fig. 6.5, to implement a systematic process in which responsibilities and information flows are clearly defined. Thus, panic and hasty action are avoided as ordered courses of action are prescribed by a target-oriented framework of action.

6.3.3 Active Risk Management

Active risk management consists of all measures aiming at the management of immediate risks the occurrence of which in the short run has a high probability.

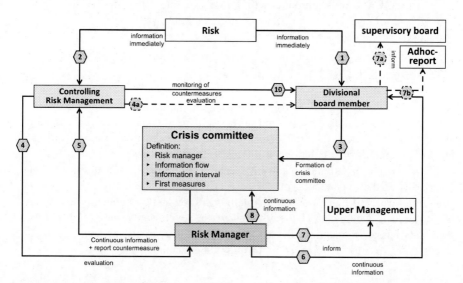

Fig. 6.5 How to handle acute risks

These risks are known and manifest without any far-reaching reviews. That is why active risk management will start earlier than reactive risk management. A concrete case example from the scope of projects and project restarts is detailed in the following "Practical Tip".

Practical Tip: Readiness Rollup
Risks for companies lurk everywhere but especially outside the home company. I would like to single out one of these by demonstrating a method of confronting these risks successfully.

Who is not familiar with the "onion-bulb effect" that will appear in almost all projects to a greater or lesser degree? This effect is not derived from the principle of putting on several layers of clothing in outdoor activities but from the bulbous form (see the following Fig. 6.6) that is very similar to the typical course of projects. The triangle shows the optimum course of the project, with the time line as the vertical axis and the needed efforts as the horizontal one. What will happen in the course of the project is known to all: At the latest, during the final phase, there will be hustle and bustle; arguments with the sales departments due to the market entrance are daily fare; and there are expensive explanations and quarrels with the controlling and the executive board as costly special measures overrun the budgets. But even more severe are the lacking profit contributions that can never be made up for and may sorely compromise the company results and even cause economic distress.

When we not a long time ago had only 6 months left before the rollup of our most important new project, I was reminded of a case I had experienced during my time in the aviation industry.

At that time, two global players competed with each other for building the world's biggest passenger aircraft. Both companies were our clients, and none of them wanted to come off second best. At the beginning, I could not understand the

Fig. 6.6 The onion-bulb effect

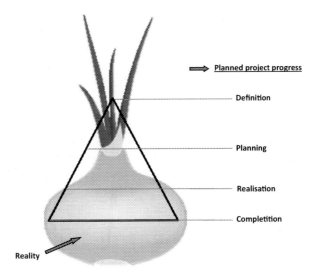

amount of efforts that the purchasing division of one of these companies put in. More than ten procurement experts spent several weeks for locally assessing our readiness and capacity to master the oncoming series production. All involved division heads and their teams had to answer a copious questionnaire and provide a presentation followed by the client's critical questions. With the benefit of hindsight, I understand that course of action: The supplier, acting in an oligopolistic market environment, by supply delays had dictated the starting curves of manufacturers and airlines (some of them were also direct clients) for years.

As I had learned in Asia, a good imitation is better than a poor original. And so I, together with my team, adapted the old questionnaire to the needs of the optical industry. Then all persons involved in the project team filtered out the most important procurement risks. The purchasing division contributed its assessment of the suppliers supposed to be critical. At the end, 10 suppliers and 25 bought-in parts had been identified (the product as a whole comprised more than 700 single parts most of which had to be procured). Now the specific risks of each of the selected suppliers and parts had to be evaluated in order to determine proactive measures. Then, the questionnaire (scorecard) was sent to the respective suppliers for obtaining their self-assessment. This measure alone galvanised some of these partners. With regard to the particular parts, the questions were divided into six categories with up to six subcategories. After the filled-in scorecards had returned in time, a plausibility check was undertaken by the project team.

An interesting fact is that the different self-assessments corresponded to the differences in mentality we had experienced during global sourcing. We made the decision to visit five of the ten suppliers at short notice to get an idea of the local situation. Our aim was to review the evaluations jointly with the suppliers and to agree measures resulting from that evaluation. We reviewed part by part, process by process; we had a look at the production equipment and identified the critical operation sequences, possible bottlenecks, as well as process risks. Afterwards, we were able to rate the complete and updated Production-Readiness-Rollup file (Fig. 6.7) precisely (a score rate of 1–5 per criterion) to prioritise the risks and implement respective measures.

But exceptions prove the rule—nasty surprises did not fail to appear before the start of the series production although their number had decreased considerably as compared to former product launches.

Conclusion While this method will certainly not be able to filter out all risks previously, their numbers will be considerably reduced. The persons applying it will have the chance of assuming the strategic role of acting in good time and no longer be confined to troubleshooting.

6.3.4 Pre-emptive Risk Management

Pre-emptive risk management encompasses all measures taken for averting and preventing risks; it is thus an important factor for maintaining the Buyer's own

CATEGORY	Supplier A		Supplier B			Supplier C			Supplier D		Supplier E							Category Stoplight
	Part 001	Part 002	Part 003	Part 004	Part 005	Part 006	Part 007	Part 008	Part 009	Part 010	Part 018	Part 019	Part 020	Part 021	Part 022	Part 023	Part 024	
1. TOOLING & CAPITAL EQUIPMENT																		
1.1 EQUIPMENT/ MACHINES																		
1.2 EQUIPMENT/ MACHINES																		
1.3 MAINTENANCE / CONDITION																		
1.4 CAPACITY																		
1.5 CAPACITY																		
1.6 CAPACITY																		

Fig. 6.7 Scorecard to evaluate critical parts

production. Pre-emptive risk management aims at receiving information on possible crises on the part of the suppliers prior to their occurrence by collecting respective evidence in order to provide for a response period as long as possible. The central question when it comes to devising pre-emptive risk management will always be how upcoming supplier insolvencies can be identified at an early time.

Supplier insolvencies do not occur suddenly—they result from a creeping process that can extend to several years. The loss of market shares or the deterioration of key data can be the first warning signals. Such symptoms that may end in over-indebtedness and impendent non-solvency of suppliers have to be identified in time and interpreted correctly. An early warning system shall help the Purchasing to reduce the response time to undesirable developments by identifying external developments and deriving maldevelopments and shedding light on internal developments in the company at an early time. Early warning signs form the basis of the pre-emptive risk management; subject to their position in time they can be grouped into three generations according to the resilience of the information.

First Generation: Early Warnings Based on Key Data
Early warnings based on defined key data compiled by the accountancy or taken from the company's annual statement of accounts. These data are of high quality; however, they are available late. Especially with regard to the aim of identifying looming risks as early as possible, key data-based systems alone will not be sufficient as these systems do not provide for enough time during which countermeasures could be developed and implemented.

Second Generation: Early Warnings Based on Indicators
These early warnings are not based on ascertained, mostly financial key data but on copious information that are chained up. Experiences from the past form the base for identifying the information on which the projection will be based. Thus, an increase of oil prices can be provoked by highly increasing demands for oil in the People's Republic of China. Prognostic data concerning the development of China's construction industry can—if the assumption proves valid—be a bellwether indicating such a price increase. The horizon of indicator-oriented early warnings extends beyond the limits of the key data approach as these warnings can integrate many fields of analysis and do not rely on data material related to the past.

Third Generation: Early Warnings Based on Weak Signals
Weak signals expand the two approaches described above by an unstructured component. This concept proceeds from the premise that discontinuities will occur that cannot be covered by indicators. Therefore, a non-directional search is deemed necessary for identifying possible signals that might indicate discontinuities. Weak signals, for that matter, are inconclusive evidence that in particular cases will require considerable time resources as well as the readiness und capacities of the involved personnel to implement this concept.

Weak signals will often announce risks before indicators work or key data unveil them. The longer a risk is away from its occurrence in the future, the more unstructured and inconclusive will be the signals pointing to that risk. Weak signals may occur even in day-to-day contacts with suppliers; as shown in Fig. 6.8, if the contact person is difficult to get hold of or if there are signs of dissatisfaction amongst the supplier's employees, this can be first hints of upcoming risks.

If these signs are accompanied by increasing prices or a conversion of the payment conditions to spot cash, this can be the first evidence of a crisis at the supplier. Additional performance deterioration in the form of delayed deliveries or quality defects should be interpreted as an unequivocal danger signal. Thus, the greater part of the information needed for pre-emptive risk management is already available in in-house systems and must only be complemented by objective data from external providers.

Company ratings especially arouse increasing interest as external information sources on the economic situation of business partners. After the introduction of the Basel II equity capital regulations, commercial banks are forced to attach higher importance to the solvency and the risk profiles of their borrowers. Thus, the rating value is decisive for the future financial margin and in consequence essentially important for the future of the company. Ratings therefore are also highly important for the evaluation of supplier risks. However, the downside is that ratings are geared to the protection of investors rather than to the evaluation of companies. Furthermore, ratings will not necessarily be available with respect to smaller companies and often the rating will be outdated. Ratings should therefore be complemented by assessments of the purchasing companies if critical supplier or product areas are concerned.

	weak signals	indicators	key data
Daily business **Supplier contact**	• Poor availability • Changing Key Accounts	• Immediate payment • Price increases	• Bad on time delivery • Low quality index
		Collect signs	
Self-disclosure **Interview**	• Strategy • Business plan	• Sales performance • Business outlook	• Earnings situation • Liquidity
		Actively ask for information	
Research **Source of information**	• Business reports • Financial rating	• Trade magazines • Industry news	• Daily press • Internet research
		Ensure data	

Fig. 6.8 Collecting information during supplier crisis

Practical Tip

The Bisnode credit enquiry agency has access to a database including roughly 200 million companies in 150 countries, which is a very high amount of available data indeed. Bisnode is one of the biggest data providers in the world. Apart from general information on companies, Bisnode provides company evaluations as well as examinations of the payment histories of companies. The Supply Management Solutions division offers diverse solutions for minimising supplier risks. These solutions include e.g. a portfolio manager that offers the opportunity of monitoring the economic development of business partners with the help of an online platform. Apart from general information and risk assessments of the respective companies, an early warning system is integrated that will be triggered by defined changes.

In a concrete case example, at first the requirements were compared against the provided services during a joint workshop. Apart from the portfolio manager that monitors the economic situation of suppliers and sends early warning messages if defined changes have been registered, a mechanism allowing for quick and effective action in the event of natural disasters was called for. For that reason, another instrument, the so-called Global Reference Solution, was integrated in the solution package. By this instrument, interdependencies of companies can be identified globally. That means more concretely that by a search function in a given region all direct suppliers as well as their production facilities and subsidiary companies with a majority interest of at least 51% can be identified. In the event of a natural disaster thus all directly affected suppliers can be identified within minutes and the appropriate measures taken. The third requirement was the need of checking the economic situation of potential suppliers prior to the initiation of business relations in order to assess the risk potential at an early stage. As this requirement is also provided for by the portfolio manager, an additional, separate application is unnecessary. Nevertheless, a further, cost-free access to a monitoring portal is integrated by which the financial division shall later have the opportunity of monitoring the solvency of particular debtors.

A method for increasing the validity of facts and figures is the Rapid Plant Assessment (RPA) developed by Eugene Goodson in the USA. This method describes a rapid evaluation of production facilities during a plant visit; the assessed key data are complemented by visual impressions.

In the course of RPA, the production as well as the processes is checked with the aid of evaluation system consisting of 11 categories. At first, the production process is reviewed with respect to these categories. Ideally, immediately after the visit the results are recorded in a standardised rating sheet. The production conditions are rated according to the following criteria:

• Customer satisfaction
• Safety, cleanness, orderliness
• Visual management system
• Planning system
• Space utilisation and production flow
• Stock inventory and work flow
• Team work and motivation
• State of the equipment and machinery
• Handling of manufacturing complexities
• Supplier integration
• Quality awareness

The rating is from 1 (bad) to 11 (best of class). To further facilitate the evaluation, an additional questionnaire is provided containing 20 questions that can be answered yes or no. Each of these questions is assigned to several of the 11 categories. Thus, the following questions will be incorporated in the evaluation of customer satisfaction:

• Are visitors bidden welcome; are they being informed on the structure and organisation of the plant, the customers, and the products?
• Are ratings concerning the customer satisfaction and product quality displayed?
• Would you buy products from this production?

RPA offers strategic purchasers the option to complement the already gathered information by visual impressions. Furthermore, this method offers a guideline as to which aspects should be taken notice of during the visit of a supplier's facility.

6.3.5 Long-Term Measures

There are several approaches for reducing risks caused by dependencies from suppliers in the long run. On the one hand, the disposal margin of the supplier can be limited by a direct stake in the equity. On the other hand, it is not only necessary to review existing potentials in the procurement markets but also to evaluate the development of new suppliers as well as the possibility of in-sourcing. The development of competencies within the home company may be suitable especially when it comes to products of strategic importance if in this way risks that may compromise the company's ability to compete can be diminished. Furthermore, measures aiming at an upgrading of one's position may enhance the importance of the purchaser in the eyes of the supplier and thus change the dependency structure. To achieve this aim, increased volumes are not necessarily the only means; unique features such as an agreement on purchasing cooperations regarding raw materials may work too.

References

Brünger, C. (2011). *Nutzenkonsistente Risikopriorisierung*. Wiesbaden: Gabler.

Fiege, S. (2006). *Risikomanagement- und Überwachungssystem nach KonTraG*. Wiesbaden: Gabler.

Gabath, C. (2011). Innovatives Risikomanagement im Einkauf. In *Innovatives Beschaffungsmanagement*. Wiesbaden: Gabler.

Grundmann, T. (2008). Der Begriff des Risikomanagements. In *Ein anwendungsorientiertes System für das Management von Produkt- und Prozessrisiken*. Aachen: Apprimus.

Meierbeck, R. (2010). *Strategisches Risikomanagement in der Beschaffung*. Lohmar: Eul.

Schatz, A., Mandel, J., & Hermann, M. (2010). *Risikomanagement im Einkauf*. Stuttgart: Fraunhofer.

Siebermann, C., & Vahrenkamp, R. (2007). *Risikomanagement in supply chains*. Berlin: Erich Schmidt.

The Risk Management Network. (2011). *Strategisches risikomanagement*. Accessed December 23, 2011, from www.risknet/126.html

Wolke, T. (2008). *Risikomanagement*. Munich: Oldenbourg.

Methods and Tools for Everyday Purchasing

7.1 Procurement Market Research

The term of Procurement Market Research has been derived from market research in general and denotes the gathering and editing of information on the market conditions that are relevant for Purchasing. Procurement market research has the task of investigating the procurement markets relevant to the company and evaluating the market development including special developments as well as the structures, risks, and potentials of the markets. In view of the increasing complexity of the goods to be procured and the growing global orientation of the purchasing activities, comprehensive and systematic procurement market research is essential for evaluating the risks and chances of the markets and for optimally procuring products and services. For that reason, procurement market research is a key task of the strategic purchaser.

7.1.1 Types of Procurement Market Research

Essentially, procurement market research can be differentiated between market analysis (related to points in time) and market investigation (related to spaces of time).

Procurement market analysis relates to the future and provides a snapshot of the basic structure of the respective procurement market at a given point in time. In doing so, the number of suppliers, the availability of materials, capacities, the competitive situations, etc., are being investigated and combined.

Procurement market investigation, by contrast, aims at revealing shifts of the markets by permanently observing factors such as market trends, price fluctuations, or changes in demand that are pertinent to the market.

However, these two types of procurement market research cannot be separated and complement each other. As a rule, market investigation will be built on market analysis and vice versa.

© Springer International Publishing AG 2017   109
U. Weigel, M. Ruecker, *The Strategic Procurement Practice Guide*, Management
for Professionals, DOI 10.1007/978-3-319-57651-0_7

When future market developments are derived from the gathered data and a coming market trend is identified, this is called a market forecast. Such forecasts may be used in the context of strategic considerations to develop long-term purchasing decisions. The reliability of market forecasts depends on the quality of the collected data and on the amount of volatility of the respective procurement market.

7.1.2   Procedure

A general, broadly defined investigation of procurement markets tends to be rather unrewarding. Therefore, at first a decision must be made with regard to which product groups specific procurement market research should be undertaken. In order to conduct targeted procurement market research, the technical key data must be known and understood including, apart from the planned use of product, its basic materials and quality demands and also the available production processes and technical peculiarities. Depending on the complexity of the respective product, this can be the first challenge to the Strategic Buyer.

In the next step, the market structure must be scrutinised with respect to the respective supply and demand situations. The analysis includes the offer available in the market with respect to availability, capacities, quality, and dynamics. When the object of investigation is a bull market (with higher demand than offer), the negotiating power of the buyer will be comparatively small. The opposite is true of a buyers' market, which is characterised by oversupply and a high degree of negotiating power for buyers. Whether a given market is a buyers' or a bull market will often depend on the macroeconomic situation of the respective industry and may change quickly depending on the volatility of the respective market. Economic indicators may provide information about future developments.

Furthermore, the competitive situation with regard to product in question must be investigated. This investigation will also provide insight into the amount of market power the Strategic Buyer commands. If there is a high quantity of suppliers and if the structure of the product is a homogeneous one, buyers will be free in their decisions concerning which suppliers will be commissioned. Thus, buyers in this market type command high negotiating powers. However, this power shrinks with decreasing numbers of suppliers and will become rather low in oligopolistic markets with only a few suppliers. Monopolies are the extreme cases. Here, only one supplier exists who can steer the price at his will. The negotiation power of the buyer tends down to zero. However, a monopolist will not exaggerate his pricing as with growing margins the interest of other market actors will be aroused.

According to similar aspects, in the next step the demand situation will be analysed. Essentially is the question how big the own demand is, compared to the demand of competing buyers. Strategic Buyers can use this knowledge to position their demands in the market. With regard to the desirability of the respective demands, one essential aspect is whether the company of the purchaser is a quantity buyer or whether it represents only a minimum share of the whole demand quantity.

Furthermore, with regard to the demand situation the availability of materials plays a key role too. Who are the quantity buyers in the market; are there any exclusive agreements; and what influence may that have on material supply bottlenecks in one's company?

Following the market analysis, the available suppliers must be scrutinised in detail. In order to limit the numbers of possible supply sources to the most suitable suppliers, diverse information on the respective suppliers' qualities and potentials must be compiled. At this point, procurement market research is providing key information for the supplier selection process. In addition to general company data, information on the current production program, technical know-how, the level of quality, and the used manufacturing processes is also gathered.

The current market price level is a further and in the end the decisive aspect that must be taken into consideration by procurement market research. In principle, all the aforementioned factors have an influence on the market price. But with the help of several methods, the market price can be scrutinised more in detail. These methods can be subdivided into analysis, monitoring, and comparison.

Price analyses aim, as will be shown below in this chapter in detail, at examining the purchase price and its composition. Price monitoring consists of investigating shifts of the market that may have a direct influence on material prices such as raw material prices or exchange rates. The comparison of prices is used in order to compare and rank the current price level of suppliers globally.

7.1.3 Sources of Information

As described in the last chapter, comprehensive procurement market research must collect a great number of market data. Different sources of information can be tapped in order to acquire these data. A commonly accepted differentiation of these sources has been derived from sales marketing, the discrimination between primary and secondary market research.

Primary market research consists of directly gathering data relevant to procurement market research on one's own. With respect to the purchasing practice, this means more concretely: requesting supplier self-assessments, visiting conferences and trade fairs, talking to sellers, and visiting production facilities. Depending on the extent and complexity of the needed information, market research institutions may be commissioned with collecting the data.

By contrast, secondary market research draws on information that is already available, e.g. publications by the supplier such as its Internet presence, leaflets describing the product, or company reports. To further explore the situation, specialist journals, trade directories, market or stock exchange reports, as well as Internet research have proven helpful.

Which sources of information will be used depends on the object to be procured. In principle, however, one should always bear in mind that the efforts invested in the research should not be greater than the benefits resulting from it. The more relevant and complex a product group is, the more intensive the efforts for gathering information may be. Furthermore, care must always be taken to safe-guard the objectivity and reliability of the information sources. Product evaluations in the Internet may come from anyone, even from competitors. And, last but not least, the used data should be as up to date as possible. If market conditions are prone to changing quickly, new data must be acquired at suitable intervals.

7.1.4   Areas of Application

Market analysis and monitoring are inevitably part of the strategic purchaser's day-to-day routine. Only by a sound knowledge of the market conditions can purchasers optimally connect the internal requirements to the external framework conditions. Procurement market research is especially necessary within the scope of supplier identification and selection. Only on the basis of procurement market, research purchasers will get the needed information for selecting from a great number of suppliers the optimum and most reliable ones for their demands.

In the context of purchase negotiations, procurement market research is a constituent part of the necessary preparation. The provision of market data helps evaluating one's negotiating power. Furthermore, procurement market research provides choices of action by identifying competitors that can be used for one's arguments in the negotiation.

The strategic and planning process is another area extensively supported by procurement market research. Especially with regard to long-term purchasing decisions, there is no other way than to gather facts, figures, and data at first on which the possible procurement options can be based.

By editing and filing the results of market research, these can be used cross-departmentally. In this way, these data will not only provide decision-making aid to the Purchasing, but other divisions such as the sales, development, or production departments will be given valuable hints for their planning. Thus, procurement market research is a powerful instrument of Strategic Purchasing that can be used company wide.

7.2   Value Analysis

Value analysis can be understood as a systematic procedure for detecting and reducing cost-intensive waste in a product or process without exerting a negative influence on features such as use, lifespan, quality, or selling power that are relevant to customers.

Value analyses start from a systematic, function-oriented point of view by isolating and analysing the function or the purpose of the object apart from the actual product. By asking for the function that the customer is willing to buy, the perspective is broadened, and new approaches for realising the function may be perceived. Value analyses will always be conducted by teams composed of members of different divisions in order to integrate different perspectives in the review and achieve the optimum conditions for conceiving ideas. The Purchasing is an active member of the team and a driving force when it comes to considerations related to the value analysis that aim at optimising the economic efficiency of products and processes. Another task of the Purchasing is to involve suppliers in the value analysis process and to tap into the know-how of the suppliers.

The essential approach of value analyses consists in assessing products and functions separately. The function is regarded as the purpose or the customer benefit, whereas the product is the way in which the function is being realised. At first, the separation of function and product is limited to original customer benefits, e.g. drawing lines in the case of a ballpoint pen or transporting goods from A to B in the case of logistic processes. Common questions for identifying the original function of an object are, amongst others:

- What does the object do and for what reason?
- To what purpose is this object needed?
- What is this object about essentially?

A detailed catalogue of question is presented in the following "Hint from Experience" chapter. In the next step, the functions of the given product are analysed with respect to their necessity. A ballpoint pen e.g. may lie well in one's hand, may write without blurs, and may be characterised by high-quality design. These functions must then be checked with regard to their relevance to the customer benefit. If the respective function is imperative for generating the customer benefit, it is classified a main function (in this case, writing without blurs). If the function is helpful for generating the customer benefit, it is classified an auxiliary function (good to handle). Functions that do not fit in either of these two categories are unnecessary functions that do not meet the market demands. Such unnecessary functions produce costs that are not rewarded by the market. For that reason, they should be eliminated in the further course of the examination, and alternative solutions should be developed. The following "Practical Tip" will show in detail how this can be done.

Practical Tip: Value Analysis
Unfortunately, the construction of a product is still the key element when it comes to cost avoidance or cost reduction. Design-to-cost is the pertinent catch-phrase in this context. But, unfortunately, the words are often not followed up with deeds. For this reason, it is all the more important that the Strategic Purchasing becomes involved at best during the innovation stage of the product creation process and at the latest during the development stage. To close the stable door after the horse has bolted—in other words, when a situation has occurred in which the waste has been built in the product ready for series production—the only, rather painful and thorny way will be to optimise the costs retroactively. All too often the solution is sought in optimising the manufacturing costs in one's company—in many cases with little success. As

the purchasing division is responsible for the lion's share of the pool of costs (depending on the respective industry, up to more than 50% of the added value), it is advised to primarily act here. Conventional purchasing, however, is no longer sufficient for effectively supporting the sustainment or increase of the company value. Modern Strategic Purchasing not only has to be a persistent driving force in this process, but it must also command an increasing degree of technical competence and management skills if the often neglected potentials of the price and value analysis (the so-called product value management) shall be fully exploited.

And there are many reasons why a targeted price and value analysis should be initiated. Drastic cost reductions may be required due to market conditions, or the corporate management may push for an increase in profit. In such cases, it is always more commendable, and also very appreciated by the corporate management, if strategists in their proactive, targeted search discover suitable candidates (such as A parts, parts with long lifespans, or parts developed under high time pressure) in their purchasing portfolio and take the initiative on their own.

In addition to the often used instruments of the price analysis, value analyses strive for systematically finding more cost-effective solutions with regard to the necessary functions of the object in question, eliminating the unnecessary functions of the product, or even for enhancing the functional range of the product if by this enhancement the commercial profit can be increased. After the object to be examined has been defined, the following procedure concerning a price and value analysis workshop has proven effective.

1. At first, a team consisting of representatives of several divisions is formed. If the added value of the product is predominantly bought in, the Purchasing should insist on chairing and managing the project. Only from a leading position, Purchasing can fully act as the driving force and additionally improve the standing of Strategic Purchasing. In any case, the following divisions should also be involved: At first, controlling. Controllers undertake the controlling of the project and apply their in-depth understanding of the costs to a target price analysis. The sound technical knowledge of design engineers will especially be needed at the value analysis stage (if possible, not only the author of the original design should be involved); detailed knowledge of processes will be contributed by the production scheduler in the context of the value stream analysis. In addition to the strategic purchaser, the key supplier (or key suppliers) should also be involved at least temporarily when it comes to optimising the bought-in parts and their supply chain.

   Value stream analysis is a microeconomic instrument that is used for improving process flows in production and also for optimising services. Value stream analysis is also called value stream mapping (VSM). Its aim is to record the current efficiency of the added value and to clearly represent the results with the aid of symbols and colours. In doing so, everything is reviewed from the customers' point of view; for in the end, the customers determine the demands on the production and consequently on each single production process.

By such an analysis, the value-adding as well as the not-value-adding processes are being identified. In the following design approach, an improved value stream is designed by minimising and, if possible, eliminating non-value-adding activities and unnecessary wait times. In the context of the services management, the particular wait times between the value-adding segments are minimised.

This method has been developed in Japan. Eliminating waste (of time) is a keystone of the Toyota Production System (TPS). The Japanese word for waste is *muda*; therefore, the procedure of waste elimination is called muda elimination.

Prior to the kick-off meeting, the project head and the controller identify the key data (parts and costs history, partial price comparison, assessment of cost drivers with the aid of an ABC analysis, and target price analysis) and prepare a presentation that shall clearly outline the motive, necessity, and chances of the project. If the object in question is an OEM product or if the added value of the product is predominantly bought in, the calculation of the supplier is also roughly assessed by this method—a nice side effect. OEMs (Original Equipment Manufacturers) are defined as manufacturers of components or products that do not market these products on their own. With excellent results I often deployed trainees for this necessary but time-consuming work; the trainees (especially the career-minded ones) enthusiastically attended to the whole process and profited enormously with regard to their training and their professional career.

2. Based on the actual designs, the suppliers are confronted with the assessed knowledge about the benchmark prices and consequently the realistic potentials to start negotiations with target prices (Fig. 7.1).

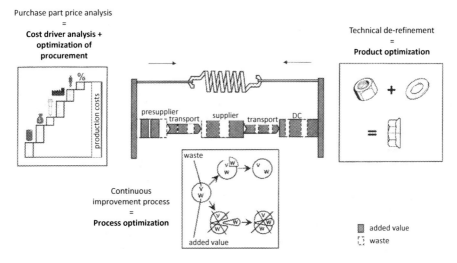

Fig. 7.1 Product and process optimisation along the value chain

The results realised in this way will, however, often be much higher than the economic costing values. For this reason, new ways of cost reduction must be found. Now it is up to the complete value analysis team including the suppliers. The following list of questions is a good guideline and repository of ideas for detecting wastes with regard to the functions and the customer benefit. Additional to purchasing price analyses, the value stream and the added value analyses are further sources of hidden potentials.

- Is the function necessary for the majority of the customers?
- Can functions be achieved by other parts?
- How can functional flaws be removed?
- Are particular attributes overdesigned?
- Which tolerances can be widened without compromising the functionality?
- Can materials be replaced by cheaper ones?
- Which materials could ease the manufacturing process?
- Can particular parts be replaced by standard parts or be made of standard parts?
- Will changes in the structural design reduce the material or handling costs?
- Will it be possible to make the part with another manufacturing process or with other means of production?
- Will it be possible to omit or shorten particular processes?
- Will in-house be more benefiting than external procurement?
- Is the prescribed surface treatment really necessary?
- Is another surface treatment acceptable?
- Will waste be diminished by changes of the construction, by changes in the manufacturing process, or by harmonisation of the raw part to the manufacturing dimensions?
- Are there others uses for the waste?
- May a particular part be made from the waste of another one?
- Will it be cheaper, if a part is composed of several single parts?
- Will costs be saved by changing packaging or mode of transportation?

3. After an extensive brainstorming process, the identified potentials are assessed and the respective cost improvements added up in best- and worst-case scenarios. The whole process runs into a realisation concept with priorities, time lines, and assigned responsibilities.

4. Realisation. Now the designed external and internal measures must be tracked by the project management with regard to their quick and effective implementation. The team and the customer must be informed on the progresses regularly—so do good and talk about it!

How the procedure works in practice, I will now describe by means of an example from my time in the automotive industry. My then employer supplied seat systems and car gearshifts to several car manufacturers as a first-tier supplier (Fig. 7.2). As a very young, fledgling technician for machine tools I was made responsible for the project

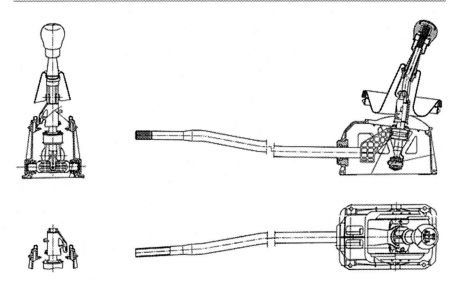

Fig. 7.2 Object of the value analysis: switching tube

after only 2 months of employment with the company. This was a difficult task for the result of a first calculation and the fixed selling price were worlds apart. A two-digit percentage quotation was missing only to break even. My then employer experienced severe economic difficulties at that time, and so the price dictate of the renowned purchaser had to be accepted according to the slogan: "We will get it done." I did not see this situation at that time as a burden but as a challenge and a chance; as the product was just at the beginning of a 4-year life cycle, all was not yet lost. I was given a free hand (which boosted my motivation enormously), and so I started with conducting the ABC analysis. Apart from several processes that badly needed optimisation, quickly a dominant A part became apparent: a shifting tube that was mounted in several car types as a platform product.

In the second step, in close cooperation with the purchasing division a global enquiry for this part was started (including, amongst others, suppliers from Germany, Italy, and China); in this enquiry, we requested that the submission of a tender should also include the figures of the separate price components (Fig. 7.3). With an annual volume of 950,000 parts, this order was very attractive for the providers, and so I received all data needed for a parts-related price comparison. Although the global enquiry brought the desired results with regard to the component prices as well as with regard to the tooling costs, the project team decided to begin final negotiations with the German provider due to its quality level and the physical proximity to that supplier.

The price comparison of the separate parts proved very helpful in the negotiation as it demonstrated, at least in theory, the possibility of massive price and cost improvements. With negotiating skills and that information, the price per unit could be reduced from 5.67 EUR to 4.93 EUR and the tooling costs from 68,000 EUR to 43,000 EUR (see Fig. 7.4).

Supplier A Germany	Supplier B China	Supplier C Italy
5.67 Euro	4.63 Euro	6.10 Euro
tooling 68,000 Euro	tooling	tooling 56,000 Euro

Fig. 7.3 Global price comparison

part / work step	Supplier A Germany	Supplier B China	Supplier C Italy	target
Ball 90235664	0.03 €	0.01 €	0.04 €	0.01 €
tube 90465459	0.95 €	0.98 €	0.99 €	0.95 €
Sheet 90465 677	0.45 €	0.32 €	0.15 €	0.15 €
Ring 90222227	0.15 €	0.14 €	0.18 €	0.14 €
Zink plating	0.60 €	0.40 €	0.75 €	0.40 €
Knurling	0.50 €	0.08 €	0.45 €	0.08 €
Reducing	0.15 €	0.10 €	0.16 €	0.10 €
Bending I	0.30 €	0.10 €	0.32 €	0.10 €
Bending II	0.28 €	0.09 €	0.26 €	0.09 €
Welding Tube	0.26 €	0.12 €	0.31 €	0.12 €
Welding Ring	0.35 €	0.17 €	0.40 €	0.17 €
Milling	0.20 €	0.01 €	0.25 €	0.01 €
Packaging	0.12 €	0.06 €	0.14 €	0.06 €
Transport	0.09 €	0.98 €	0.40 €	0.09 €
Profit & Contribution	1.24 €	0.80 €	1.30 €	0.80 €
Complete price	5.67€	4.63 €	6.10 €	3.27 €
Tooling	68,000.00 €	16,000.00 €	56,000.00 €	16,000.00 €

Fig. 7.4 Results of the parts-related price comparison

But, sadly enough, the result was not sufficient for the project going into the black. In close concert with the supplier, and our customer as well, within 1 year we succeeded in reducing the price of the shifting tube to 4.30 EUR with the aid of value analysis measures, and we could at the same time also considerably reduce the weight of this component (a comparison of the shifting tube before and after the value analysis measures is given in Figs. 7.5 and 7.6). Especially for automotive manufacturers, weight reduction is a very important customer benefit that—in contrast to the situation at that time—will nowadays be financially rewarded by customers from that industry.

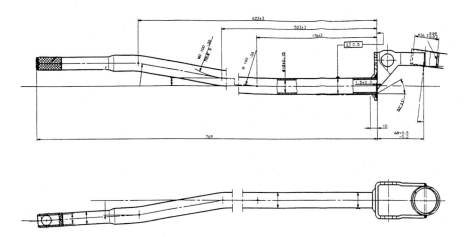

Fig. 7.5 Switching tube before value analysis

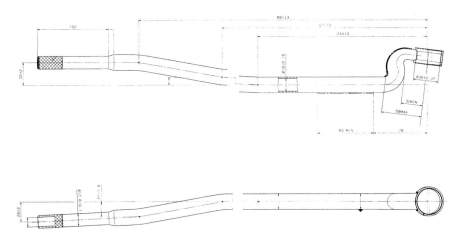

Fig. 7.6 Switching tube after value analysis

The resulting savings of 1.54 MM EUR greatly contributed to the profitability of the system. And I had found my lifelong love of Purchasing, as I had learnt that Purchasing is a powerful leverage that is becoming ever more important.

Conclusion Price and value analyses are an efficient instrument if significant cost reductions must be achieved. And never forget to involve the suppliers with their great optimising know-how!

7.3   ABC Analysis

As already described above, the purchasing division assumes many, in part new tasks in the company. In order to counter the danger of overwork and to safeguard an efficient resource management, the use of a management method is advised by which important things can be separated from unimportant ones.

The ABC analysis is a microeconomic analytical method for classifying given quantities of objects according to their quantity–value ratio. The principle describes the statistical fact that a small number of high values within the value pool contributes more to its total value than a big number of small values. The separate values of the value pool are ranked and prioritised according to a particular criterion by classifying the positions with respect to their economic importance.

The ABC analysis was originally used in the materials management for evaluating the values of inventories of particular kinds of goods. Transferred to other applications, ABC analyses can generally be used for separating important and unimportant values. Thus, activities can be concentrated on a small area with high economic significance. By a targeted use of ABC analyses, the efficiency of management measures can be enhanced.

To understand the ABC analysis procedure in detail, in the following will be shown how the bought-in parts of a final product can be classified according to their acquisition values with the aim of deriving from that analysis courses of action for the respective categories. For conducting the ABC analysis, it is advised to use a spreadsheet program giving a diagram similar to the one in the following figure.

At first, the single components and their purchase prices are listed e.g. in a parts list. Subsequently, the list is screened for bought-in parts, and the quantity of the respective component that is incorporated in the final product is multiplied by its purchase price. Thus, a monetary value is found for each bought-in part. These monetary values are now sorted in descending order resulting in a value-based ranking of the single components. In another column, these values are now being accumulated resulting in a total sum at the lowest component.

At the next stage, the value share of the single bought-in parts is assessed as a percentage. The assessed percentage is accumulated in another column. This procedure is then repeated for the respective quantities of the single bought-in parts resulting in a chart of which an example is given in Fig. 7.7.

The columns showing the accumulated value percentages and the accumulated quantity percentages are now crucial for further analysis. Here, the positions are separated in A, B, and C parts. The boundaries of this separation should be drawn sensibly and may differ case by case. As a rough guide, the boundaries may be set at roughly 80 and 95% of the accumulated value percentage. Putting the results into graphs (see Fig. 7.8) may provide a clearer understanding. The graphical representation can now be interpreted as follows:

- A parts: Include 12% of the parts, representing a value share of just under 80%
- B parts: Include 13% of the parts, representing a value share of roughly 15%
- C parts: Include the last 75% of the parts, representing a value share of 5%

material	price / 100 pcs.	quantity	total (Price x quantity)	total cum.	% value	% cum.	% quantity	% quantity cum.
385-000	6018.30 €	1	6018.30 €	6018.30 €	12.31%	12.3%	0.2%	0.2%
210-009	2950.00 €	1	2950.00 €	8968.30 €	6.04%	18.4%	0.2%	0.3%
345-000	2020.00 €	1	2020.00 €	10,988.30 €	4.13%	22.5%	0.2%	0.5%
640-010	1951.26 €	1	1951.26 €	12,939.56 €	3.99%	26.5%	0.2%	0.7%
580-000	1733.00 €	1	1733.00 €	14,672.56 €	3.55%	30.0%	0.2%	0.8%
025-000	1667.00 €	1	1667.00 €	16,339.56 €	3.41%	33.4%	0.2%	1.0%
361-014	1480.00 €	1	1480.00 €	17,819.56 €	3.03%	36.5%	0.2%	1.2%
405-000	1374.00 €	1	1374.00 €	19,193.56 €	2.81%	39.3%	0.2%	1.3%
003-022	1370.57 €	1	1370.57 €	20,564.12 €	2.80%	42.1%	0.2%	1.5%
020-000	1222.00 €	1	1222.00 €	21,786.12 €	2.50%	44.6%	0.2%	1.6%
030-015	1175.00 €	1	1175.00 €	22,961.12 €	2.40%	47.0%	0.2%	1.8%
...	...	...	...	...	...	...	...	...
...	...	...	...	...	...	...	...	...
...	...	...	...	...	...	...	...	...
456-802	0.14 €	3	0.4200 €	48,869.88 €	0.0009%	100.0%	0.5%	99.7%
451-913	0.10 €	1	0.1000 €	48,869.98 €	0.0002%	100.0%	0.2%	99.8%
454-703	0.08 €	1	0.0800 €	48,870.06 €	0.0002%	100.0%	0.2%	100.0%

Fig. 7.7 Extract of an ABC analysis

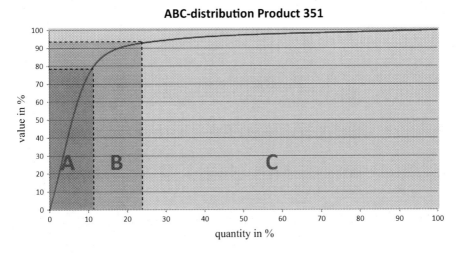

Fig. 7.8 Graphic representation of the ABC analysis

From the completed analysis, now recommendations for actions can be derived, e.g. comprehensive procurement market research, monitoring, and analysis measures with regard to the identified A parts. The implementation of consignment warehouses or a just-in-time delivery schedule may result in a significant reduction of the stock value with regard to these parts. Furthermore, A parts may provide starting points for cost-cutting programs or be made the subject of value analysis investigations. Thus, by focusing on the key positions efficient management measures can be taken. B and C materials must, however, never be completely neglected. Here, it is necessary to minimise the management efforts by standardisation and automation, e.g. by standardised procurement market research, automated ordering processes, or the arrangement of collective billing. From this approach, C parts management has been developed as a purchasing discipline providing a standardised procedure for the procurement of sundries with a low value percentage.

As the example has shown, the procedure of the ABC analysis focuses on a quantitative evaluation of the net value in order to concentrate on the key parts. However, one must always bear in mind that for parts that have been classified as B or C parts in some circumstances, certain management efforts may be necessary due to qualitative criteria (such as risk, complexity, or image). Nevertheless, the ABC analysis offers an approach for deliberately managing the purchasing and realising greater efficiency in the purchasing activities.

7.4   Portfolio Technique

The portfolio technique has originated in the financial management; there, the composition of the investment portfolio with the aid of portfolio analyses has been represented according to the factors of return and risk. Nowadays, this technique is used in modified form in diverse areas of business administration and has become one of the most widely used instruments of the strategic management. Thus, schemes such as the growth share matrix of the Boston Consulting Group, the growth share matrix of McKinsey, or the market-product life cycle matrix have been established.

Basically, the portfolio technique can be applied to different questions in the purchasing area. Applying it will always be sensible when one or more objects shall be related to two criteria. With regard to strategic considerations, often a company criterion (internal) will be singled out as the key factors. These two criteria form the two axes of a two-dimensional coordinate system. The coordinate system is then divided into four fields, and generic and standard strategies are being defined for each of the fields. Thus, a general scope of action is created.

In the next stage, the objects to be examined are being analysed and evaluated according to both criteria. By the evaluation the position of the object within the coordinate system is determined; all objects will in the end be found in one of the four defined fields. Conclusively, the selected generic and standard strategies can be specified and elaborated. Thus, the portfolio technique provides for a clear and simple visualisation of complex circumstances from which concrete courses of action can be deduced.

For better understanding, two usual examples of the use of the portfolio technique in purchasing are given below.

7.4.1 Commodity Groups Portfolio

Establishing the commodity groups portfolio is a familiar and usual application of the portfolio technique in purchasing. The commodity groups are analysed according to the criteria of purchase volume and supply risk. The purchase volume is the company criterion and can be equated with the relevance of the commodity group for one's company. The supply risk on the other hand is the environmental criterion and represents the availability of the material and the complexity of procuring it.

The commodity groups are evaluated with respect to the criteria with the help of a grid diagram. A fixed classification scheme is used to safeguard the objective positioning of the commodity group. The groups can then be classified according to four categories (see Fig. 7.9), and generic strategies be applied to them.

With regard to leverage commodity groups, it is advised to make use of the existing market power in order to realise long-term savings e.g. by sourcing in best-cost countries. With regard to strategic commodity groups, the focus should be laid on supplier development and close cooperation with the suppliers, while with regard to non-critical commodity groups, bundling, standardisation, and automation should be the key strategies. With regard to bottleneck commodity groups, especially risk management and material substitution will be called for.

Fig. 7.9 Portfolio technique to display the purchasing program

7.4.2   Supplier Portfolio

The supplier portfolio (Fig. 7.10) represents an approach to make clear different constellations of market power by a comparison of the supplier's supply power and one's company's demand power.

The individual suppliers are positioned as circles in the supplier portfolio according to the respective market power constellation. As the third parameter, the size of the respective purchase volume can be shown by the diameter of the respective circle—the bigger the circle is, the higher is the purchase volume. The diagram thus not only shows the power constellations with regard to the individual suppliers but also the purchase volumes they represent.

To the four categories, generic and standard strategies can be assigned that determine the basic orientation of the strategic measures:

A. The supplier has a strong position of power with regard to the buyer. Emancipation will be the strategic target in this case—the dependency on the supplier should be reduced by targeted internal and external measures; materials should be substituted if possible; and one's attractiveness as customer should be better exploited.
B. Both the supplier and the buyer have strong positions of power. Both depend on each other, and both have many opportunities to exert influence on the other. In this power constellation, a close partner-like cooperation is advised in which the interests of both parties are being preserved.

Fig. 7.10 Positioning of suppliers based on market power position

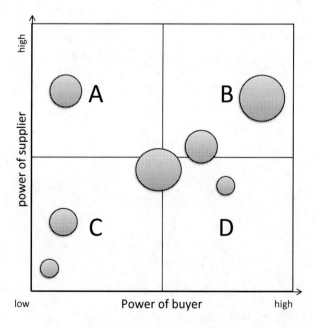

C. Two weak and insignificant market partners meet. Both do not need the other, and normally their business relationship is loose and impersonal. Strategic considerations will, if at all, only be applied selectively as suppliers of that kind can be replaced at any time.

D. The supplier has a comparatively weak power position with regard to the buyer. In this market constellation, the strategic considerations will focus on realising chances. Such chances may include generating savings but also the development of the supplier targeted to one's needs. This market constellation is especially favourable to that aim as such suppliers are easily malleable because of their weak position.

As these two examples have shown, the portfolio technique can be applied variably if complex situations should be visualised in a clear form. By positioning different objects strategically, the portfolio technique is useful to the planning process but also to daily questions.

7.5   Price Structure Analysis

The instrument of price structure analysis tries to track the pricing of suppliers. The price of the product is broken up into its individual cost and gain components in order to identify the supplier's negotiating range as well as optimisation potentials. In this procedure, at first the relevant cost components of the project are being identified and evaluated. This is the most difficult task in a price structure analysis. By adding the individual cost components, the approximate unit cost value can be established. The difference from the offer price is the margin which will be subject of the ensuing price negotiation.

A price structure analysis based on the absorbed costs uses the generally accepted product costing scheme; the individual costs and the overhead costs are established separately (Fig. 7.11).

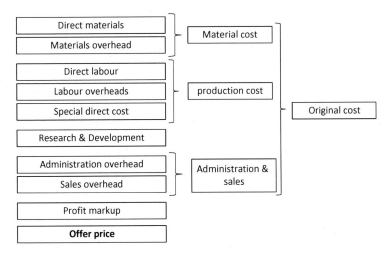

Fig. 7.11 Components of full costing

Individual costs are measurable costs that can be directly attributed to a cost object: the most important cost components in this category are material and labour costs. A purchasing division should be able to comparatively accurately assess the costs of the production material; only the type and volume of the material to be deployed must be determined in advance. These costs can be established by breaking up (also literally) the product into its individual components. This process will result in a parts list in which the individual components are listed according to their types of material. By weighing, measuring, and counting the individual volumes can be included; percentages for scrap and clippings must be taken into account. In order to calculate the merchandise value, one's own experience concerning prices may serve as a guideline. If no reference prices are available, they must be assessed by research in the markets in which the suppliers source their own supply, e.g. by concrete quote requests of sub-suppliers or by analysing market reports and price statistics. For assessing the material costs, it is advised to estimate medium prices in order to factor price fluctuations in.

At the next stage, the direct labour costs are assessed. Here, the two factors of time exposure and hourly wage have to be factored in. After establishing the needed qualifications of the employees deployed to the manufacturing process, the customary wage rates are assessed. As a basis for doing so, company-owned data from the human resources department or trade-specific publications such as pay scale tables may be used. The time exposure, however, is more difficult to estimate; for doing so, the production process must be known in detail. To break up the production process into its individual steps and to allocate the times, the support of departments such as production, development, or process planning may become necessary. If no clues to the production process are available in-house, a visit of the supplier's plant may be helpful for understanding the production process in detail. The resulting manufacturing costs are the product of wages and time exposure.

In the further course of the analysis, one has to ascertain whether other cost components can de directly attributed to the product apart from the material and manufacturing costs. Such individual production costs include, amongst others, the costs of special tools, models, or special devices necessary for the manufacturing of the product. As these costs are often displayed separately in the respective offers, there will, as a rule, be no problems to assess them. Much more difficult, however, is the estimation of research and development costs. The only clues are provided by the development time that is estimated subject to the complexity, novelty, and unusualness of the product. As a rule, one will be reliant on the supplier's information.

In contrast to individual costs, overhead costs cannot be attributed directly to a cost object. In company cost accounting, these costs are broken down with the aid of overhead rates that may differ greatly depending on the structure of the company. Material overhead costs include all costs arising from the procurement, examination, transport, and storage of materials. As an accurate assessment of these costs is hardly possible, normally a surcharge rate of 5–10% of the direct material costs will be estimated. Production overheads represent a much bigger pool of costs. These include all production-related costs (imputed depreciations, occupancy and energy costs, wages, etc.). These costs can only be estimated roughly; a clue may be the supplier's machinery in operation. Hardly any clue is available to the estimation of the administrative and selling overheads. These costs depend on the size of the administrative organisation and the number of different products these costs are apportioned among.

As for the given reasons assessing the overhead costs is difficult, in Germany normally cost statistics of the Statistisches Bundesamt are used. This agency assesses and publishes the cost structure of manufacturing companies sorted by industry and size of company in an annual report that provides clues to the customary overhead rates.

From all these collected data, now the supplier's calculation can be reproduced and the original costs of the product can be estimated. The difference from the offer price is the margin for the negotiations in which a suitable mark-up must be conceded to the supplier.

Although the assessed original costs will never exactly coincide with the supplier's actual costs, price structure analyses provide for a high degree of transparency in the price negotiations. The breakdown of the individual cost components gives facts and figures for discussions in which individual cost drivers can be identified and optimised. The key factor, however, is that the supplier is compelled to disclose information. If the assessed calculations do not meet the actual costs, the supplier will justify this discrepancy and thereby disclose valuable information, especially concerning the structure of the overhead costs. This information can be used for future price structure analyses. Thus, the accuracy of the price structure analysis increases the more often this instrument, which is very valuable for price negotiations, is applied.

References

Arnolds, H., et al. (2010). *Materialwirtschaft und Einkauf*. Wiesbaden: Gabler.
Wannewetsch, H. (2010). *Integrierte Materialwirtschaft und Logistik*. Heidelberg: Springer.

The Purchasing Negotiation

8

8.1 The Principles of a Purchasing Negotiation

A negotiation in the tradition sense is a situation in which persons or parties represent different interests and aim at the realisation of reciprocal benefits, e.g. by the exchange of services for means of payment. The prerequisites of a negotiation are the existence of mutual dependencies, a relative balance of power between the parties, and the willingness of both parties to reach an agreement. If one of these conditions is not met, a negotiation will, as a rule, end in one party dictating the exchange conditions with the other party being forced to either accept these conditions or terminate negotiations.

Negotiating is a matter of everyday life. It occurs whenever two or more parties have different positions that must be reconciled. Typical examples of such conflict situations are negotiations with one's superior concerning a fair payment, negotiations with friends concerning the question where to spend the next holidays, or negotiations with one's life partner concerning the selection of the TV programme. In all these cases, our own position must be reconciled with the position of others. In most cases, the reconciliation will be achieved intuitively without thinking. We do not reflect on how to conduct the negotiation or what negotiation strategy we should use. And such reflection will often be unnecessary indeed. However, reflection will be necessary in cases where decisions of great significance have to be made and much money is at stake—situations strategic purchasers are confronted with often. Every day, strategic purchasers must reconcile the position of their respective company to that of suppliers, and in doing so, they must always try to achieve the optimum results for their respective company. Thus, their success in negotiations has a direct bearing on the purchasing division's value contribution to the company's business success since every sum that has been negotiated badly will reappear in the company's profit and loss account at the latest. Thus, purchasing negotiations are one of the core tasks of Strategic Purchasing.

In many cases, however, the starting position of purchasers is worse than the position of their negotiation partners for sellers, in contrast to purchasers, as a rule

© Springer International Publishing AG 2017
U. Weigel, M. Ruecker, *The Strategic Procurement Practice Guide*, Management for Professionals, DOI 10.1007/978-3-319-57651-0_8

represent a limited range of products and are adequately trained in conducting sales talks. Special negotiating trainings for purchasers are relatively rare even today, so the available negotiating know-how will often be confined to personal experience. For that reason, mistakes in the conduct of negotiations that have not been perceived and analysed may be repeated in other situations. The situation can be compared to exercising a type of sport without the instruction of a coach. While progress may be registered as success on a personal basis, there will be no objective judgement regarding the question whether techniques and motion sequences have been applied correctly and efficiently.

For that reason, abstract basic knowledge should be available that has to be supplemented by practical experience afterwards. In the following section, some approaches are introduced by which purchasers will be enabled to reflect on and optimise their conduct in negotiations in order to enforce realistic demands within the scope of a purchasing negotiation.

8.1.1   Motives for Purchasing Negotiations

Negotiating is day-to-day business of strategic purchasers; myriads of situations arise in which negotiating becomes necessary. Negotiations are already necessary in in-house conflicts concerning e.g. the right way to handle questions that have a bearing on purchasing in the context of projects or the cross-departmental implementation of strategies.

But negotiating with external suppliers and service providers is the crucial task. The most important element in this area is negotiating prices—whatever topic has been scheduled for a negotiation, at some point in the course of the talks costs will have to be discussed.

Price negotiations may be conducted for the following reasons, amongst others:

- Negotiations concerning the acceptance of a bid
- Prevention of price increases
- Realisation of price reductions
- Volume bundling
- Reallocation of expiring framework agreements
- Negotiations concerning one's own salary

Practical Tip: What to Do in Suddenly Arising Negotiation Situations
How can one react in situations such as an unexpected telephone call in which the caller (who will, by the way, in most cases have an advantage over the person called) demands an unpostponable negotiation and an immediate decision? Or—a case I experienced many years ago—if a member of the executive board without any advance warning suddenly presents a former schoolmate as his preferred supplier with whom a "quick" negotiation should be conducted on the spot?

As an aid for such awkward situations, the "supplier negotiating chart" has been developed. This chart, which will be detailed below, provides at a glance all key information on a supplier including its quality and supply reliability, the current risk score, its trading volume, its A-parts and their respective price development, all business conditions, etc. Additionally, general argumentation aids and a field dedicated to the previously defined targets are also given.

I never leave my ring binder at home although some people may think this habit to be old-fashioned (of course, a tablet computer will also do). Thus, equipped with many empirically established figures, checklists, and current market and procurement data, I am always and wherever I may actually be ready for impromptu negotiations without the need for special preparation. In many cases, I could make my presence felt in quite diverse meetings and enhance efficiency thanks to these up-to-date data. By way of example, two of these checklists are given now.

Checklist Concerning Work Contracts and Work and Delivery Contracts

1. Subject of the order
   - Has the subject of the order been defined?
2. Scope of supply and scope of work
   - Has the scope of supply, work, and services been described completely and precisely?
   - Have the warranted qualities been adequately described?
   - Have packaging and shipment been specified?
   - Has the scope of test and approval procedures been defined exactly?
3. Bought-in or spare parts
   - Does the producer also supply bought-in or spare parts, if necessary?
4. Quality requirements on the producer
   - How and by whom will the acceptance processes be performed?
5. Deadlines
   - Have all single steps and milestones important to the purchaser been defined?
6. Prices
   - Is the producer obliged to provide evidence of the marketability with regard to additional or reduced costs (by disclosing the calculation, if necessary)?
   - How are travel costs in the context of the project accounted for?
7. Payment conditions
   - Have events been fixed that will prompt payments, e.g. demands?
   - Acceptance of order
   - Acceptance protocol
   - Are advance payments or warranty bonds required?
8. Contractual penalties
   - Have contractual penalties been agreed (in % of the contract value, in concrete sums, in material supplies, or other services) with fixed maximum prices?
   - Has the time of tolerable delay been defined?
   - Can additional compensation for damages caused by delays be claimed?

9. Warranty
   - Has the scope of warranties been precisely defined?
   - Which qualities are warranted?
10. Liability and other claims
11. Secrecy, property rights, documents
12. Termination, suspension, avoidance, publication of contract
13. Cession, pledge, rights of third parties
14. General order processing
15. Place of performance, place of jurisdiction, applicable law
16. Options
    - Is there the option of possible future orders that could be negotiated at the same time?
17. Machinery guidelines
18. General terms and conditions of purchase
    - Have the General Terms and Conditions of Purchase been accepted?
    - If not, have at least the conditions according to the applicable law (in Germany, HGB/BGB) been agreed?

Checklist: Framework Conditions Concerning Direct Materials or Production Materials

1. Prices and price components:
   - Long-term agreements (falling prices)
   - Quantity scale discount
   - Special offer discount
   - Special offer prices
   - Bonuses
     - Volume increase
     - Diversification
     - Reliability
     - Special deals
     - Marriage bonus
   - Discount for increased productivity (learning curve)
   - Discount for long-term contracts
   - Has the price been broken down into its components?
   - Bull-and-bear clause for cost drivers
2. Payment conditions:
   - Discount
     - Longer time for payment
     - Compensation
     - Bill/cheque—bill/prolongation
3. Incoterms:
   - Ex works
   - Free buyer's store
   - Free buyer

4. Stock:
   - Delivery times
   - Stockpiling at the supplier
   - Preferably consignment stock at buyer's domicile
   - Kanban/just in time
   - C parts management
   - Direct delivery to purchaser
5. Follow-up costs:
   - PPM rate or 100% good parts
   - Procedure in cases of default (return/rejection/replacement)
   - Hourly rates, carrying costs, handling, loss of sales and profits
6. Terms and conditions of purchase:
   - Have the terms and conditions of purchase been accepted?
   - If no other agreement has been met, HGB and BGB have always to be applied amongst German business parties
7. Warranty:
   - Has the scope of warranties been defined precisely?
   - Which qualities have been warranted?
8. Quality assurance agreement:
   - Can a quality assurance agreement be reached?

8.1.2   Negotiating Strategies

Basically, three types of negotiating strategies may be chosen: the cooperative, the fair compromise, and the competitive negotiating strategy.

The cooperative negotiating strategy aims at close cooperation with the negotiating partner in order to jointly achieve solutions. In these cases, the establishment of long-term partnerships will often be the ultimate target of the negotiation.

The fair compromise strategy is based on rational aspects. Both sides make mutual concessions in order to reach a just and fair deal.

The competitive negotiating strategy shares the same basic structure with the fair compromise; however, the aim is to achieve as much for one's own and as less for the other party's position as possible by a one-sided exchange of concessions. This negotiating strategy (which will often be accompanied by negotiation wiles) is often applied in the case of one-time deals as one of the parties is bound to be the loser of such negotiations.

A good negotiator must have all three negotiating strategies at his or her command in order to be able to use, but also to fend them off in different situations.

8.2   Preparation

An in-depth preparation for a negotiation is often neglected in business practice—mostly because of lacking time, unstructured lines of action, or ignorance of its importance. Nevertheless, the preparation is already one of the key stages in the negotiating process. Regardless of motivation, initial position, and strategy, a major part of the negotiation success will always be achieved by sound preparation. The preparation can be compared to a film script. Experienced purchasers tend to devise a common thread by previously deliberating different scenarios. This offers the opportunity to flexibly address different topics in the course of the negotiation without losing sight of the main questions. Many potentials and risks can be considered previously and will thus offer room for manoeuvre. A clear structuring of the course of the negotiation and the devising of different options and approaches will have a positive influence on the negotiation time and help to avoid lengthy and tough negotiation marathons. The more difficult it is to anticipate the course of a negotiation, the more careful the preparation should be. As a rule of thumb, one might say that double the time planned for the negotiation should be spent on the preparation.

8.2.1   Organisational Preparation

At first, the organisational framework conditions for guaranteeing a smooth course of the negotiation must be realised. To achieve this, at first the location, the date, and the time frame of the negotiation must be arranged with the negotiating partner. Conducting the negotiations in the company's own premises will—apart from the home field advantage—have the positive side effect to make alternative use of the time otherwise spent on travelling. Colleagues from other departments can be called in flexibly, and all resources of the own workspace are available. Furthermore, the purchaser has the host role, which means that he is in control of the framework conditions of the negotiation. However, the advantage of negotiations at the supplier's is that the purchaser will get a personal idea of the supplier's production flows, process steps, and potentials. The place of negotiation should therefore be carefully selected according to the background and aims of the respective negotiation.

The timing of the negotiations is also important as the performance capacities of people vary in the course of the day. So-called morning persons reach their highest performance capacity around 10 a.m. while evening persons will perform best only in the afternoon. But one thing both types of persons have in common: noonday is always the time of lowest performance. Therefore, midday is always the worst time for starting negotiations. It is important to know one's own performance curve and plan the timing of negotiations accordingly. And it is of course only sensible to also consider the length of the negotiation and take care that it can be conducted in the regular working hours.

The timing should be done in a way that all individual points can be discussed without unnecessary time pressure. Depending on the foreseeable length of the negotiations, pause times should also be planned in.

Apart from place, time, and duration, the subjects of the purchase negotiation should also be agreed beforehand. To do so, one party will compile a subject list in writing that is then amended by the other and thus becomes the agenda. In this way, both parties have the opportunity to prepare the negotiation specifically, which in turn ensures an efficient course of the negotiation. In reality, it often happens that decisions must be postponed because some documents are missing or speciality departments must be consulted—this situation would have been avoided by a subject-oriented preparation.

If the negotiation takes place in the company's own premises, the next step is to create the general framework conditions. These include e.g. the visitor registration at the reception. It is a sign of professionalism when the supplier is welcomed by name on a display board at the reception, and this will also give him or her the impression of being appreciated. A tour of the facility may be included to provide the supplier insight into the processing of the delivered products. Aspects such as tidiness, process reliability, and quality management should be emphasised especially.

With respect to the ever-increasing amount of meetings in the day-to-day activities of the company, it is essential that an appropriate conference room be arranged. Furniture, fixtures, lighting conditions, and air ventilation should be appropriate for the negotiation as the room in this case is representative of one's company. If necessary, devices such as laptop, beamer, or flipchart that may be needed during the course of the negotiation must be organised and placed in the conference room.

Finally, an appropriate catering must be provided. The basic principle is to offer at least these things that one would expect if one were the guest. Coffee and soft drinks should be offered standardly regardless of the visitor and the length of the meeting. If the negotiation is planned to take a longer time, a lunch may also be organised. If due to the distance the supplier will arrive the day before the negotiation, it has often proven helpful to invite him or her to dinner that day. A shared dinner may help to break the ice on the personal level, and that can only have positive repercussions on the course of the negotiation. But in this, one imperative must not be forgotten: to listen carefully and to disclose prudently.

After the framework conditions for a smooth negotiation process have been set, the next step is the preparation with regard to contents by means of a standardised checklist, the so-called supplier negotiation form.

8.2.2 Supplier Negotiation Form

The supplier negotiation form (Fig. 8.1) is a tried-and-tested checklist for preparing negotiations with suppliers as far as contents are concerned. This list consists of several subject areas that must be researched in the run-up to the negotiation. Essentially, the following three questions shall be answered:

- What is the concrete topic of the negotiation?
- What information is needed to make decisions within the scope of the negotiation?
- Will the supplier be capable of fulfilling the required demands?

At first, the business relations between the supplier and the customer are depicted in a clearly arranged way. Usually, the result will be a number of starting points and possible lines of reasoning that may become useful during the negotiation. The list especially includes actual company data such as its legal form, its capital resources, its branch of trade, the size of the company, its market position, references as well as the deployed production procedures, and the number and location of the production facilities. The necessary information can be gathered by

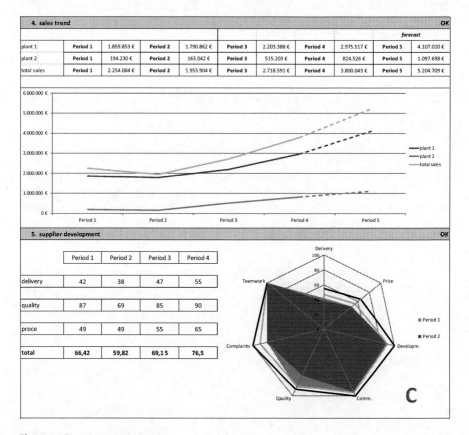

Fig. 8.1 Supplier negotiation form

procurement market research, a supplier self-assessment, or other research methods.

At the next step, the current market trends of the supplier's branch of trade are being evaluated. Up-to-date business indicators, exchange rates, or the development of commodity prices may strengthen the purchaser's negotiating position. If the negotiation partner is a regular supplier in the next step, the history of the business relationship can be scrutinised. The development of sales is a good indicator of whether the supplier is gaining in significance for one's home company or whether the supplier is increasingly losing purchasing volumes to competitors. Apart from the development of sales, two key figures of the supplier rating can also be helpful: delivery reliability and quality. These two figures do not only provide aids to push one's negotiation goals but can also be introduced in the negotiation by linking the agreed result to a specific target value (see Chap. 5). Thus, the supplier commits itself to a direct improvement in performance. However, the measuring method for ascertaining the key data as well as the consequences for non-fulfilling the target values must be defined clearly to preclude the possibility of later conflicts.

In the next steps, the products are listed that are bought from the negotiation partner. Depending on the respective volumes, the list can be limited to only the most important positions and those with the highest turnover. For the listed parts, the history of the prices is ascertained in absolute numbers and percentage. This shows on the one hand how steady the prices of the parts bought from the supplier are and on the other whether not only increases but also reductions of costs are passed on to the customer.

If the negotiation is concerned with new parts, the previously offered prices of the suppliers can be recorded in the list. By adding the prices of competitors, a simplified comparison of the bids is compiled although additional costs such as freightage, tolls, packaging costs, etc., must always be taken into account for a meaningful comparison of the prices. From this information, a price should be formed the realisation of which will be the target of the negotiation.

At the end, the participants of the negotiation should be considered. Who will take part in the negotiation; which interests do these persons pursue; and to what extent are they entitled to make decisions? If the person in question is a managing director or sales manager, there will often be the possibility of making decisions during the negotiation. If engineers take part in the negotiation, the supplier's arguments may quickly divagate to technical details—the purchaser must be prepared accordingly, either by in-depth know-how of the subject in question or by calling in technical advisors from other departments of the company. For planning a structured course of the negotiation, one must always know who takes part and which direction the course of the negotiation may take under their influence. Furthermore, there must be no doubt about one's own authority to decide; if there are any doubts, the necessary backing of the management level must be demanded.

In this way, all information necessary for the negotiation is integrated and clearly represented in the Supplier negotiation form. Depending on the complexity and extent of the negotiation, it may be advised to peruse the form jointly with the involved departments. Thus, a second or third perspective is provided, and further starting points for the negotiation may be opened up.

8.2.3   Negotiation Targets

In any case, targets should be defined at the end of the preparation for the negotiation. Minimum and maximum targets may serve as the corner posts of one's own room to negotiate. In this way, the danger is prevented that during the negotiation—driven by pressure or euphoria—hasty concessions are made that will be rued afterwards. For setting the targets, the application of the SMART rule is advised. SMART stands for the attributes: specific, measurable, accepted, realistic, and time-phased. The more of these qualities the defined target fulfils, the more tangible and precise this target is.

The BATNA method may be applied as an orientation guide with regard to the minimum targets. BATNA ("best alternative to a negotiated agreement") is derived from the "principled negotiation" method devised by the Harvard Negotiation Project that will be detailed in the course of this chapter. This method takes the approach that the result of a negotiation is satisfying only when it is better than all available alternatives. That means that within the scope of the preparation, realistic alternatives must be identified which could be taken should the negotiation fail. The better the alternative, the higher the minimum targets can be set. Thus, BATNA is strengthening one's own negotiating position enormously, for only those who have good alternatives up their sleeves need not be afraid of the collapse of the negotiation.

Maximum targets can be set in a similar way by estimating and evaluating the negotiation partner's BATNA. The opponent's pain barrier will in this case be the optimum negotiation result.

Since in many cases the negotiation partner's BATNA will only be vaguely assessable, recourse can be made to a method of competitive negotiating, the so-called MPP phenomenon. MPP ("Maximum Plausible Position") takes the approach that a negotiation should start with the highest, barely justifiable demand. The demand need not be justified but only sound plausible. This approach is based on the fact that as a rule the true pain barrier of the opponent is not known. For that reason, the negotiating power and interests of the negotiating partner may have been overestimated grossly, and thus a theoretical chance for success may be given. Furthermore, the bar of one's own negotiating range is raised by this approach which will often bring better results as a higher opening bid provides the opportunity of concessions. This in turn will have positive repercussions on the course of the negotiation as the negotiating partner—spurred by the success of having beaten down his opponent—may now be ready to make his or her own concessions. As a rule, an agreement will be achieved in the area where the negotiation ranges of both parties overlap. If e.g. a purchaser has a 20,000 EUR budget available for buying an installation and the supplier must at least obtain a price of 15,000 EUR to break even, the span between 15,000 EUR and 20,000 EUR is the area in which an agreement can be found that will satisfy both parties. This area is called the "Zone of Possible Agreement".

By applying the MPP rule, the purchaser can e.g. reduce his opening bid to 10,000 EUR with the hope that the course of the negotiation may end somewhere near the minimum price acceptable for the supplier. The less information on the object of the negotiation is available, the higher the initial demand should be set. By using mellow words, an orderly retreat without loss of face will still be possible. However, the initial demand must not be set so high that it may result in the immediate termination of the negotiation. For this reason, many purchasers prefer to submit their demands in a restrained and appropriate way for avoiding the impression of being rude or impudent.

Apart from concrete and measurable targets, goals of a superior nature may also be sought within the framework of a negotiation. These goals can be defined on substantial or personal levels and may include e.g. an exchange of information or forging a strategic partnership.

At the end, priorities are set with regard to the collected targets. By doing so, the negotiator has the possibility of making concessions in a systematic way during the course of the negotiation. The prioritisation ranges from "painlessly dispensable" up to "must be reached at all means". For negotiating is always a give and take, and without concessions negotiations are bound to quickly come to a deadlock, a situation in which no further steps can be taken. For that reason, good negotiators must act flexibly and be able to give. Ideally, concessions with low priority for one's own company should be exchanged for concessions with high priority. To deploy concessions strategically and systematically, their use should be planned during the preparation.

Practical Tip: Good Preparation Is More than Half the Battle Won

It is well known that negotiating is one of the core competencies of Strategic Purchasing, but even an operative purchaser will fare better in the struggle for dates and volumes when he has the respective know-how and talent. Naturally, this also applies to the other party although the number of clients and articles sellers are in charge of is usually smaller than the number of suppliers and bought-in parts that purchasers have to manage. For that reason, sellers are often better prepared too. And therefore it is very important that purchasers are able to stand up to them and try to surpass them. For negotiating, success is always a combination of good preparation and clear negotiation targets that comply with the strategy and aim at influencing and convincing the other party. The success in a negotiation can be accredited by up to 80% to a sound preparation—so one should force oneself and one's colleagues to do the necessary preparation if need be.

But how to prepare in the right way? At first, one's own negotiating position needs to be analysed, for those who have the power can afford a failure of the negotiation. For that reason, it is very important for one's negotiating strategy to correctly assess one's own position and to weigh the alternatives. To do so, information needs to be collected. In doing so, the efforts made should be appropriate to the potential gains. The more difficult the subject in question seems to be, the more profound the preparation should be, and the more potentials or risks seem to be involved, the more intense the preparation should be. One's personal efforts, however, may be manageable as this kind of routine work can easily be delegated to trainees or students. In many cases, these persons then supported the complete negotiating process very interestedly. As case example I will now detail the preparation for a negotiation in which an increase of prices had been the impending threat. The procedure has proven very well in practice:

Step 1 As a rule, almost all price increases are based on price increase rates of individual price components such as material costs, labour costs, etc. Therefore, the first step will be checking whether and to what amount the alleged increases of costs have really taken place. With reference to the price structure, it can then be ascertained which influence on the total price the respective price increase rates have and also whether the demanded price increase is justified.

Step 2 In the next step, the total and percentage increase of prices is evaluated in its 12-month effect in order to represent the impact of demanded increase.

Step 3 Now, the history of the price is examined in order to see whether the supplier has also passed on cheaper purchase prices in times of recession. The important point is to identify the actual price increasing forces as compared to the price agreement in the past.

Step 4 Depending on the supplier's position of power and the life span of the article, actual enquiries are started preferably in Low-Cost Countries as suppliers from those countries usually submit offers very quickly and with good conditions. Even if in the end no recourse may be made to these sources, they provide excellent arguments for the forthcoming price talks and may also serve as a benchmark.

Step 5 To realise volume effects, it is checked with regard to which articles no framework agreements exist. The potential volumes of these articles are included in the subjects of the negotiation.

Step 6 A considerable enhancement of the buyer power can be achieved by negotiating product roadmaps. These are an easy way to instigate the supplier's interest and thus lead him to make more concessions. Most of all, this is about potential sales volumes that the supplier has not been aware of previously. These are being visualised for the coming years as shown in Fig. 8.2, differentiated according to the substantiality of the possible agreement. But be careful: The supplier will remind you of your words later.

Step 7 Which gains in productivity have been achieved by the supplier in the last months or years, and has he passed them on to his customers? If this has not been the case, a notional customary annual gain in productivity can be used as bargaining chips in the negotiation.

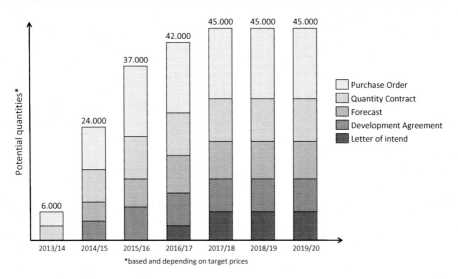

Fig. 8.2 Showing sales potential to raise the greed of the supplier

Step 8 Now, a check must be made whether and in what way the supplier has failed in the past. This includes an analysis of the adherence to schedules and prices as well as of the delivery quality—as a rule, something "useful" will be detected. The database of the actual score development will also deliver ammunition for the negotiation. Furthermore, the actual margin conditions will be compared to the strategic aims in order to find another bargaining point.

Step 9 After that, minimum and maximum targets will be defined—these should not be excessive, for here the general motivation curve (shown in Fig. 8.3) applies. If the line is crossed discouragement may follow—in the worst case, the negotiating partner may withdraw meaning a loss of one's face.

Step 10 The final negotiation planning will be the last step. The place of negotiation should be chosen advisedly; negotiating on one's home ground will always be easier. The time factor should be exploited, and the maximum and minimum performance curves in the course of the day should also be considered. The method of negotiation must be adequate to the topic discussed (e.g. price, complaint, demand negotiation or initial analysis talks), but there should be enough flexibility to react on the course of the talks. And there are quite a few methods and measures, as will be detailed later in this chapter. From utilising the MPP phenomenon (Maximum Plausible Position), meaning "demand the impossible to achieve the best possible", to result-oriented competitive negotiating, to using the BATNA (Best Alternative To a Negotiated Agreement) method, up to the Win-Win approach of the Harvard Concept, several negotiation tactics can prove successful. After an agreement has been reached internally, a plan B for the course of the talks should be developed and even rehearsed (when the expenditure of time is reasonable). Now, the agenda proposal is completed and should be discussed and agreed

Fig. 8.3 Motivation curve

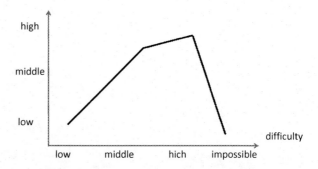

upon with the negotiating partner previous to the actual negotiation. This procedural approach should become second nature to all purchasers.

8.3   Communication and Body Language

Apart from meticulous preparations, the key factors of successful purchasing negotiations are the purchaser's communicative competence and his negotiating skills, for the actual negotiation is characterised by a high degree of interaction, and in this, the relationship aspect plays an important part. This has been described very colourfully by communication scientist Paul Watzlawick in his iceberg model of communication. According to this model, only a small part of the interaction can be seen above the water surface—amongst others the words spoken, the figures, data, and facts as well as the written offers. The by far greater part of the interaction, however, happens below the water surface, on the level of the relationships between the people involved in the negotiation. Thus, the needs, motivations, emotions, and feelings of these persons will significantly influence the negotiation results.

Therefore, creativity, flexibility, and interpersonal intelligence are as much in demand as are quick-wittedness and authority. Some of these qualities can be gained by learning, but a lot is based on intuition and knowledge of human nature. For this reason, a short digression to the field of communication and body language will be inserted, from which starting points and behaviour patterns for purchasing negotiation can be deducted.

8.3.1   The Communication Square

The Communication square or Four-Sides Model by Friedmann Schulz von Thun is a familiar concept by which the question shall be answered in which way communication problems may turn up. According to this model, every message has four sides generally (see Fig. 8.4):

- *Factual information*: It delivers the facts and contents of the information.
- *Self-revelation*: What do I reveal of myself? This aspect delivers hints of my thoughts and feelings as well as of my understanding of my role.
- *Relationship*: How is my relation to the receiver of the message? This aspect delivers hints concerning my relation to that person and what I think of him/her.
- *Appeal*: What do I want the other to do, accept, or understand? This aspect is about the influence I want to exert on the receiver and which wishes, advices, or acting instructions I want to give him/her.

Misunderstandings often originate from the fact that the sender wants to address a specific side with this message while the receiver notices another side.

For illustration, a simple example from everyday purchasing activities may be chosen. During a purchasing negotiation, the purchaser says: "The offered price is too high." Now, there are several possibilities how the supplier may understand this sentence.

Taken as factual information, he or she will simply understand that the offered price is considered too high. Maybe, there are other providers offering cheaper prices, or maybe the offered price is really beyond the predetermined target price of the purchaser.

If, however, the message is taken as a self-revelation of the purchaser, the supplier will begin to draw conclusions regarding the personal motivations of the sentence: Maybe, the purchaser wants to distinguish himself by pressing out the last Cent in order to make an impression with his superiors. If the message is understood this way, the supplier's reaction will be neutral or even negative.

If the message is understood on the relationship level, the supplier might begin to consider the given business relationship. Maybe, the purchaser and the supplier have been business partners for long years and the purchaser wanted to give hints on

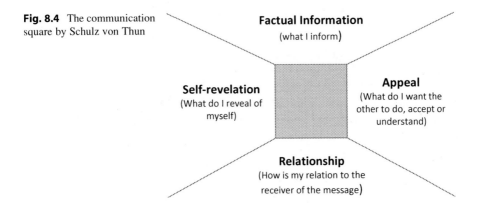

Fig. 8.4 The communication square by Schulz von Thun

Factual Information
(what I inform)

Self-revelation
(What do I reveal of myself)

Appeal
(What do I want the other to do, accept or understand)

Relationship
(How is my relation to the receiver of the message)

the competitors' price calculations. But it may also be that the purchaser has no interest in any further cooperation and wants the negotiation to fail.

If understood as an appeal, the supplier could feel prompted to lower his price and make a new offer immediately.

Thus, there are four perspectives that—depending on the actual situation—will allow numerous conclusions as to how the message should be understood. This pattern illustrates that communication will in all cases be unsuccessful when the receiver understands another side of the message than that intended by the sender. But people who know that these four sides exist can—in cases in which a misunderstanding has occurred—try to find out whether the receiver has understood the side of the message one had intended or—vice versa—whether one (as receiver) has understood the side of the message the sender had intended. For in many cases, one reacts angrily or with disappointment on words uttered by a colleague or business partner only on the grounds of having understood the false side of the message.

8.3.2   Nonverbal Communication

According to Paul Watzlawick's well-known theory, it is impossible to "not communicate". Communication does always happen when persons take notice of each other since all human behaviour has a communicative nature. That means that human beings are always communicating nonverbally by facial expressions, gestures, or visual signs.

Nonverbal communication is the oldest form of interpersonal understanding and is normally already mastered by newborn babies. By this means, human beings either express their feelings and emotions or support the content of a verbalised message. The range of interpretation may differ widely, and in all cases a situation-related, objective view is called for. Nevertheless, it is still useful to know some fundamental rules of nonverbal communication and to respect them:

Etiquette encompasses an adequate behaviour and a fitting appearance within a given social situation. The social situation considered here will normally be the meeting with a supplier. A purchaser who looks untidy in such a context will not only cause repudiation but does also demonstrate a low esteem of his negotiation partner. Tardiness and an inadequate attire will also convey the impression that the purchaser does not consider the meeting to be of greater importance.

Eye contact is one of the most important means of nonverbal communication. With it, the hearer signals interest and gives the speaker a feedback as to whether the spoken words have been understood, while on the other hand the speaker by means of eye contact adds authority to his/her message and underlines its importance. A long eye contact can also cause different reactions by the negotiation partner: It may signal sympathy or importance, but the partner may also feel being cornered or intimidated. Staring is always perceived as impolite, uncomfortable, and derogatory.

Gestures are communicative moves of hands, arms, shoulders, and the head. These moves serve to underline, intensify, regulate, or replace verbal messages.

Normally, these gestures occur naturally and spontaneously, for instance by using the hand to underline the importance of an argument or by counting with the fingers while giving an enumeration. Gestures should never convey the impression of being unnatural or forced, and they should be appropriate to the contents of the message. Perceived discrepancies of this kind can signal insecurity or poor credibility. The negative effect is often aggravated by scratching one's neck or nose and by avoiding eye contact. Since gestures are often used spontaneously and naturally, they need not necessarily be in accordance with the contents of the words. Rubbing one's hands may for instance convey pleasant anticipations, while scratching one's head may convey insecurity or embarrassment. Putting one's hand together will however signal ease and self-assurance.

Facial expressions mean visible movements of the face and are considered emotional forms of expressing one's moods or affects. Facial expressions thus reflect a human being's feelings and thoughts. In certain situations, laughing will be an adequate means of overcoming barriers as it reduces the distance between the speaking and the listening person. Laughing conveys openness, cordiality, and confidence.

The Voice is an indirect component of nonverbal communication as by varying one's voice certain contents can be conveyed better and more understandably. The voice, for that matter, is characterised by quality (adaption to the contents), articulation (pauses, phrases, and grammar), as well as variety (pace, sound intensity, and stresses).

8.4 Negotiating Stages

With regard to the general stages of a negotiation, there is an easy to memorise mnemonic: the English acronym "NEGOTIATE". The single letters represent a logical sequence of the negotiating process.[1]

Names and Niceties The negotiating process starts with exchanging names and niceties: The participating persons introduce themselves and begin to build up interpersonal relations by small talk. In the Western business world, this process step will only take a few minutes while in other cultures it may take several hours. *Especially in regions in Asia building up personal relations is vital for successful deals in the future.*

Establish General Conditions Establishing general conditions means a joint agreement on the negotiation framework. Who shall keep the minutes; what expectations do the negotiating parties have; and which target shall have been reached at the end of the negotiation? At this stage, it can also be cleared whether

---

[1]Cf. Portner (2010, p. 67 ff).

the participants have the authority to make decisions or whether the approval of persons with higher authority must be sought subsequently.

Get Standard Points Exchanged In the next negotiation step, the positions, demands, and wishes of the parties are exchanged.

Normally, a discussion will ensue in which the parties will try to understand the wishes and interests of the respective other party. In this context, it is important that one's own demands are being articulated precisely and unambiguously. Phrasing one's position too weakly will only offer points of attack and signal the other party room to negotiate.

Observe and Identify Common Ground After both parties have exchanged their positions, one quickly understands how far both parties differ. Prior to any attempt at closing the gap, it is advised to summarise the standpoints and to identify common ground which will help to find joint solutions later.

Take Note of Differences In the next step, one must try to understand and recognise the differences of both positions. Recognising in this context does not mean to accept the other party's demand. At this stage, it is important that the negotiation does not come to a standstill and the atmosphere remains relaxed.

Initiate Negotiation Now, the negotiation really begins. Several different strategies may be followed. Irreverent of "hard" or "weak" negotiating, the main task at this stage is to exchange concessions and work out approaches for a solution. In this context, concessions should be placed strategically and exchanged effectively.

Agreement Should Be Reached If the gap between the two positions could have been closed by an agreement, the negotiation results are being summarised. This ensures that both parties have the same understanding of the result and support it.

Tasks Should Be Distributed Then the negotiated fields of action are distributed to the participants. Which steps must be initiated next, and who will do what up to what date? This ensures that there is no lack of clarity with regard to the responsibility assignment and that the collected points of action are timely implemented.

End, Celebrate, and Say Farewell At the end, the other party is bidden farewell. In normal cases, this will mostly involve small talk and take only a few minutes. According to cultural practice, however, the negotiation result may also be celebrated by a shared dinner or by visiting a cultural event—here again, personal relations play an important part.

Practical Tip

With me, the following course of action in negotiations has always proven—and still proves—most successful:

After greetings and the enquiry for daily targets and the wishes of the other party, the own view is given. In a superior but friendly and not arrogant way, the other side is confronted with numbers, data, and facts that shall ideally bring him or her in a defensive position. My former English-speaking boss called this method "grounding". But, beware: the arguments must be cast-iron, and there must be a B plan. The weakest argument should be used in the middle and the strongest at the end of the exchange. Everything must be clear and true. Efficiently and targeted experts from the own enterprise (e.g. from the material planning or quality assurance departments) are deployed as "bad guys" to provide—in a frame that has been concerted previously—seemingly irrevocable evidence. These evidence on the table—e.g. a defective part or a poor delivery statistics from the ERP system—cause immense pain and weaken the other side's position. Afterwards the supplier is slowly propped up again partly by introducing artificially construed complexity from diverse fields of negotiation as part of the bargaining chips. Following a holistic approach, oneself and the other side should at first get the overall picture. Thus, one will be able in the further course of the talks to give something without too much pain. For on the surface, negotiating is always give and take, and so it becomes easier to assert one's true targets. After all topics—especially the technical ones—have been concluded finally, the most important point of the negotiation is saved up to the end, and then it is time to take. During the whole negotiation body language should be used purposefully, e.g. by creating a faithful atmosphere by mirroring (Figs. 8.5 and 8.6).

In this, one assumes a posture similar to that of the negotiation partner—that will make him feel comfortable and thus have a positive effect on the relation level.

In the further course of the negotiation, one should always keep a keen eye on the negotiation partner. One should intervene whenever one gets the impression that something has not been understood or misunderstandings have occurred.

If the partner scratches his nose (Fig. 8.7) or neck (Fig. 8.8) repeatedly, this conveys uncertainty and may be a hint to doubts or even untruthfulness. If one observes such behaviour patterns, one should repeat one's statements in order to dispel mistrust and insecurity.

Another gesture that signals scepticism or lack of interest is resting the chin on the hand (Fig. 8.9). If one observes this posture, it is best to interrupt one's speech for asking the partner whether you have expressed your ideas clearly.

One should always take account of the spatial territory as shown in Fig. 8.10. On could use this knowledge for an attack (when appropriate to implement one's strategy), e.g. by placing a ballpoint pen on the table directly opposite to the negotiation partner.

When certain boundaries are transgressed, especially the intimate sphere, the dialogue partner will feel embarrassed and pushed. To infringe in someone else's sphere may be seen as a statement of trust but also as a threat and may trigger

Fig. 8.5 Different body postures indicate different content-related position

Fig. 8.6 Mirroring indicates consensus

aggressive reactions. Not in all cases a negotiation will aim at reaching an agreement and to continue business relations with the other party.

How insecure and uncomfortable one may feel—on the outside, one should demonstrate strength and self-confidence.

8.5   Negotiating Methods

There are, as has already been shown, several methods for reaching the present aims within a negotiation context. In theory, there are basically three ways of negotiating: cooperative negotiating, fair compromise, and competitive

Fig. 8.7 Scratching nose
conveys uncertainty

negotiating. According to the respective situation, each method has its advantages
and disadvantages. If a long-term, close partnership is sought, the cooperative
method is advised, while the competitive method may be used with regard to
one-time deals and an unequal proportion of power. Good negotiators should be
proficient in all three methods in order to make use of them in the right situations
and also to be able to react sensibly when the other party uses these methods.

8.5.1   Competitive Negotiating

Competitive negotiating in general is the approach of driving a hard bargain. In
cases where a long-term partnership is sought, this method should be used restrict-
edly for in most cases there will be a clear winner and a clear loser. Nevertheless,
good negotiators must also be proficient in this method in order to realise when hard
bargaining is necessary and to be able to react on the other side using this method. It
is not always obvious and clear that the other side is negotiating competitively.
There are of course tough-minded negotiators who are pushing their demands

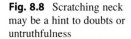

Fig. 8.8 Scratching neck
may be a hint to doubts or
untruthfulness

strictly and threaten all the time to cancel the negotiation. Good competitive negotiators, however, will never let their partners know that they are taken to the cleaners, for these negotiators know that at the end of the negotiation an agreement will only be reached by a compromise that is satisfactory for both parties. For that reason, such negotiators will use the subjective satisfaction with the negotiation for fine-tuning their own negotiation success (Risse 2007). Competitive negotiators make a difference between the satisfaction with the negotiation results and the satisfaction with the course of the negotiation. Inexperienced negotiators often draw their satisfaction from the methodical course of the negotiation. Competitive negotiators use this fact by making the other side content with the course of the negotiation so that they will forget to concentrate on the real results.

8.5.1.1 Basic Pattern of Competitive Negotiating

Competitive negotiating is based on the plausible assumption that the subject of the negotiation is always a scarce good that must be divided optimally. Optimal in this context means as much as possible for one's own benefit. Thus, competitive negotiations will always follow the same basic pattern. Both parties start by presenting their maximum demands. In the next step, there will be a bargaining for concessions in order to reconcile the standpoints. In this process, one party always loses what the other one wins. The aim of the negotiator is to win as much as

Fig. 8.9 Resting the chin on the hand signals scepticism

possible and to lose as little as possible. After both sides have made their respective concessions, at some time a compromise is found and an agreement concluded.

Competitive negotiators often use the highest demand that can be justified in any way as their opening bid. This so-called MPP phenomenon (Maximum Plausible Position) is justified by the fact that theoretically there is a chance for success—it is possible that the negotiating power of the other party has been overestimated previously. At the same time, the opening demand has the purpose of keeping the room to negotiate as great as possible and to lower the expectations of the negotiation partner. However, if the opening demand is much too high, there is the risk that the other party will cancel the negotiation immediately. For in our culture, excessive demands are considered impolite and impudent. For that reason, the opening demand should be justifiable in some way, and it should be phrased in friendly words to signal a genuine willingness to negotiate.

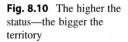

Fig. 8.10 The higher the
status—the bigger the
territory

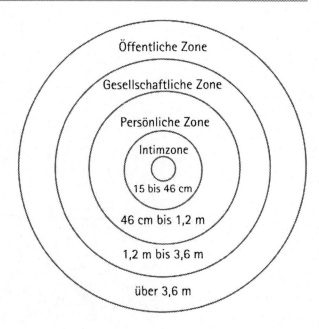

8.5.1.2 The Power Factor

The power factor plays an important role for successful negotiations, and this fact is
known to all participants in the negotiation, for those who have power can move
things in the direction of their own targets. Thus, many manoeuvres applied during
negotiations aim at influencing the power relationship to one's own benefit.

As a rule, all parties in a negotiation command a certain power potential in the
eyes of the other side. Otherwise, there would be no reason to negotiate. Prior to the
actual situation, one should get things straight concerning one's own and the other
side's power position. Why is the other party ready to negotiate; which are our
assets; and who can afford to terminate the negotiation without an agreement? For
to have negotiating power means to be able to say "No," and to be less dependent on
a successful conclusion of the negotiation than the other party. For that reason, one
should previously make oneself aware of the risk of the negotiation breaking off
and assess whether this risk can be taken. If the risk is too great to be taken by one
person alone, colleagues and superiors may be involved to split the risk. Producing
alternatives with the help of the BATNA method may also be very helpful for
lessening one's risks and thus for strengthening one's negotiating power
effectively.

Power, however, can also be built up with the help of a conclusive chain of
arguments. Being able to represent one's position conclusively will always change
the power relation on one's own behalf and will make it much easier to induce the
other side to give in. In this context, however, one has to bear in mind that the full
power of arguments unfurls only in the run-up to a negotiation. If arguments are
being introduced in the negotiation—which is a stress situation—they can easily be
understood as attacking the other party's position. As in negotiations it is important

to defend one's position, new arguments will in most cases trigger defensive reactions. The more plausible the argument is, the quicker the negotiation partner may feel cornered or bullied. Thus, arguments introduced during the negotiation will rather be an encumbrance to a course of the negotiation that is experienced positively than facilitating a good result. For that reason, the other side should be informed about these arguments previous to the negotiation and in writing. Thus, the other side will have the opportunity of considering them objectively and at ease and prepare answers. This will facilitate an adaption to one's own position, and fervid discussions will be avoided.

8.5.1.3 The Time Factor

The time factor has a key position in competitive negotiation for normally negotiations will adhere to a time frame that has been agreed beforehand. If no agreement has been reached, many negotiators will become uneasy with the approach of the set time limit. If no agreement is reached, the negotiation has failed. Thus, agreements are often reached just before the end of a negotiation when the participants are more prone to make greater concessions. For that reason, it is advised never to disclose one's own time limits, for instance the time of the reserved flight. To use the time factor effectively, one should know the other party's time limit and discuss the subjects that are most important for one's own position only near the end of the negotiation. This will exert greater pressure on the other party and help to induce the other side to make greater concessions.

But time is not only a means for exerting pressure; it also means expenditure and hence money. The more time has been invested in a negotiation and its preparation, the more probable the conclusion of an agreement is. That is the reason why in many negotiations at first a lot of lesser important points will be discussed and ticked off. The longer the negotiation takes, the greater the relevance of the subjects becomes and the more time has been invested. If a lot of time has already been invested, it becomes much harder to say no. Thus, many negotiators are prone to make greater concessions the more time they had invested already.

The invested time does also include the time of the journey. Thus, negotiations on one's own premises offer an additional advantage: The other party at the beginning of the negotiation has already invested time and is therefore interested in reaching an agreement.

8.5.1.4 The Information Factor

The most important instrument during a negotiation is handling information. The more information has been gathered, the more power a negotiator commands, for, basically, each party wants to become acquainted with the other party's limit without disclosing one's own limit. Therefore, collecting information thoroughly during the run-up to the negotiation is of enormous importance for getting an idea of the negotiating partner's probable limit previously. At the same time, information to the other party may be given selectively in order to conceal one's own limit.

During the negotiation, it is essential to collect as much information as possible and to disclose as little information as possible. For that reason, good negotiators will speak one-third of the time only and listen two-thirds of the time. This can be achieved by an appropriate technique of asking questions—open w-questions (probe questions) encourage speaking and thus disclosing information.

8.5.1.5 The Complexity Factor

Complex negotiations in which a multitude of positions are discussed tend to overwhelm the participants quickly. For that reason, in classical negotiations many single solutions are summarised under one negotiation subject the monetary value of which is negotiated in exchange for concessions. To break up this negotiation subject may however be helpful in order to generate complexity. By building up additional positions on the one hand, room for manoeuvre concerning the exchange of concessions will be opened up, and on the other hand the complexity can be used for one's own benefit as inexperienced negotiators sometimes have difficulties in assessing values in the non-price sector and will thus make great concessions ignorantly. In this context, it is essential to structure the generated complexity previously for oneself—in order to prevent being overwhelmed by the complexity as much as the other party.

8.5.1.6 "Dirty Tricks"

Competitive negotiating is not always a clean and fair affair. There is a whole slew of so-called "dirty tricks" to reach intended targets by bluffs or false promises. Good negotiators should know these tricks, react competently when being confronted with these methods, and even use them from time to time. One must, however, never forget that sellers have a long memory and one might get one's own back when the situation is convenient. The following list gives a short overview of established methods used by tricky negotiators[2] and the appropriate reactions according to one's power position.

Salami Technique Little by little, concessions of seemingly little relevancy are wrested from the other party that on the whole prove to be considerable.

  | **Hint** Never give away important concessions, but demand an equivalent for every concession.

Jumble of Figures By introducing a jumble of figures confusion and insecurity is generated.

  | **Hint** Collect and structure these figures in a flip chart to keep track of the full picture.

Good Guy/Bad Guy This method is known from detective stories: The other side assumes different roles. While the "Bad Guy" is unrelenting, the "Good Guy" seemingly supports the negotiation partner. Thus, trust is built up, and the "Good Guy" will finally wrest concessions from the negotiation partner.

---

[2]Cf. Portner (2010, p. 170 ff).

| **Hint** In this situation, it is essential to be strict and consistent, and to win the "Good Guy" for achieving one's own aims and/or to use one's own "Bad Guy" for delivering bad news (see Grounding).

Change of the Chief Negotiator By replacing the chief negotiator the other side tries to revoke already granted concessions or negotiate them afresh.

| **Hint** Here, only tenacity and the determinedness to keep the negotiated concessions can help. Otherwise, the negotiations will start again from the beginning. If tenacity does not prove successful, the termination may, according to one's power position, be an option.

Limited Authority The negotiation partner lacks the authority to conclude an agreement. Often, the approval of the management has to be obtained.

| **Hint** An agreement upon which decisions shall be made and upon the fact that the negotiators shall have the necessary authority or be able to get the approval during the negotiation telephonically should be reached during the run-up.

Arouse Compassion Another popular trick is arousing compassion. By emphasising the difficult economic situation and by invoking the long-term partnership negotiators, try to exert emotional pressure on the other side.

| **Hint** Assistance should only be an option when there is a real emergency situation. Otherwise, the principle of the Harvard Concept should be applied—to be friendly to the person but stand firm as far as the factual level is concerned.

Director or Superior Bonus Quite often, a superior or even the executive director of the other company will show up at the end of the negotiation and demand some more concessions although an agreement had already been reached.

| **Hint** Stick to the agreement by emphasising that the result can only endure with all its parts; compliment the other party for having reached the optimum irrespective of whether this is true or not.

Flaws By singling out flaws the position of the other side is denigrated in order to strengthen one's own negotiating position.

| **Hint** In such situations, remember your own BATNA and counterattack, for the other party has its flaws too.

Visualising Demands By visibly writing down the price psychologically a mark is set that is almost a fact.

| **Hint** Let not yourself be affected by this manoeuvre but "obliterate" the written figure by writing your own figure alongside.

Compliments Compliments, appreciation, and praise make the negotiating partner feel comfortable and incite him to make quick concessions.

| **Hint** Experienced negotiators understand this psychological manoeuvre, interrupt it, and direct the discussion quickly to the subject of the negotiation.

Time Pressure   Very often by setting a time limit pressure is built up artificially in order to come to an agreement quickly and to wrest further concessions from the negotiating partner.

| **Hint** Question the time limit and clarify from the beginning which consequences exceeding the time limit shall have.

Added Extras   When at the end of the negotiation an agreement in all points has been reached, there will often be a handshake to seal the agreement. On this occasion, one could use the chance of getting an extra bonus by a demand of minor importance.

| **Hint** ... and you will deliver carriage-free, o.k.?

8.5.2   The Harvard Concept

The Harvard Concept is an alternative approach of task-oriented negotiating in which controversial issues are resolved according to their importance and their material content and not by bargaining.[3] By this concept, all parties shall be enabled to reach a positive result in a negotiation. The Harvard Concept has been developed in the context of the Harvard Negotiation Project at the renowned Harvard University by Roger Fischer and William L. Ury, two American scholars of jurisprudence, who introduced the concept in 1981 in their book *Getting to Yes*. The aim of the method is to find a constructive, peaceful agreement even in difficult negotiating situations without one of the parties losing its face. In this context, one often speaks of creating a win-win situation or of cooperative negotiating meaning a method by which both parties can be satisfied with the negotiation results.

Especially in view of the increasing importance of close and trustful partnerships with suppliers, the Harvard Concept offers the possibility of developing solutions in concert with suppliers that will enable long-term and lasting negotiation results.

The Harvard Concept consists of five principles in logical order that shall lead through the negotiation process:

Principle 1: Separating Persons from Problems   Negotiating partners are always persons with two basic interests—the negotiation subject and the personal relations. According to the Harvard Concepts, it is essential to separate these two interests from each other at first. Relation problems must have no influence on the content level. However, a functional relation is the prerequisite for working out efficient solutions for factual problems. In this respect, mutual trust and acceptance are essential. The principle is to be friendly to the person but stand firm as far as the factual level is concerned.

Principle 2: Interests Are Important, Not Positions   The second principle asks why. Not the other person's position matters but his/her interests and motivations.

---

[3]Cf. Fisher et al. (2004).

For, as a rule, interests can be realised by several possible solutions. Widening the acting horizon may enable open negotiations and avoid bargaining for positions. In this context, it is important to know and understand the interests of the negotiation partner and to make clear one's own interests.

Principle 3: Collecting Possible Solutions "Creative people normally will find different options." According to this principle, at the next stage possible solutions are compiled together with the negotiating partner. This may happen by brainstorming as this step focuses gathering as many different and creative solutions as possible, especially options that will bring advantages for both sides.

Principle 4: Agreeing on Objective Criteria At the next stage, the collected solution options are being evaluated. It is important that the results of the evaluation shall be based on general and objective decision criteria, e.g. court decisions, expertise, or moral criteria. Thus, it is ensured that both parties share the same understanding and no party feels disadvantaged afterwards. By evaluating solution options according to objective criteria, there will be better chances for a convincing and viable solution.

Principle 5: Comparing the BATNA If the two negotiation parties will agree on a solution package will depend on whether the result is better than the best existing alternative (BATNA). Only if this is true, an agreement will be sensible, and both parties will leave the negotiation table as winners.

8.6 Peculiarities in International Negotiations

In Scandinavia, Danes are considered shirt-sleeve and direct and Swedes as business-like, matter-of-factly, and fair, while in Finland negotiations may be sweaty sauna affairs, and in Norway caution is advised as almost everybody knows everybody else. In Russia, one should especially bear Lenin's saying in mind that trust is good but control better.

These, admittedly generalised assumptions concerning the characteristics of some European countries nevertheless often hold true as the following comparison of cultural ways of behaviour between Chinese, Japanese, and Koreans shows that has been condensed from experience gathered over many years.

Practical Tip: Global Negotiations Using the Example of China, Japan, and Korea
Although the Japanese, the Koreans, and the Chinese think of themselves as fundamentally different, during many years I have realised similarities that are more or less pronounced, beginning from the ritual of exchanging business cards to the principle of seniority to the process of decision-making, to mention but a few. That is why I summarised these three cultures in the following reflections on the conduct of negotiations.

Around 70% of all European–Chinese joint ventures fail due to different ways of behaviour and business conduct of the involved partners while only 30% of the problems are caused by financial problems, false strategies, judicial mistakes, or false assessments of the market.[4] Several studies confirm this fact which proves once again Henry Ford's saying: "The secret of success is based on the ability to understand others and to see things with their eyes."

8.6.1 The Ritual of Exchanging Business Cards

Globally acting purchasers especially should intensely look into the cultures of their business partners. For the saying is: "Different strokes for different folks." And this already starts at the reception with the ritual of exchanging the business cards. In China, the custom is known since the times of the Han dynasty, the second century BCE. At the time, the cards consisted of thin wood or bamboo slats and were called *ye* (plea for reception). Normally, these cards were used by subordinate or younger persons when being invited for audience by the authorities. On these cards, only the name and the point of origin of the card holder was written; data concerning his social status or his title only rarely were given. This historical custom afterwards had been forgotten for many centuries and reappeared only at the beginning of the 1980s. Since the beginning of China's economic boom, it has become more and more popular not only in the business world but in all sectors of social life. Celebrating the exchange of business cards is especially pronounced in Japan, but also in Korea and China it is still of very high importance. For that reason, one should observe the following procedures:

At first, the person highest in rank or the oldest is greeted. The business card is held with both hands, and one bows while the cards are exchanged. During the handing over of the card, the side with the text in Chinese, Korean, or Japanese should be turned towards the receiver. Furthermore, it is advised that the respective translation is printed on the back side of one's business card.

The business card one receives in exchange will often only be in Japanese, Korean, or Chinese, respectively. It is important that all information such as title, function, and contact data are clearly printed on one's own card so that the business partner knows which status one has in one's organisation (for example, see Figs. 8.11 and 8.12). Because of the enormous importance of the card exchange ritual one should invest in high-quality paper and best print, and always carry sufficient copies in mint condition with oneself. Under no circumstances should one simply put the received cards in one's pocket. Instead, the cards should be regarded with interest and spread before oneself (ordered according to the seating arrangement) during the meeting. In China and in Korea, a handshake follows, and one learns from the intensity of the handshake who is still part of the "old guard" and who has been trained in Western manners. Only decades ago, handshakes were

---

[4]Wieland (2006, p. 3).

邬　利
采购经理

Hailo-Werk   电话：+49-(0)27 73-8 24 30
Postfach 1262   传真：+49-(0)27 73-8 24 50
D-35702 Haiger   手机：+49-(0)1 51-12 64 38 30
www.hailo.de   e-mail:uweigel@jlu.de

Fig. 8.11 Chinese business card

ライカカメラAG / オスカーバルナックストリート11
D-35606 ソルムス / www.leica-camera.com
Telephone +49(0)6442-208-565
Fax +49(0)6442-208-271
Mobile +49(0)175-2266348
ulrich.weigel@leica-camera.com

ウルリッヒ・ヴァイゲル
購買部部長/代理権保持者

Fig. 8.12 Japanese business card

totally unusual, especially in Japan. For that reason, members of the elder generation up to now shake hands very softly. Alternatively, the guest is greeting by bowing.

After the end of the meeting, one puts the business cards carefully in a special wallet or a portfolio. It is always better to bring too much than too less business cards on the voyage. Especially for Japan, the rule is to carry at least thrice as many business cards as usual—if you have no business card you can exchange you could also stay at home.

8.6.2 The Beginning of the Talks

Partners from Japan and Korea invest a lot of time in the preparation of the talks and will show up considerable time before the agreed date. They expect the same regardful behaviour on the part of the other side. To come exactly at the time agreed is almost considered rude. In China, at the first meeting with foreigners preferably some standard questions are asked to get in touch with each other. What is your name and where do you come from? Persons of higher age are often asked: "How old will you be this year? How old are your children?" or "Are your children already in business?" Younger persons may be asked: "You are still younger than thirty, I presume?" or "Are you married, do you have children?" and even: "What do you earn per month?" As a rule, praising words concerning the culture (language, script, art, nature, as well as sports or sports legionnaires) will prove helpful for the further course of the discussion.

These questions may seem strange to Europeans, but in China they are quite normal and express politeness. The ensuing negotiation process, as a rule, in Japan, Korea, and also China will proceed as follows: After the small talk subject-related information is exchanged. Afterwards, business persons from Asia tend to explain their standpoints at lengths and to repeat them in all variations in order to convince the negotiating partner. At the end of the negotiation, however, willingness for compromise or for considering the arguments in good faith is expressed.

8.6.3 Laughing: An Asiatic Means of Managing Conflicts

Inapt or awkward statements by a foreign negotiation partner will sometimes cause the negotiator from Asia to become taciturn but sometimes such statements will also answered by laughing loudly. Such a laugh is to be understood as a means of conflict management. In the Chinese conversational behaviour, laughing can be used to avoid or ease conflict situations. For that reason, a critical expression of opinion is also often accompanied by laughter. This is an important technique of leading a conversation that is called "zhuangxie bingju" in Chinese. Successful discussions depend on a harmonious atmosphere for which there is the following Chinese saying: "When meeting a close friend, a thousand glasses will not be enough; when meeting someone with whom you do not share the same language half of a sentence will already be too much." As important and serious the subject may be, negotiators from China will always discuss it even-tempered and easily. The most character features are derived from Confucian teachings and can be described as follows:

– Showing modesty and reservation with respect to oneself and one's accomplishments.
– The targets of companies or departments are regarded as personal aims; individual needs or wishes are subordinated to the need of the company or common welfare.
– The person has a strong sense of belonging to his company or group and is rather uncritical in his belief of the authorities.
– As a rule, he has a strong sense of honour and self-esteem.
– His sense of justice is rather based on emotions than on rational thinking.

– In interpersonal contact, he tends to act warily but also sneakily.
– Due to his self-control he always aims to leave a favourable impression in his social sphere.

8.6.4   Lose One's Face

The "loss of face" ("diu mianzi") for many people from Asia is a dramatic event. It may be caused by the person's neglect of social rules but also by other persons' unwillingness to allow him to save face in such a situation. Losing one's face calls the character of the concerned person into question. The damaged or lost face can only hardly be mended or restored. The reputation of the person is damaged and can only painfully be regained and heightened by good deeds. For just that reason, one should avoid singling out specific persons in the view of their group (in confidence, there is no problem) either negatively or positively. In the last years, there is a tendency to break away from this tradition; especially in some Korean companies, a rude conduct can be observed.

8.6.5   Other Peculiarities

According to my experience for Europeans, it is much easier to learn the "right" way of dealing with people from China and Korea than with people from Japan. Koreans, however, think their manner more akin to Japan as to China.

The Japanese are decidedly afraid of conflicts. Neither in a letter nor in a meeting, they like coming to the point immediately. For the same reasons, people from Japan do not like to give direct answers. As a rule, one must allow long time for small talk before coming to the point. From a European point of view, one needs exceptional patience and stamina during a negotiation as Japanese but also Chinese people are used to discuss anything in their group intensely and at length. Koreans in this respect are much different from their Asian neighbours, which is one of the keys for their actual success. With strategies such as that of the smart pursuer, they outpace one Japanese corporate group after the other. An actual example is the family-managed conglomerate (also called Chaebol) Samsung that is by now the fifth biggest enterprise in the world. Palli, Palli (quickly, quickly) is lived and practised by Koreans almost excessively. Combined with quick decisions (rather untypical of Asia) and seven workdays a week at least at the top management level (from the 55th year of life onwards the salaries are reduced continually and many Koreans go into retirement then), Korea is unbeatable at the moment.

Almost all meetings with partners from Asia bear the risk of interpreting their gestures wrongly. Due to the language barrier, Europeans soon get the impression of consent while their Asian partners only wanted to show that they were listening attentively. The Japanese do not like to say "No" plainly—for the very good reason to avoid their negotiating partner losing his face. For that reason, one must observe the Asian partner's nonverbal communication precisely. It is best to ask questions in the way that they can only be answered by "Yes" or "No". Decision-making and consensus within the group are important values for Asians. Japanese will often fall in silence for some time. In such situations, one must be patient and must try to find out whether the negotiation partners have really understood what had been discussed. The Japanese, Koreans, and Chinese count on broad agreements and mutual understanding for solving arising problems flexibly. Some people from Japan even shut their eyes when listening intently. They seldom make concessions immediately and expect that both parties come with their best offer to the negotiation table. They do not consider contracts as final agreements so that renegotiations are always possible. This is, by the way, one of the biggest potentials for conflict in intercultural business relations. While Western business people as a rule come with full deciding authority, put their cards on the table immediately, and signal an instant give and take by dominant negotiating, Japanese especially have only limited negotiating authority. He tends to achieve a long-term mutual give and take and tries to reach it by his restrained conduct of negotiations. How difficult a negotiation may become, one should never lose one's temper or raise one's voice.

8.6.6 Conclusion

Be friendly, confident, but never arrogant in dealing with your global partners. Show adequate appreciation for their accomplishments even if these are not yet perfect. Show interest in the culture of your business partners and their families; eat, drink, and celebrate with them as much as you can answer for or tolerate but be careful with regard to political statements. Develop a feeling for the language (I personally took lessons in Italian as well as in Chinese) and thus for the culture and offer presents to your hosts (but with caution—in China, for instance, never give a watch for that means as much as "Your time is over"). Respect the ritual of exchanging business cards and do not—especially at the first meeting—press too quickly to discussing business details. These will be discussed later or on a lower level. Observe the seniority principle and show sensitivity in interpreting your business partner's nonverbal signals. Ask closed questions whenever you got the impression that your negotiation partner does not understand you or wants to react elusively. Take part in the time-consuming analyses and discussions of the other party—that will create a sense of togetherness and thus the base for an optimum course of the negotiation. Build contacts and foster them especially when the joint business activity is over.

But the attention for other cultures and the adaptation to them should also have its limits: The German way in which business is done is quite appreciated globally and especially in Asia, and the "new" generation of Asian business people is—according to my experience—well prepared for that way.

8.7   Evaluating the Success of Negotiations

Whether the result of the negotiation is considered a success depends on the expectations and the negotiation parties' priorities. Basically, there are three dimensions for evaluating the success of a negotiation: efficiency, effectiveness, and the atmosphere of the talks. How the success of a negotiation can be evaluated in practice shall be illustrated in the following Hint from Experience.

Practical Tip: How to Evaluate the Success of a Negotiation?
In hardly any other company department the own performance can be as easily made transparent and expressed in Euro as in the Purchasing. One should make use of this chance although it heightens the pressure—for not all results are, and will be, positive throughout. But only things that can be scaled can also be managed, compared to planning, and, if need be, be amended in time. Figure 8.13 shows exemplarily how the value proposition can be shown graphically.

Another example documents the complex negotiation result concerning the purchasing of two machines. The summary in Fig. 8.14 is very suitable for informing all participants in the negotiation as well as the superiors about the result. Again, the saying is true: "Do well and talk about it", for this will increase the Purchasing's standing continuously. Keep an annual account of the successes in

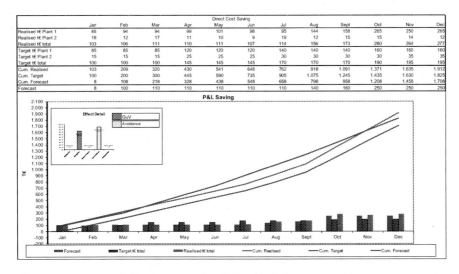

Fig. 8.13 Value contribution by cost saving (P&L effective) or cost avoidance

	Object of negotiation	Initial offer	Agreement	clause
1	Prototypes	-	50 prototypes included	§ 1 (2)
2	Promised characteristic	-	circle times	§ 2 (2)
3	Price for 2 machines + tools	827.000,- €	775.000,- €	§ 6 (1)
4	Option	same discount for the next two years	same discount for two additional machines	§ 6 (3)
5	Payment terms	30% - 60% - 10%	20% - 60% - 20%	§ 7 (1)
		-	45 Tage	§ 7 (3)
6	Bank guarantee	-	+	§ 7 (1/4)
7	Transport insurance	-	+	§ 10 (4)
8	Relocation	-	Abbau + Wiederaufbau, ohne Transport	§ 14
9	Warranty	12 month	24 month + extension to 30 month in case of rectification	§ 15
10	Vertragsstrafe	-	penalty bei Liefer- bzw. Produktionsverzögerungen	§ 17
11	allgemeine Versicherungen	-	+	§ 19
12	Geheimhaltung	-	+	§ 20

Fig. 8.14 Overview negotiated result

which all your successes are registered in Euros. Not only you but also your superior will be surprised when the sums are added.

Conclusion Invest twice as much time in the preparation as in the actual negotiation. Be flexible with regard to your negotiation style. The less information you could collect on the product, the more you should demand but without going too far. Always have a B plan at hand for cases in which the negotiation takes quite another course due to circumstances previously unknown. Update your market and supplier data regularly, and always have them at hand. Use your gestures purposefully, for that conveys authority. As a rule, stay friendly for those who smile will win. But also show your teeth from time to time.

Observe the body language of your negotiation partner incessantly and react, if necessary, by questions. Bring as much negotiation areas as possible into play in order to artificially generate complexity that can easily be dispensed with. By this, you will achieve considerably more in the points that are important to you. Set the agenda previously in concert with the supplier. "Be credible and good to the other party but stay firm as far as the factual level is concerned"—this advice should be taken to heart. Paraphrase the other party during the negotiation—that means repeat important words of the other party with your own in order to create a mutual, identical understanding. At the end, a contract, an agreement, or at least a written, undersigned amicable record shall result in which is stated WHO shall do WHAT up to WHEN. Collect, scale, and cluster your successes and thus hold an up-to-date documentation of your performance and the profit contribution of the purchasing department.

References

Fisher, R., Ury, W., & Patton, B. (2004). *Das Harvard-Konzept*. Frankfurt: Campus.

Portner, J. (2010). *Besser verhandeln – Das Trainingsbuch*. Gabal: Offenbach.

Risse, J. (2007). *Verhandlungsführung – Kann man verhandeln lernen?* Workshop auf dem 14. Syndikusanwaltstag. Berlin: Baker & McKenzie.

Wieland, J. (2006). *Tugenden in der chinesischen Kultur*. KieM 21(2006), Konstanz.

Personnel Development in Purchasing

9

9.1   The Principles of Personnel Development

The field of personnel development represents a central task of personnel management and aims to establish and expand the personnel resources required for achieving a company's objectives. This comprises, on the one hand, the preservation and development of employee skills in order to secure employability in a changing working environment. The necessary skills need to be fostered through, for example, training and further education, while incentives need to be created through employee loyalty, motivation, and perspective. On the other hand, personnel development involves recruiting skilled employees and managers through what is known as Recruitment and Talent Management. Personnel development could thus be described as an organised learning process, taking place within the company's social environment, from which it is triggered, designed, and managed. Both the personal and professional interests of the employee need to be taken into consideration in order to effectively perceive current and future tasks.

As shown in Fig. 9.1, it is not just the personnel management and disciplinary management level that are responsible for personnel development but primarily the employees themselves.

Personnel development can take place within the company, externally, or as a mixture of the two. Various concepts have been developed for this purpose:

Personnel Development: Into-the-Job
- Vocational training: Training in an officially recognised skilled profession
- Induction: Technical and social integration into the working environment
- Trainee programme: Systematic assembly of university graduates through coordinated assignments in various company divisions
- Dual study: Higher education with firmly integrated practical elements in company

© Springer International Publishing AG 2017
U. Weigel, M. Ruecker, *The Strategic Procurement Practice Guide*, Management for Professionals, DOI 10.1007/978-3-319-57651-0_9

Fig. 9.1 Personnel
development as a cooperation
task

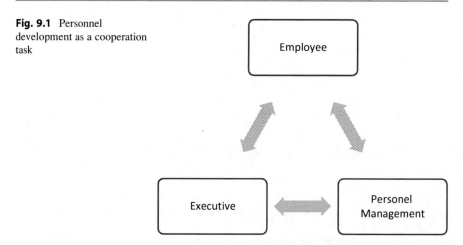

Personnel Development: On-the-Job
- Coaching, Mentoring: Personal transfer of knowledge between experienced people (Mentors) and, in this case, inexperienced employees (Mentees)
- Job Enlargement: Increasing the variety of tasks and content to the same required level of performance
- Job Enrichment: Expansion of skills through assumption of new areas of responsibility, for example through project work or the role of representative
- Job Rotation: Systematic job rotation with the aim of mastering a new work situation and broadening competencies

Personnel Development: Near-the-Job
- Quality circle: In-house work groups, for activating the creative and knowledge potential of employees while improving the quality of products and services
- Learning workshop: Learning environments with extensive material, where employees can gather their own experiences through practical and active learning

Personnel Development: Off-the-Job
- Seminars: Learning and teaching events, where knowledge is interactively shared and consolidated within small groups
- Study: Academic learning and researching at universities and vocational academies

A prevailing shortage of skills makes the task of personnel development even more difficult, and this has long been an issue for Purchasing too. Particularly as, even today, there are still relatively few academic opportunities, such as apprenticeships or study paths, that are specially tailored to its requirements. The company buyers are thus often career changers with varied qualifications who require additional specialised training, making it particularly difficult to find qualified purchasing personnel who meet the higher requirements. And this trend looks set to continue as a result of the changing demographic structure.

There is often no way around the internal development of personnel as a method for nurturing existing employee potential and generating enthusiasm among new purchasing talent. Because only highly qualified and well-trained purchasing personnel will be more than able to effectively deal with the challenges faced.

9.2   Requirements for the Modern Buyer

With purchasing playing a far greater role in a company's success, and the networking of internal departments taking a more process-oriented approach, the profile of requirements for the modern Buyer has changed dramatically.

While the operational buyer requires, for example, in-depth knowledge of the logistics and procurement processes, the strategic buyer must have extensive market knowledge, as well as international negotiation skills. The Buyer participates in projects as a team player while respecting all interests relevant to purchasing.

It is clear that the tasks of the purchasing employees, and how they are organised, are becoming more comprehensive and increasingly complex. The Buyer is thus taking on new and previously unknown roles in the company, as indicated in Fig. 9.2.

In addition to the higher professional demands, sociocultural and personal skills of the purchasing employee are becoming increasingly important. While the focus in the past was on coordinating orders and safeguarding communication with suppliers, the Buyer is today faced with a far greater density of interaction. With the increasingly networked internal departments, Purchasing is now playing the role of interface manager between internal company departments and the external suppliers. In this context, as illustrated in Fig. 9.3, management skills, as well as communicative and intercultural capabilities, will become central fields of competence for the Buyer.

One particular skill to be practised by the modern Buyer is the art of defence. This is an important aspect when it comes to protecting company-wide purchasing interests. The following practical tip should help to explain this further.

Fig. 9.2 The Buyer career profile—from administrative employee to talented all-rounder

former	today
Administrator	Service provider
Order processor	Purchasing optimizer
Role specialist	Supply Chain Manager
Lone fighter	Team player and moderator
Data administrator	Know how facilitator
Agent	Manager

Fig. 9.3 Fields of competence for the modern Buyer

Expertise	Soft skills
• Product competence	• Appearance
• Research competence	• Entrepreneurial skills
• Bidding competence	• Intellectual skills
• Supplier management	• Communication skills
• Negotiation competence	• Leading skills
• Controlling competence	• Emotional skills
• Value analysis	• Compliance
• Strategy development	• Internationality
• Risk Management	
• Process Management	

Practical Tip: The Art of a Clear-Sighted and Ready Defence

As Buyers, we know the situation all too well: an important meeting becomes the scene of a sudden reproach or attack. For it is in the nature of things that earlier failings first become apparent at the end, and this all too often in the form of missing purchased parts. In layman's terms, this often means: "Purchasing has once again failed to procure the parts on time, parts that are too expensive or that do not meet the standard of quality". That this is often only the symptom for failings in other departments is of interest to no one in the millisecond it takes to deliver the damning verdict. *Failure is an orphan after all!* The criticism generally comes from those departments with competing objectives, such as Sales, Quality Assurance, Project Management, or Production. And, of course, there is also the regular threat from those less than friendly "colleagues". As Buyers, we are certainly not looking to be everybody's darling. Which is why now is the time to immediately counter. But words fail, you are left floundering and would like nothing better than to deliver a hard-hitting response. And this is what the situation calls for, as an appropriate reaction to the attack delivered verbally or unexpectedly during a presentation. Because otherwise your speechlessness and uncertainty will be seen as a weakness and you will lose this round. If you are not capable of delivering a professional response, doubt will be cast over your managerial skills as a logical consequence. And this must be avoided at all costs.

But what exactly constitutes a quick wit? One of the main characteristics of a quick wit, without which you won't come far in life, is the self-assured and unwavering air of confidence, or at least the appearance of one. Always able to hold your own, baffling opponents at every opportunity with a retaliation that hits the mark. There is an immediate answer to almost every question, possibly delivered with humour and thus triggering helpful sympathies. Quotes are occasionally used, a selection of which have been rehearsed beforehand. Arguments are often laced with irony or even sarcasm. This the ideal anyway.

Not everyone is naturally talented in this way, however. Yet this trait can be learned and constantly improved upon. Lessons often learned the hard way in early childhood, however also the successes that everyone has experienced in some way or the other, are the basis for what is known as the thumb pressure method. How does this work, a method derived from the world of acupuncture? Pressing the thumbnail into the tip of the index finger creates a painful sensation, at the same time triggering memories of success or happiness. The release of these "happy hormones" brings with it a new burst of sorely required energy. Practised over a long period, the artificially created pain will be enough to power the imminent counterattack. Just the reminder of personal success is enough to briefly restore self-confidence.

It is always good to be well informed, making it easier to respond convincingly. In most cases, rhetorically gifted people also have a better than average general education or extensive expertise. Forward planning (see Preparing for Negotiations) is another important success factor and is not as difficult as it may initially suggest. Have a selection of quotes at the ready, and be familiar enough with each one to ensure it can be used at the right moment. You will generally be aware of which meetings are likely to cause conflict. It is thus advisable to prepare your responses to potentially uncomfortable questions. And here it is important that your team has been schooled in the importance of transparent communication. There is nothing worse than being the last to know about bad news from your own field, and then hearing this from others too. This early warning system should not only be supported from within your own ranks. Your "real" friends are just as important, who ideally include stakeholders (and by "stakeholders" we mean "interested parties" or project participants, also seemingly uninvolved persons such as customers or employees) from all important areas, however also from the company's opposing camps. Cultivate and maintain these important contacts. Invest your time and energy in this network, provide tips, and keep allies informed. It is also important to defend any colleagues who are not present during meetings. In doing so, you are demonstrating social competency and earning respect and can expect the favour to be returned.

Relevant key data and the latest information should always be on hand and ready to use. Information that can be used to fend off potential attacks and opponents should also be saved. This bolsters self-confidence and gives courage to deliver the necessary counterarguments. Questions for your opponent also provide you with valuable time to prepare your own response. Provide factual answers as a rule, add humour, or contribute quotes on occasion; however, don't be afraid to take a more aggressive approach where necessary. A successful comeback will often leave a lasting impression, as well as discourage other opponents. You will not always win, however, especially if the appropriate response fails you at the decisive moment. Here, you need to reflect on how to avoid a repeat occurrence.

To conclude: Think ahead. Establish an early warning system both within and beyond the confines of your department. Update your information regularly, and always have it to hand. If you are unable to immediately respond, ask a question to buy time. Use humour and include famous quotes. A smile can also provide protection, or even unsettle your opponent. Remind yourself of previous successes or special moments, and make the most of the strength this gives you. Defend colleagues and regularly provide tips or information you deem important. Do not shy away from conflict and set examples where appropriate and if confident enough to do so. If you do lose the war of words, then remember the following:

A *"good" enemy is often more valuable than a good friend. They will challenge you, keeping you alert and always thinking.*

9.2.1   Identifying Potential with the Transactional Analysis

Identifying and fostering employee potential is crucial for an effective development of personnel. The approach often taken here involves what are known as "potential analyses", structured investigations into the existence of certain employee skills. It allows weaknesses to be identified and strengths systematically developed, with potential analyses benefitting both management and employees.

The transactional analysis is one method that may be used to identify potential. This originates from humanistic psychology and is based on the assumption that every person has three different "ego states": the Parent ego state, the Adult ego state, and the Child ego state. These states of consciousness describe patterns of behaviour displayed by the person when communicating in various situations. The respective ego state refers to overall behaviour and how any given moment is experienced by a person.[1] The various ego states generally feature typical behavioural patterns:

- *The Parent ego state* takes two forms: the Critical Parent ego state and the Caring Parent ego state. A typical mother/father figure can be found in both. However, while the Critical Parent ego is characterised by reproach, criticism, and giving orders, the Caring Parent ego comforts and supports.
- *The Parent ego state* is characterised by rational behaviour and objective decisions. Behavioural patterns in this ego state are generally neutral, matter-of-fact, and lacking emotion.
- *The Child ego state*, in turn, appears to have two forms: on the one hand, the Natural Child ego state, characterised by carefree, spontaneous behaviour, and, on the other, the Adapted Child ego state, with its adapted and hesitant behaviour.

The analysis comprises a comprehensive questionnaire, the results of which can then be represented in an ego gram. The results show the frequency and intensity of the various ego states over the course of the employee's working day. The practical tip in Sect. 9.3 outlines a specific case.

---

[1]Cf. Henning und Petz (2007, p. 28).

9.3   Purchasing as a Managerial Function

Considered an essential requirement, today's Buyer is expected to be able to lead others. Not every Buyer will be directly assigned managerial duties; however, this strategic role requires a considerable degree of leadership competence. This is particularly evident in the Buyer's role as Supplier Manager, in which he selects, assesses, develops, and possibly controls suppliers. This means nothing other than actively managing suppliers, whether by stipulating target agreements, providing systematic support, or enforcing sanctions.

Furthermore, the Buyer is faced with conflict situations involving other internal departments on a daily basis. During the early phases of product development in particular, it is the task of the Buyer to drive down costs, which often requires impressive communicative skills, assertiveness, and a high degree of social intelligence.

The modern Buyer can thus only do justice to the role's growing importance in the company when he assumes, to a certain extent, managerial responsibilities. The following practical tip should provide some enlightenment here (Fig. 9.4).

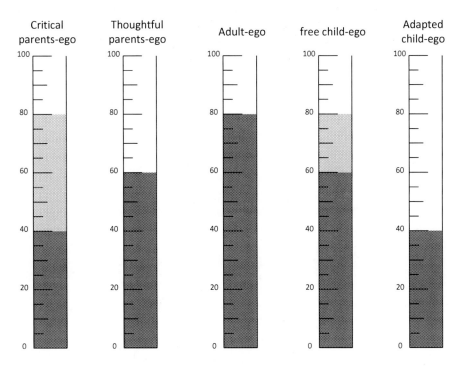

Fig. 9.4 Evaluation of transactional analysis with leadership qualities

Practical Tip: You Are Not Just Managing Employees, You Are Managing Suppliers Too

For years, I just didn't know where to start with the term "Management". I was thrown in at the deep end from early on, whereby I learned quick enough that here was a key to professional success and thus to a better income. I always viewed the assessments (a must for many companies when employing anyone above the level of divisional head) as an opportunity for personal improvement, and thus answered the extensive questions honestly, whether it was a "Potential Check" according to the "Bepa System" or a Transactional Analysis that was 143 questions long. The results corresponded in an astonishing way. An ego gram is used to represent the results of the transactional analysis, showing whether the person in question has any managerial talent and how one's psychic energy compares to the average value compiled from 3000 German-speaking candidates.

And there it was, in black and white: I had a talent for leadership, however tended to set the pace too fast, meaning not every employee could keep up. I knew what I was dealing with now, and had the chance to develop the necessary sensibility. This demonstrates the importance of knowing who you are as a person, the impression you make on others, and how you react to situations, particularly stressful ones. It can be very helpful (for both parties) during management talks, as well as for negotiations with suppliers. The transactional analysis is also a superb tool for making objective, recruitment-related decisions. As head of a strategic purchasing department, you are not only managing people within the company, but also taking on a managerial role in your dealings with suppliers. Leadership qualities and concepts, for both employees and suppliers, thus come into play here too. My 25 years of managerial experience in Procurement were not only influenced by former superiors, but I also gradually adopted important leadership concepts and principles. These qualities form, in my experience, the basis for a high standard of management. Success here fundamentally depends on having a positive self- and public image, as well as personal authority. Other distinguishing characteristics include *integrity (walk the walk, talk the talk)*, a distinctive talent for organisation and communication, as well as the ability to delegate. Sound judgement and an instinctive understanding help just as much as conflict management and, above all, fearless leadership. To be able to admit to your own mistakes, to personally support your own employees in critical situations, and to always defend them against others. If there are failings to report, then this needs to be discussed one-on-one. These characteristics differ from person to person, of course; however, I always keep them in mind and try to make the most of existing potential.

Just as Important as the Leadership Qualities Are the Leadership Concepts

Lead with SMART (cf.), ambitious, and yet achievable aims, derived from the long-term, strategic planning of the company or department (cf. Chap. 2). Encourage your employees to take an entrepreneurial attitude and give them the freedom they need to let this play out. Look for innovative solutions together, ones that will increasingly turn reactions into actions, and enable you to adopt an approach less process-oriented and more focused on results. As a manager, generalisation should always take preference over specialisation. I have never followed the advice of Lee Iacocca, former Chrysler Executive, to "take only the best", but instead always reminded myself that "there is something for everyone". Being able to recognise these strengths within a team, correctly utilising its members, motivating them, and successively reinforcing the unit with external talent also represents leadership for me. When putting together a team, always remember to ensure "compatibility before suitability". Don't just make demands, actively foster employee engagement. In Sales, for example, on average there is up to nine times more investment made in training and further education than is generally the case in Procurement. Recognise the strengths of your employees and expand on them. Strength = Knowledge (gained from third-level education) + Experience (gathered over the years) which can both be learned + Talent (which cannot be learned, however). The greatest potential for success then exists when the job encompasses strength, character, and passion. Employees need to feel that they are doing something worthwhile and that they belong. Under normal circumstances, they shouldn't have to worry about anything happening to them. Not everything is sweetness and light however and, as a manager, you need to be able to lay off employees. This, of course, should be taken as a last resort when dealing with low performers. Then it is a question of finding out whether the person is willing yet unable, or able yet unwilling. In order to be able to assess work in terms of quality and quantity, workplace, and job descriptions, along with target agreements, must always be kept up to date. If discussions and coaching remain unsuccessful, then the situation is serious. Any one-on-one meetings deemed necessary must be documented and signed. If possible, proof must be provided of any damage caused to the company. If this is the case, warning must be given; however, the following also applies here: Sometimes less is more. Focus on serious, specific incidents and include the HR department and the works council in these meetings as soon as possible. *You also need to separate yourself from chronic complainers; some people are simply not happy until they are unhappy.*

To conclude: One this is certain: Your employees (this equally applies to suppliers) will always be watching you, particularly during difficult situations. *Therefore, make sure you do the right thing at all costs.* It is very easy to see how authentic and reliable your behaviour is. "Walk the walk, talk the talk": this is what should guide your role as leader both within and outside the company, *because this is what will generate the essential ingredient of trust.*

9.4   A Career in Purchasing

Unlike other departments, such as Marketing, Sales, or Controlling, there is no conventional training for the role of Buyer. As a rule, career changers from other departments are individually nurtured to meet the relevant demands. Apprenticeships or trainee programmes can be used here to make the transition easier. Apprentices and student trainees are ideally suited to advancing the department's strategic development as they can explore methods and processes as part of their own projects for which there may otherwise be no time. The company thus benefits directly from their work while, at the same time, has the opportunity to encourage new talent to join the ranks of Purchasing.

In order to make it easier for young professionals to get started, many companies go down the route of offering trainee programmes. These programmes generally last around 12 months and provide the trainees with an insight into how the company is run. The focus here is on gaining experience, particularly with internal customers such as Design, Quality Assurance, and Production Planning who make an appearance down the line. Becoming acquainted with procurement parts and suppliers in an distinct phase of operational purchasing is an essential element.

This may also be where the first "battles" take place and where the main areas for subsequent strategic activity are identified and understood.

This is also a chance for young professionals to carry out their own projects for the first time, looking at, for example, the development of a commodity group strategy or optimising purchasing processes. Providing the trainees with a mentor is helpful here, someone to provide support in the execution of the project and who is on hand to answer any questions. Specific opportunities for further training may also be offered, or the chance to spend time abroad. In addition to the general requirements for a career in Purchasing, such as personal initiative, good communication abilities, and leadership skills, a healthy mix of commercial and technical expertise is also a must.

Practical Tip: From Apprentice to Strategic Buyer (M. Ruecker)

Having completed school and a standard 3-year course in industrial management, I was ready to start my professional career. The first few months were spent in the Purchasing department, which was to considerably influence my working life. Initial experience was gained working through order processes, compiling queries, and exchanging information with suppliers.

Once the final examination was successfully completed, there were two positions within the company to choose from. I decided on the position of Junior Buyer. I was mainly responsible for the operational support of non-production materials, as well as the implementation of smaller projects. It quickly became apparent to me, however, that my purely commercial training would not suffice for the more extensive tasks in Purchasing. I lacked the technical, social, and methodical expertise. After a year as Junior Buyer, I thus decided to start my bachelor's degree in industrial engineering. The company supported me in this and I was able to complete the course as part of the current "StudiumPlus" dual programme of study at the Central Hesse Technical University. I attended lectures during regular semester times for the next 3 years, and completed various company projects during the holidays. Support was provided by both the company and the university, with mentors who oversaw my projects. I was able to complete a large part of the projects here in Purchasing, for example implementing systematic cost reductions, designing a supplier evaluation process, or setting up an early warning system for the management of supplier risks.

Once completed, the projects were documented in a report, presented, and assessed by the mentors. I was thus able to systematically work through practical purchasing topics with basic theoretical knowledge.

Following the successful completion of my studies, I took up the position of Strategic Buyer within the company, which I still carry out today. In this role, I am responsible for the transfer of complex assemblies, strategy and process development, as well as organising risk management in purchasing. In order to further develop my skills, I am also completing the 2-year dual master's programme in process management alongside my full-time job, which is particularly helpful when it comes to shaping and optimising processes. A comprehensive knowledge of purchasing is really only obtained through a lifetime of learning, and by adapting to the changing requirements.

Reference

Henning, G., & Pelz, G. (2007). *Transaktionsanalyse*. Paderborn: Junfermann.

e-Procurement

10

10.1 Basics of e-Procurement

The digitalisation of business processes has become an increasingly important method of driving modern business organisation. Because with the emergence of the Internet and the potential it offers, not only were new economic structures created, the handling of electronic business processes was made possible with new and innovative forms of transaction. This has led to intensive networking and a collaboration across departments and companies. Mobile scenarios and cloud computing determine today's organisational development and provide companies with completely new opportunities.

Electronic procurement, also referred to as e-Procurement, opens up major potential for companies when it comes to reducing process, product, and inventory costs in conjunction with greater speed and higher quality. Electronic procurement provides businesses with the opportunity to design faster and more cost-efficient processes with greater transparency. Many companies have recognised this potential and are increasingly turning to electronic aids in order to optimise their procurement processes. Catalogue systems, tendering tools, and electronic supplier evaluations are just a few of the applications making day-to-day work easier.

These approaches are nothing new, however. IT solutions for Purchasing have been offered for the past 15 years. Back in 1998, software gurus predicted that e-Procurement would quickly become one of the main standard technologies used by companies, in both large concerns and medium-sized enterprises. Yet the big breakthrough never came. Although, according to a study from the German Association for Supply Chain Management, Procurement and Logistics (BME) regarding the use of electronic solutions, more than 70% of companies asked were using at least one e-Procurement application, the intensity of use has stagnated for several years, however, at a rather low level.[1]

---

[1] Cf. Bundesverband Materialwirtschaft, Einkauf und Logistik e.V (2014, p. 16).

© Springer International Publishing AG 2017

U. Weigel, M. Ruecker, *The Strategic Procurement Practice Guide*, Management for Professionals, DOI 10.1007/978-3-319-57651-0_10

According to this study, the main reasons for not using e-Procurement were:

– Internal resistance (35%)
– Poor project resources (33%)
– Suppliers cannot or will not support IT system (19%)
– Technical requirements not met (16%)
– Lack of know-how or qualifications (13%)
– Management is reluctant (8%)

From this, it appears that e-Procurement solutions are generally viewed positively. Difficulties arise when putting them into practice. This is a fundamental issue highlighting the fact that installation of the purchasing software is not the problem.

In order to be able to take a closer look at electronic procurement, several basic principles will be outlined first below. In addition to classifying the standard terms used, current developments will be explored and an overview provided of the various objectives for e-Procurement solutions.

10.1.1 Conceptual Definition

e-Business Electronic-Business (e-Business) is generally understood as the use of digital information technology for the initiation, arrangement, and processing of business processes between economic partners via innovative communication networks.[2] The service providers and service consumers can be companies, public institutions, or private consumers. The focus should be on generating an added value from the electronic business relationship, either in the form of a monetary contribution or an intangible one.[3]

When transforming traditional value-added chains, the boundaries between internal departments and between the company and its business partners are reduced, while old hierarchical structures are simplified and a more efficient flow of information and communication is aimed for.[4]

Basic e-Business technology constitutes the world wide web, as it facilitates cost-efficient information and exchange processes at local, regional or global level, whereby every user, regardless of time zone or location, is able to use electronic services or do business.

Common e-Business models include:

– *Content Models* for the processing and provision of new information
– *Commerce Models* for the management of business transactions

---

[2]Cf. Kollmann (2013, p. 51).
[3]Cf. Meier and Storner (2012, p. 2).
[4]Cf. Wöhe (2008, p. 189).

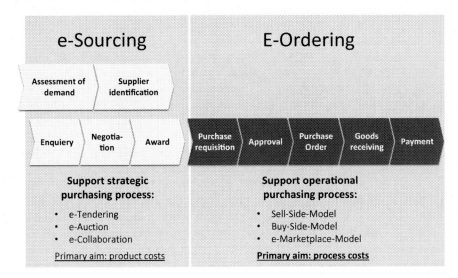

Fig. 10.1 Subareas of e-Procurement

- *Context Models* for the aggregation and evaluation of existing information
- *Connection Models* for the provision of channels for exchanging information

e-Procurement is a subarea of e-Business and generally stands for the electronic purchasing of products and services by companies via digital networks. e-Procurement thus electronically supports both strategic and operational procurement to such an extent that the procurement process, in terms of process costs and process result, is optimised.

As shown in Fig. 10.1, e-Procurement can be divided into two basic subareas: e-Ordering and e-Sourcing. These terms accordingly represent the electronic support of strategic or operational purchasing.

e-Ordering is aimed at operational and administrative tasks and is used to reduce process costs, for example through the use of electronic catalogue systems or online shops for corporate customers, for the handling of low-value requirements.

e-Sourcing, on the other hand, describes the strategic approaches taken, the sole aim of which is to reduce cost prices and where the reduction of the internal process costs is regarded as more of a side effect. Examples here include the use of databases for identifying new suppliers, electronic requests, and tenders or electronic procurement auctions.

10.1.2 Basic Types of e-Sourcing Models

While models assigned to e-Ordering mainly focus on operational and administrative tasks during the procurement process, e-Sourcing is focused on strategy. The aim here is to improve the process result, whereby the focus is not on process costs, but instead the product costs or process result. Electronic marketplaces (e-Marketplace solutions) form the basis here as platforms for trading goods and services. The marketplace operator is aiming to offer both buyers and sellers access to as many potential business partners as possible and to support successful business transactions.

The use of a central platform increases the transparency of market structures and prices, whereby platform conditions come close to an ideal market. This effect stops short, however, of automatically providing the "ideal price". Special pricing procedures are required, which differ according to their method used.

10.1.2.1 e-Tender

Tenders are used as part of the strategic procurement process to find suitable suppliers and to prepare for the negotiations that follow. Several suppliers on the market are selected, requirements formulated in a tender, and this is then communicated to those taking part. Once the participating suppliers have submitted their offers, these are assessed and compared.

With an electronic tender (e-Tender or Electronic RFQ), suppliers are requested to submit their offers for a tender to an Internet platform. Access to this tender can be open or closed. With an open tender, the relevant documents will be freely accessible on the platform and anyone interested can submit a corresponding offer. This type of tender is often used as a means of identifying new suppliers. With a closed tender, only selected suppliers receive access to the tender documents. The advantages here include better protection of company know-know and less effort required in evaluating the submissions made.

Open tenders generally receive a greater response as they have a far wider appeal, while the quality of the submissions is better for closed tenders as the participants have already been pre-selected by the company issuing the invitation to bid.

The aim of tenders is, once a particular requirement has been determined, to establish the current market situation, identify new suppliers, make the suppliers comparable with each other, and build up price pressure for subsequent negotiations. The advantage to electronic tenders is that the technology can accelerate, standardise, and simplify the process.

10.1.2.2 e-Auction

If, unlike the e-Tender, pricing needs to be more dynamic, auction procedures can be used. Auction principles are applied here when determining the price. The auction thus takes the place of conventional price negotiations, whereby far greater pricing pressure can be built up during an auction as the participants are forced to react immediately to competing offers. While there may be difficulty gathering all participants at the one location for a conventional auction, this is not an issue for the electronic tender.

There are various auction models to choose from, with different result profiles. Four popular models are described below:

- The *English Auction* is the oldest and most well-known form of auction. Suppliers submit offers for a predetermined order, each offer better than the previous one. The supplier who submits the last and thus best offer wins the auction.
- The *Japanese Auction* is based on rounds. In each round, the supplier with the worst offer must underbid the best offer or leave the auction. The pace is generally determined by the buyer. The rounds continue until there is only one supplier left.
- With the *Dutch Auction*, the prices go up and not down. The Buyer puts forward an unrealistically low starting price and this then gradually increases until a supplier is ready to accept the price quoted.
- The *Brazilian Auction* also involves increasing bids. The Buyer discloses what he is willing to pay before the auction starts. The suppliers then compete for the order by gradually increasing the services they are prepared to offer for this price. The supplier who offers the most for the price specified is awarded the contract.

An important requirement for the e-Auction is that offers from suppliers can be made comparable and the price is the only remaining award criterion. If this is not the case, the result of the auction may be distorted; in other words, it won't be the best offer that wins, but the bidder with the cheapest price. In order to ensure comparability, a tender is often issued before the auction in which product details and specifications are set out.

The use of e-Auctions creates two decisive effects: cheaper cost prices and increased buyer productivity. Because with reduced negotiation phases, Buyers can process more procurement transactions or the time saved can be used for other activities.

A further point of criticism for e-Auctions, however, is that they can negatively influence supplier relationships. Due to the increased transparency and pressure to react to competing bids, suppliers are left to deal with a considerably higher price pressure. With the classic negotiating process, the supplier bids without the influence of others or it is unclear to him, at least, how much his own offer differs from the competition. As a result, it is highly likely that he will not entirely reach his lower price limit. Furthermore, there is a risk that unqualified bidders will distort the market situation or drive down the market price with artificially created bids. Consideration should thus be given to the fact that e-Auctions are not suitable in all situations. Particularly if the aim is to establish long-term partnerships, the use of auctions is not recommended.

10.1.2.3 e-Collaboration

Unlike other e-Sourcing solutions, e-Collaboration does not use the competition between suppliers to achieve the best possible results, instead focusing on a particularly intensive collaboration with the suppliers. e-Collaboration is thus not product oriented but supplier oriented. This collaboration can play out on both a commercial and technical level. On a commercial level, the most frequent e-Collaboration integrations take place between the back-end solutions of the partners with the aim of optimising requirements planning and supply. In terms of technology, suppliers are incorporated into development projects at a very early stage in order to utilise supplier know-how as soon as the product development phase is established. This type of e-Collaboration involves systems for the exchange of design data, documents, or project plans. As a high degree of integration depends on the technical support provided, the development of such solutions is generally very time-consuming and cost-intensive for the purchasing companies and suppliers.

10.1.3 Basic Types of e-Ordering Models

e-Ordering aims to support operational, administrative, and market-oriented activities during the procurement process. It is generally used in areas where the traditional procurement process demands a lot of time and resources for routine work and administration. In particular, with the procurement of what are known as MRO Goods (Maintenance, Repair and Operations), often neglected due to their low merchandise value, this type of electronic procurement boasts a number of options for the automation of order processing. e-Ordering solutions are generally based on electronic product catalogues, from which the consumer selects the required goods and places an order. The order is automatically sent to the supplier, registered, and paid for. These solutions cover the entire operational ordering process, including availability check, approval, receipt of goods, and invoice verification.

Three approaches can be taken to implement an e-Ordering concept, depending on catalogue responsibility: an external purchasing solution (Sell-Side), creation of own solution (Buy-Side), or purchasing via a catalogue-based marketplace (Intermediary).

10.1.3.1 Sell-Side Models

Sell-Side e-Ordering solutions are widespread, primarily among sellers looking to use the Internet as a channel for transaction and distribution thanks to the development of online trade. Both purchasing software and the online catalogue are provided by the supplier with this option. Access to the online catalogue can either be open, for example in the form of an online shop, or closed, meaning only certain people will have access. The buying company, once registered via the supplier website, has access to the products on offer. While there are no special agreements in place with open access, closed access involves negotiated conditions and framework agreements. As the supplier controls the catalogue's entire content management, there can generally be no changes made to product descriptions and classifications.

As illustrated in Fig. 10.2, there is a considerable disadvantage to Sell-Side solutions, namely that the consumer is left to grapple with the various designs and navigation structures of the respective suppliers. Furthermore, integration into the existing procurement processes is only possible to a limited extent. Depending on

Fig. 10.2 Procedure for implementing sell-side solutions

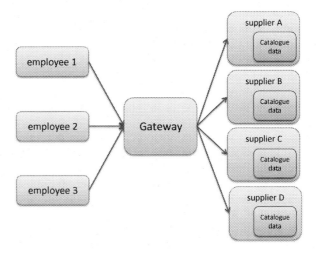

the maturity of the e-Ordering solution, however, various products can be pre-configured by the supplier and specifically offered according to customer requirements.

The main advantages to Sell-Side solutions:

– Configuration of complex products is possible
– No investment costs for an order system
– No operating costs for maintaining current product lists and prices for the buying company
– Shorter delivery times thanks to direct placement of order in supplier's system
– Real-time request of current availabilities and prices

The disadvantages to this solution include:

– No option of automatic product comparison
– Only restricted support of procurement process from Buyer
– Consumer must use different information system for every supplier
– Restricted integration of procurement process in operational information systems of customer

10.1.3.2 Buy-Side Models

The counterpart to systems on the supplier side are solutions on the buyer side, also known as Buy-Side Models. The purchasing software and a large part of the online catalogue are run by the buying company. Here, the Buyer combines various items from several suppliers in an individually defined Multi-Supplier Catalogue and makes this accessible to his consumers. This often takes place using Desktop-Purchasing-Systems (DPS), which allow the individual consumers to generate orders via a standard user interface on their own computer. The shopping basket

Fig. 10.3 Procedure for
implementing buy-side
solution

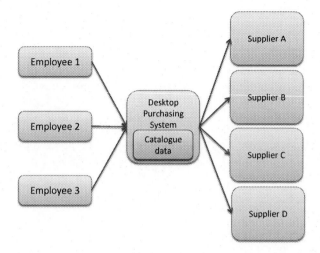

is sent to the individual suppliers via the DPS. The Multi-Supplier Catalogue may
be created, where necessary, by a third-party provider (Content Broker) who
specialises in this area.

The standard product view makes user operation considerably easier, while clear
procurement rules may be individually defined, for example with individual
approval procedures.

As shown in Fig. 10.3, many of the processes for this solution are run by the
company, such as user management and administration, for example. The Multi-
Supplier Catalogue may also be supplemented with offers from other suppliers and
thus gradually expanded. Furthermore, Buy-Side solutions may be integrated into
the existing software environment and connected to ERP systems.

The main advantages to Buy-Side solutions:

– Products from all suppliers may be represented in one system
– Procurement process may be designed according to specific company
  requirements
– Internal authorisation and approval procedures are supported
– Process lead times can be reduced
– Central administration of products already negotiated
– Consumer can operate system independently

Disadvantages to Buy-Side solution:

– Investment costs for information systems rest with procuring company
– Operating costs for Content Management incurred
– Not all suppliers have an electronic product catalogue
– Suppliers sometimes deliver poor-quality product data
– Purchaser and supplier must coordinate exchange format

10.1.3.3 e-Marketplace Models

e-Marketplace solutions are, in principle, just like Sell-Side solutions; only here not every supplier separately offers catalogue data. Instead, this data is collected, prepared, and published online by an independent marketplace operator (Intermediary). Access to this platform may be either open or closed, just like a Sell-Side solution.

Unlike the other e-Marketplace models, catalogue-based marketplaces are aimed at the procurement of C-goods and are thus oriented more towards e-Ordering than e-Sourcing. The bilateral business relationship is generally concluded individually between the buying and selling company, often including blanket and bulk orders. When compared with Sell-Side solutions, e-Marketplace solutions provide additional value with their multi-supplier availability of the products on offer, as well as the use of a standard user interface. There is no optimum integration into the buying company's existing system solutions, however.

Advantages of e-Marketplace solutions:

– Standard user interface
– Display of current and detailed market offers
– Efficient transactions
– Comparability of various offers
– Anonymous procurement option
– Bundling of supply and demand

The disadvantages include:

– Poor integration into ERP systems.
– Intermediaries generally only cover a narrow product range.
– Only large companies can negotiate better prices.
– Classified directories are often not up to date.

10.1.4 Aims of e-Procurement

As shown in the previous section, the main aim of e-Procurement is to optimise results in the procurement process. The following target areas all lead back to this primary objective.

10.1.4.1 Financial Objectives

It is the "leverage effect of materials management" that makes e-Procurement so attractive, as all savings generated in Purchasing can be directly added to the commercial profit. Product costs offer the most obvious opportunity to achieve savings. Dynamic pricing mechanisms in particular, such as with e-Auctions for example, allow for lower cost prices to be realised. Procurement goods with high product values are particularly suitable as this is where the greatest savings can be made. Standardisation mechanisms from catalogue systems also encourage the reduction of suppliers. Thanks to the resulting bundling of requirements and the negotiation of larger volumes, considerable price reductions can also be achieved.

There is further potential for saving in the reduction of process costs, as well as the optimisation of storage and inventory costs, which can be achieved through the faster and more flexible processing of operational and strategic procurement processes.

These potential savings are particularly relevant before the introduction of e-Procurement solutions, if the question is how long before a Return on Investment (ROI) will be seen. A brief payback period is a crucial selection criterion here.

10.1.4.2 Process Objectives

In addition to the financial objectives, the simplification, support, and automation of business processes is a central objective of e-Procurement solutions. On the one hand, to achieve savings through the reduction of process costs and, on the other, to increase process quality and reduce susceptibility to errors.

With automated processing and no paper used, orders are considerably faster and simpler to process. Particularly with idle periods, authorisation procedures, and transaction types, a considerable amount of time is saved, shown below in Fig. 10.4. e-Procurement systems thus facilitate the reduction of processing times by 83% on average.

The shortened order processing times have a proportional effect on the entire replenishment time, whereby safety stocks can be reduced.

Furthermore, through the use of e-Procurement solutions, existing capacities can be optimised to such an extent that purchasing employees are relieved in their operational tasks and given greater freedom for strategic tasks, or for the supervision of more important requirements and projects, because the use of electronic catalogues, for example, allows company consumers to identify their own requirements and to place orders without needing to check in with the Purchasing department first.

e-Auctions can also help reduce process costs as negotiations, often lengthy and sequential, can be parallelised and shortened.

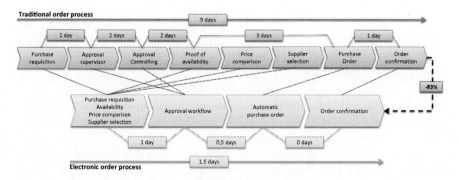

Fig. 10.4 Reduction of process times through e-Procurement

10.1.4.3 Information Goals

The use of e-Procurement solutions considerably improves the scope of information provided. More information is available to the buyers at a faster rate as the information acquired and evaluated from the existing material is simplified considerably. The transparency then created generates considerable advantages in terms of available information. A targeted product search in the e-Ordering area, for example, is far less of a task than the paper-based processes, saving a considerable amount of time and costs. Furthermore, the transparency acquired facilitates an easier bundling of requirements, for improving market position and harnessing more attractive conditions.

Also, the flow of procurement processes is made considerably more transparent through the use of e-Procurement solutions, with weak points more easily identified and improvements implemented faster.

10.1.4.4 Market Objectives

The use of e-Procurement solutions can considerably improve a company's purchasing position. On the one hand, the transparency achieved can be used to bundle requirements and thus secure a more attractive position on the market. The bargaining power gained from this can then be used to reduce cost prices or improve conditions. On the other hand, the transparency of electronic tenders or actions intensifies competition among suppliers, thus increasing the price pressure on suppliers.

Finally, automated order processes help combat the use of shadow processes, such as "Maverick Buying", in Purchasing. Maverick Buying describes the acquisition of goods and services by an unrelated department without the involvement of Purchasing. Enormous damage is done here to the company each year, due to the absence of a systematic supplier selection or professional price negotiations. The use of e-Ordering solutions specifically reduces these negative tendencies, with consumers able to process orders independently within a defined set of rules. Purchasing selects the suppliers and negotiates conditions beforehand.

10.2 Practical Application of e-Auctions

The electronic auction is one of the core elements of e-Sourcing. The extent to which this tool can be used in practice will be explained below. A structured and well-thought-out approach should be taken the first time around to keep the rate of error to an absolute minimum. Because if the very first auction turns out to be a failure, any further use will take some convincing.

One option for systematically introducing an auction tool is the problem-solving process "PDCA", familiar from the management concept Kaizen. The PDCA cycle comprises the following phases:

- Plan: Project implementation must first be planned. During this phase, the current situation is recorded and analysed, and the implementation concept worked out.
- Do: In this phase, there is no widespread implementation or introduction; instead the concept is tested and optimised with quickly realisable means. The first test auction takes place here.
- Check: In the check phase, the results are checked and assessed. The criteria necessary for a successful and long-term introduction in existing company processes are derived from this.
- Act: In the final introductory phase, the new standard is introduced across the board for long-term implementation in the company. As part of this phase, approaches need to be developed that facilitate the emergence of a structured e-Sourcing process.

10.2.1 Preparing for the e-Auction

As shown in previous chapters, e-Procurement solutions can support the procurement activities of a company in various ways. Here, it is crucial to know which type of tool is required for which demand, because not all e-Procurement solutions provide blanket coverage. Preparations should thus give consideration to potential procurement fields, differentiated according to the portfolio concepts described in Sect. 7.4. Here, procurement requirements are categorised according to their relevance for corporate success (purchasing volume) and, according to the complexity of the procurement market (supply risks), compiled in product groups and assigned to one of four superordinate product groups, from which general strategic approaches are then derived:

- *Non-critical commodity groups*: These commodity groups are characterised by a low purchasing volume, as well as a high availability or low material complexity. This group typically comprises what are known as "C-items", such as screws and standard parts or indirect materials such as office supplies. With these commodity groups, the strategy is focused on optimising cost prices, while at the same time reducing the support required. Electronic catalogue systems from e-Ordering would be suitable here for automating order processing, or even electronic auctions to conclude framework agreements for lower-value goods and thus obtaining favourable purchase prices.
- *Bottleneck commodity groups*: Bottleneck materials are characterised by a low purchasing volume combined with a high supply risk, for example due to poor availability or a high material complexity. The purchasing volume does not generally suffice to attract the interest of suppliers, nor to trigger internal measures that would lead to an improvement of the situation. The materials in this group are also not generally suitable for e-Procurement. The strategic focus here is on risk minimisation measures, for example through the introduction of safety stocks.

– *Leverage commodity groups*: These commodity groups have a high purchasing volume, a high material availability, and a low component complexity. Due to the high purchasing volume and the high number of suppliers, these commodity groups are the easiest for making savings. They are suited to electronic auctions, for utilising the competition among suppliers and optimising purchase prices.
– *Strategic commodity groups*: Strategic commodity groups may have a high volume, yet their material availability is very low or the procurement risk very high. These commodity groups require intensive support, permanent procurement market research, as well as a comprehensive risk management. In terms of e-Procurement, these commodity groups may involve the use of open tender tools for the identification of new suppliers.

Looking at these four commodity groups in relation to the applicability of an electronic auction, the following recommendations are made:

– Non-critical commodity groups: Only applicable with sufficient volume
– Bottleneck commodity groups: Inapplicable
– Leverage commodity groups: Well applicable
– Strategic commodity groups: Only applicable on condition

The initial criteria for a successful electronic auction can be derived from this. On the one hand, the highest possible volume must be used in order to generate interest among potential bidders. Furthermore, there must be sufficient supply sources available in order to create the necessary competition. And, last but not least, the requirement may not be too complex.

When selecting a suitable requirement for a pilot auction, ask yourself the following questions:

– Is there sufficient competition for the subject of the tender?
– Can the subject of the tender be clearly specified?
– Is there a willingness to change supplier?
– Is the price an important decision-making criterion?

Ideally, all four questions can be answered with Yes. If there is a chance a requirement cannot be sufficiently specified, or the price is not enough as an exclusive selection criterion, special consideration must be given to this, for example by adding an e-Tender with subsequent technical coordination.

10.2.2   Supplier Acquisition

The key to success lies in selecting the "right" suppliers. The first question you need to ask yourself is thus whether the auction should be open or closed. While an open auction allows for more suppliers to take part, there is a chance with the closed auction that the quality of the bids made will be higher, as suitable suppliers are selected and approved for the auction by Purchasing beforehand. A closed auction is thus recommended when first carrying out an e-Auction as it can be assumed that the quality of the bids made will be higher. First, potential suppliers need to be found and identified. Depending on the procurement object or supplier structure, input can come from the existing supplier base, from the specialist departments, or from procurement market research. When first carrying out an auction, the suppliers selected should initially be contacted by telephone and informed of the plan. The aim here is to gather initial feedback about whether the suppliers are fundamentally interested in participating in an auction. Furthermore, making personal contact is a way of breaking the ice and introducing the supplier to this new form of order placement, thus increasing their readiness to take part.

10.2.3 Creating an Electronic Invitation to Tender

In order to ensure the e-Auction runs smoothly, all requirements first need to be compiled in an electronic tender and made accessible to potential suppliers. The various platform operators generally provide support here in the form of a coach, who accompanies the entire tender and auction process. This should guarantee the best possible chance of success.

When creating an auction event, several basic rules first need to be determined for the tender and auction process.

– *Auction procedure*: The type of auction procedure needs to be selected here. The English Auction is the oldest and most well-known form of auction. Suppliers submit offers for a defined order, each offer better than the previous one. The supplier who submits the last and thus best offer wins the auction.
– *Auction design*: If non-monetary criteria also need to be considered when the auction is over, this must be determined beforehand when designing the auction. This means that if the lowest bid is not automatically granted the tender, but instead the order will be placed conventionally to the most suitable bidder after the e-Auction, this must be communicated in the tender. The most suitable does not necessarily have to be the lowest.
– *Scope of requirement*: The scope of the order must be described in detail and a corresponding specification drawn up. Ancillary services such as delivery and assembly services must be described.
– *Schedule*: Depending on the complexity of the requirement, the suppliers need to be given enough time to become acquainted with the specification and possibly clarify any queries. A deadline is set for submission of the initial bids. These are the starting bids for the actual auction, which is the next step and generally doesn't take longer than 30 min. The shorter the auction, the greater the dynamic of the bids. If verification needs to take place between bidding and the auction, this must be taken into consideration when planning the schedule.

- *Bidding rules*: The participating bidders can amend their bids to any amount. However, in order to restrict bidding activities to a reasonable level, minimum limits should be set for amending bids, for example a 0.5% reduction of the current offer. In order to avoid a rush of bids in the last seconds of the auction, an extension can be set up for when a bid is entered shortly before the auction ends. The others then have a chance to respond.
- *Transparency*: Depending on how transparent the auction should be, what the bidder can and cannot view during the auction must be determined. It must be decided here whether the bidders can only see their current ranking in the bidder list or even the difference between the most favourable bid to their own.

If these rules are defined and the auction event created accordingly, content must be added to the tender. This can be compiled in a logical sequence using the following bullet points.

- *Non-disclosure agreement*: Depending on the sensitivity of the specifications provided, the conclusion of a non-disclosure agreement with participating suppliers is recommended. This kind of agreement can be stored in the auction event and defined as a mandatory confirmation field. The participants only then have access to further stages of the auction once they have accepted the non-disclosure agreement.
- *Support information*: Contact information for the company issuing the tender is given for any clarification of technical or content-related questions, as well as contact data for the platform operator for clarification of questions or problems relating to the tendering tool.
- *General terms and conditions of purchase*: The supplier is involved from this step onwards, once he has gone through the specification and wishes to enter a bid. Similar to confirmation of the non-disclosure agreement, the acceptance of purchasing conditions can be defined as mandatory fields, whereby the participant can only submit a bid once these fields have been accepted.
- *Voluntary supplier disclosure*: Particularly when new suppliers wish to take part in the auction, a request for company information during the tender stage is highly recommended. In addition to general information about the company and the contact partners, selected balance sheet information such as equity, turnover, or expected growth rates should be requested. A corresponding questionnaire can easily be integrated into the auction event.
- *Technical feasibility*: At this stage, all requirements can be stored as Yes/No questions. The supplier now answers every question with "Yes" or "No", and also has the opportunity to enter user-defined text, making evaluation of the tendering results at a later stage far simpler.

Once all content has been added, the suppliers and their contact information are saved. With the announcement of the auction event, all suppliers will then receive the relevant notification per email, as well as access to the contents of the tender.

10.2.4 Executing an Auction Event

A fundamental step towards the success of an e-Auction is the instruction of the participants. This will ensure that the event runs smoothly. Instruction can involve the provision of a guide that describes how the tender platform is dealt with. The participants should then also be contacted by telephone after the tender has been launched, in particular to clarify whether:

- All suppliers have received the invitation by email
- All participants are able to use the tender platform
- There are any problems in viewing the documents
- Any initial ambiguities can be cleared up

Once the deadline for submitting bids has expired, the bids need to be verified. It can then be determined whether all requirements have been described intelligibly and in full, or whether the participants sufficiently meet these requirements. As all the relevant information has been stored in the auction tool, there is little difficulty in contacting the suppliers individually. The aim of this phase is to clarify all technical details and to make the bids submitted comparable. In order to guarantee a fair competition, unqualified bidders should be excluded from the final auction in order to prevent distorting the process.

The culmination of the process is the actual e-Auction. The previously rejected bidders should be blocked from participating in the auction in order to avoid invalidating the result. Only authorised participants may submit a bid during the auction. Once the auction has been launched, the suppliers receive a defined time period during which they may place a live bid.

When starting the auction, phoning the participants one more time to ensure they have access to the auction and everything is in place to make a bid is recommended. Extension mode may be activated towards the end of the auction, meaning the time will be extended if a bid is entered just before the auction is due to end. The remaining participants then have the chance to react to this bid.

10.2.5 Verification of Auction Results

The findings gained from the auction should be assessed and evaluated before their wider use in the company. The potential derived here can be used to introduce this procedure to the company in the long term. As the core aim of the electronic auction is to optimise product costs, the greatest potential is expected here. The sample e-Auction process illustrated in Fig. 10.5 is particularly suited to displaying the results and supports evaluation of the auction's success.

Reducing the process costs is not the primary aim of e-Sourcing, however represents a positive side effect. The e-Tender facilitates a simplification of the bid appraisal as the bidders enter their bids in a predefined format. Lengthy and nerve-wracking price negotiations can also be condensed into a period of 30 min,

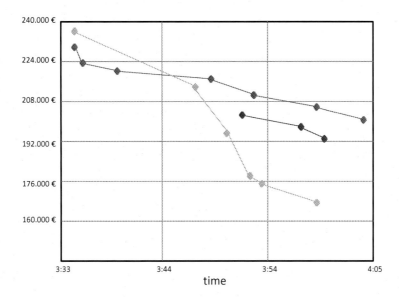

240.000 €

224.000 €

208.000 €

192.000 €

176.000 €

160.000 €

3:33   3:44   3:54   4:05

time

Fig. 10.5 Sample e-Auction process

saving a considerable amount of time. Contractual agreements such as a non-disclosure agreement or general purchasing conditions may be incorporated into the e-Tender and concluded without any additional effort.

e-Sourcing has an entirely positive impact on the competitive situation. Thanks to the electronic support of the tender process, a far greater number of suppliers may be considered and thus a far broader view of the market. As the bid appraisal is also supported, those suppliers best suited can be selected beforehand. The concluding auction generates far greater cost pressure for the suppliers due to the high degree of transparency, which can lead to better results when compared with more conventional negotiations.

10.2.6 Long-Term Implementation of e-Auctions

In order to use an e-Sourcing solution as described, simply providing the software or access to a platform will not suffice. Understanding and acceptance first needs to be established amongst the employees for these new methods. Only when the employees recognise the potential for improvement, and know-how to use the tools, can it be employed within the company over the long term. Therefore, e-Sourcing workshops should be organised for employees during implementation. In order to be able to systematically and uniformly determine whether an auction is suitable in a given situation, checklists are recommended. These will allow Purchasing employees to decide themselves whether an e-Auction makes sense and when a conventional procurement procedure should be used. In order to establish the long-term use of auctions, a yearly planner is recommended in which auctions can be systematically collected and scheduled.

10.3   Determining the Potential of e-Ordering

Traditionally, the purchasing process consists of a number of decisions that are closely interrelated and, in addition to the purely process-oriented execution of an order, demands consideration be given to a variety of factors. The most important aim will always be to achieve optimum results with regard to materials management, which means the procurement of the right goods, in the right quantities, at the right time, and at the right location, in due consideration of the price.

As shown in Fig. 10.6, the procurement process can be subdivided into strategic and operational elements, whereby the strategic tasks generally precede the operational ones.

The tasks in the respective phases can be further subdivided into the following subtasks and described as follows in simplified terms:

– Determination of demand: Definition and specification of required products or services
– Request: Obtaining binding offers for the specified requirement
– Supplier selection: Comparing and assessing the incoming offers
– Placement of order: Placement of orders with selected suppliers
– Order monitoring: Tracking and ensuring deadlines are met
– Incoming goods: Checking and booking delivered goods
– Invoice verification: Checking the purchase invoice against the order data
– Payment: Payment instruction for invoice amount

The subtasks described are not always required and not always applied with the same intensity. The procurement process has actually proven to be quite varied in practice, with circumstances depending on the type of product being procured.

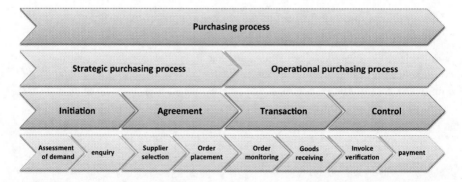

Fig. 10.6 Steps of the procurement process

While goods that flow directly into the production process are generally obtained using automated and clearly defined processes, non-production materials mostly involve manual or undefined processes.

A distinction is made here between structured procurement involving the automated processing of requirement identification, ordering and delivery, and unstructured procurement, characterised by a non-automatic procedure. Unstructured procurement processes generally feature a variety of product- and employee-specific options, which provide the consumer with a greater degree of freedom. With unstructured ordering processes, the large share of administrative and repetitive routine tasks in particular, as well as the relatively high process costs in relation to low requirement values, is viewed as problematic. Furthermore, with unstructured processes, "Maverick-Buying" tends to crop up, whereby prevailing procurement guidelines are deliberately or unknowingly disregarded by consumers and products are obtained independently and without the involvement of Purchasing.

The main problem areas for unstructured procurement processes can be summed up as follows:

– Routine work: More time spent on recurring tasks
– Purchasing regulations: Non-compliance with existing purchasing regulations
– Procurement time: Major time resources of procurement process
– Procurement costs: High process costs, particularly when compared to low-value materials

e-Ordering systems promise to provide relief in these difficult situations, the benefits of which should be considered more closely. These solutions are particularly suited to the purchase of low-value goods or to what are known as non-production materials such as office supplies or equipment. In many places, this is driven half-heartedly and with lacking professionalism or poor resources, as the impact on the company's success here is very small. Serious cost savings cannot be achieved due to the low purchasing volumes. The result is often escalating process costs caused by complicated processes, carried out often unnecessarily over the years, as well as media discontinuities and the well-known Maverick-Buying. Electronic catalogue systems offer promising approaches here to simplifying purchasing processes, to automation, and thus to considerably reducing procurement costs.

10.3.1 Requirements and Supplier Analysis

A paradox frequently observed in companies is that with requirements critical to success, such as camera sensors for example, there are conscious dependencies on monopolistic suppliers, whereas smaller requirements and standard components are distributed amongst a number of suppliers, thus unnecessarily tying up resources or giving away volume effects. To what extent this situation affects

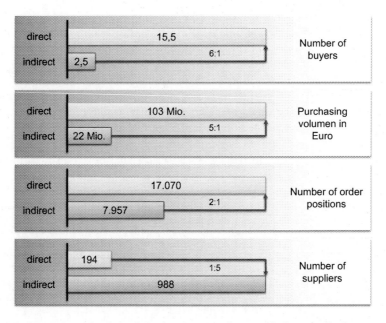

Fig. 10.7 Comparison of ordering behaviour between direct and indirect purchasing

one's own company can be determined using a requirements and supplier analysis. Ordering behaviour during a prior period is assessed and there is a comparison of the structured procurement of direct production materials and the unstructured procurement of indirect goods and services. Both of these areas are clearly differentiated at the start and compared with one another on the basis of various characteristics.

For situations like the one illustrated in Fig. 10.7, the initial potential of an electronic ordering process is already realised, as there is a clear disparity between the supplier relationship established and the order items or determined purchasing volume. The fundamental causes of this phenomenon are generally the non-existent standardisation of commodities, as well as the lack of coordination between consumers. The consumers thus carry out their own research into products and suppliers and pass this information on to the Buyer. The Buyer, under time pressure or lacking capacity, often has no other option than to order the product in question from the preferred source.

As the use of e-Procurement systems is only ever recommended for situations where substantial product and process costs can be expected, consideration also needs to be given to requirements. The aim here is to form and select commodity groups that have a high degree of standardisation and are thus particularly suited to an electronic ordering process. Reference can be made here to the database and the observation period of prior analyses.

A precise classification of the ordered products into product groups can be tedious work depending on the quality of the data and may require manual input. Particularly suitable for the first step:

– Office materials
– Clothing and industrial safety
– Tools and workshop supplies
– Magazines/Books
– Packaging

When first selecting catalogue-based product groups, it should be noted that the mix of products must not be fixed. Instead, a development trajectory for future product procurement can be outlined and thus the catalogue quota successively increased.

10.3.2 Consideration of Representative Market Solutions

In order to gain an overview of the various systems, representative suppliers can be contacted to help decide whether the respective model suits the company structure. The representative suppliers can be separated from each other using the criteria system complexity and integration, as shown in Fig. 10.8.

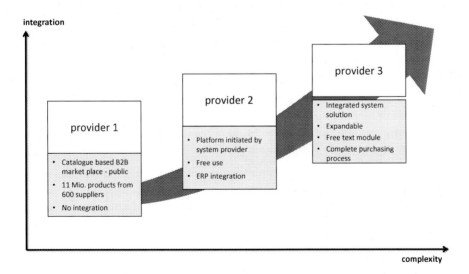

Fig. 10.8 Classification of representative market solutions

10.3.2.1   Marketplace Solution: Mercateo

One of the best-known catalogue-based marketplace solutions for business customers is the Mercateo procurement platform, named after the company running it. Based in Bavaria's Taufkirchen, Mercateo employs a workforce of around 250 and generated turnover to the tune of 135 million euros in the 2013 financial year, with average annual growth rates of over 25% in the last 5 years.[5]

Mercateo is targeting companies who wish to electronically process their low-value C-item requirements without investing in their own procurement solution. The business model is thus based on a multi-supplier catalogue comprising more than 11 million items from 600 suppliers. It should be noted that Mercateo does not just function as an intermediary for electronic transactions, but as a genuine trader who assumes proprietary rights for goods traded via the platform, and also issues invoices.

One considerable advantage for the customer is that only one creditor needs to be created and managed in order to gain simultaneous access to 600 affiliated suppliers. Furthermore, the use of the platform for purchasing companies is free of charge. When it comes to a lean ordering process, there are however several disadvantages. Due to a lack of integration into the customer's own IT infrastructure, the customer needs to ensure that the order transaction data is transferred to his inventory control system. Even then, the internal ordering process is only partially supported.

10.3.2.2   Simple-System Procurement Platform

Simple-System GmbH &amp;amp; Co. KG from Munich provides a free B2B procurement marketplace for the processing of low-value C-item requirements. It has continued to develop since its establishment in 2000 by companies Hagemeyer Deutschland, Hoffmann Group, Keller &amp; amp; Kalmbach, and Kaiser + Kraft, generating 82.4 million euros turnover in the 2013 financial year. The online platform is available in ten languages and pools C-items valued at more than 25.4 million euros from approx. 430 suppliers.[6]

Registered customers are granted online access to the platform, with users able to log in directly and access the various product catalogues. In addition to the supplier catalogues already stored in the platform, the users' own suppliers can be integrated into the system, leading to the platform's steady growth. A distinction is made here between public product catalogues that can be accessed by all users and company-specific supplier catalogues. Furthermore, the platform operator has secured the right to veto any new supplier, thus ensuring that those companies in direct competition with the operating companies are prevented from offering their goods via the platform. This move is understandable from the point of view of the

---

[5]Mercateo (2014, p. 4).
[6]Simple System (2013, p. 3).

operator, however restricts the competitive environment and the customer becomes dependent on the operator when using the platform.

Unlike a pure e-Marketplace solution, Simple-System provides a protected administration area in which individual users can be created and ordering guidelines stored. Here, for example, individual catalogues or catalogue areas can be hidden for users, order value limits determined, or a cost centre assignment created. Furthermore, users have the option to connect the platform to their own ERP system. Using an interface, the ordering data created via the platform is transferred to the ERP system, where a formal order is created. This then leads to a wider support of the procurement process.

10.3.2.3 Pool4Tool System Solution

Pool4Tool AG from Vienna describes itself as a leading innovative company providing e-solutions for purchasing optimisation. Since its foundation in 2000, the owner-managed company has provided its customers with systems and solutions for the sustainable reduction of process costs in purchasing. The product portfolio has a modular-based design and, according to company reports, supports more than 40 processes from Operational and Strategic Purchasing, Supplier Management, Supply Chain Management, Quality Management, and Product Cost Calculation.

Each of the modules offered can be individually licensed and gradually combined to form a central online platform with ERP integration. Furthermore, communication with external companies is possible via a connected supplier portal.

The module offered for the processing of catalogue requirements is similar in its main features to the procurement platform described in the previous section. The scope of operation is considerably greater, however, when it comes to the individualisation of customer requirements, and permits more adjustments to one's own company structure. Thus, in addition to the processing of catalogue requirements, free-text orders are also supported, whereby specific individual requirements or special requests can be represented. With the free-text order, the consumer triggers an order request, which is processed by the Buyer following the approval process. Requirements that are not represented in the connected catalogues can thus also be processed via the platform. Combining free-text orders with one's own input masks or forms opens up potential for standardising non-catalogue goods and for processing via the procurement platform. For example, a form for commissioning IT advisory services can be stored, which permits employees to act independently where necessary while, at the same time, enabling them to refer to centrally negotiated daily rates.

Pool4Tool thus clearly sets itself apart from the previous suppliers looked at, as not just individual subprocesses but instead the entire procurement process is supported by this solution. Through the modular design of the product portfolio, upstream and downstream processes such as supplier selection and assessment can also be connected, whereby the individual modules complement each other.

10.3.3 Cost-Benefit Analysis

Once the internal requirements and supplier situation have been determined, and initial consideration given to the e-Procurement systems available on the market, a cost-benefit analysis will assess the respective systems from an economic perspective, thus supporting the decision-making process.

10.3.3.1 Cost Analysis

Benefit and cost are the two main criteria when deciding for or against the introduction of an electronic ordering platform. The value of an e-Procurement solution is calculated from the sum of the price and process cost benefits, minus the initial costs incurred during implementation. These primarily include the following:

– *Investment costs* for purchasing or leasing the system
– *Consultation costs* for support during implementation
– *Programming costs* for adjustments to the system solution
– *Project costs* for one's own employees during implementation
– *Follow-up costs* for administration, maintenance, and use of the software

If orders are placed via the supplier's online shop, there will initially be no additional costs. The higher the degree of system integration, the more cost pools will need to be considered when determining value.

10.3.3.2 Potential Benefits in the Procurement Process

Unlike costs, the benefits gained are considerably more difficult to determine. Particularly important aspects include:

– *Reduction* of process costs for the order
– *Time saved* and relief of employees
– *Improvement* of purchasing conditions
– *Optimisation* of demand management

These aspects can be generally formulated and plausibly represented; however, ascertaining concrete figures is not easy. The precise determination of process costs, due to the wide variety of product- and employee-specific options, is difficult to implement in practice. However, as we can assume the optimisation of process times represents a clear benefit, this should be given greater consideration, in approximate terms at least. For the purchasing process, a complete breakdown into individual subprocess steps is recommended in order to be able to realistically estimate the average time taken in minutes for each subtask. This estimation is then offset against the internal cost rate. The resulting value represents the process costs incurred when an entire procurement process is carried out.

In order to determine the respective benefit of the e-Procurement solutions considered, the impact the respective system has on the current procurement process is represented (as indicated in Fig. 10.9).

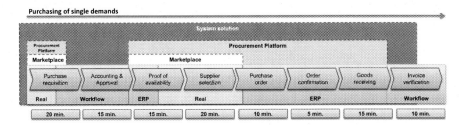

Fig. 10.9 Process times for current procurement process

process steps	Process 'old' (minutes)	Marketplace (minutes)	Procurement platform (minutes)	System solution (minutes)
Purchasing requisition	20	10	5	5
Accounting & Approval	15	15	15	5
Proof of availability	15	9	9	9
Supplier selection	20	0	0	0
Purchase order	10	5	0	0
Order confirmation	5	3	3	3
Goods receiving	15	15	10	10
Invoice verification	10	5	5	5
Sum	110	62	47	37
Valuated with internal cost rate	80.00 €	80.00 €	80.00 €	80.00 €
Sum of costs per Order	146.67 €	82.67 €	62.67 €	49.33 €
Saving per order	- €	64.00 €	84.00 €	97.33 €
Saving in %	0%	44%	57%	66%

Fig. 10.10 Saving potential for the individual systems

As shown, the marketplace solution supports the consumer in determining requirements, as well as the buyers in checking availability and selecting suppliers. The administrative processing of the requirement request, approval, and order, however, continues in the previous workflow and ERP environment. The procurement platform also supports order processing through the connection to the ERP system. Order data does not need to be created twice. The system solution has the biggest influence, which can not only be connected to the entire procurement process, but also upstream and downstream processes.

From this, the potential for savings can now be determined for the respective systems. Here, as illustrated in Fig. 10.10, the individual process times are reassessed, assuming that it is possible to reduce the process times using e-Procurement solutions. Depending on whether the respective activity is influenced by the system or not, the time determined is reduced or remains unchanged.

The "requirement request" process step, for example, is thus shortened considerably in all systems. Activities such as collecting price information, sending queries to the respective buyers, or searching through paper catalogues are replaced by the research carried out directly in the e-Procurement system. The separate creation of a requisition note is only required for the marketplace solution.

The "Approval" process step remains unchanged for two of three systems. The system solution permits the creation of approval limits, as well as the definition of cost types, whereby manual classification does not apply in some cases.

The suppliers are not separately selected during the electronic procurement process, but instead when determining requirements using the catalogue data available. The same applies when creating the order. This step is carried out automatically. Only for the marketplace solution does a separate order need to be created in the ERP system. Due to the fact that no new creditors need to be created, this step may take far less time to complete. There is also an impact on the processing of order confirmations. Fixed framework conditions have generally been agreed with the catalogue suppliers, and no adjustments need to be made here. Furthermore, the catalogue goods are warehouse goods that are commissioned and delivered directly after the order is made, often making any separate order confirmations unnecessary. The process steps "Incoming goods" and "Invoice verification" are indirectly influenced by all systems. Here, a higher quality of data used for delivery notes and invoices in particular leads to less errors being made, whereby a reduction of the process times can also be assumed in these areas.

In order to determine the overall potential of minimising costs, the order frequency is added to the newly determined process cost rates. This is identified when determining catalogable product groups during the requirements analysis, whereby it is assumed that the historical values determined here are also suitable for future calculations.

What results is an overview of the respective saving potential, as shown in Table 10.1. When considering the overall potential, a start-up curve is taken into account initially. It can be assumed here that, during the first year, the use of an e-Procurement solution cannot achieve 100% coverage. As expected, individual systems with an increasing degree of integration offer greater potential. However, the costs increase too. Therefore, a final analysis of costs and benefits should determine which approach can best meet internal requirements and is best suited to the financial situation.

10.3.3.3 Further Potential

The introduction of an e-Procurement system has a far-reaching impact on the overall procurement process, the organisation, as well as relations with external

Table 10.1 Saving potential for process costs over 36 months

Relevant purchasing volume				
Purchasing volume	1,000,000.00 €			
Number of orders	1500			
	Present process	Marketplace	Platform	System solution
	146.67 €	82.67 €	62.67 €	49.33 €
Purchase orders per year—considering start-up curve (100% = 1500 orders)				
Transactions (year 1): 60%	900	900	900	900
Transactions (year 2): 90%	1350	1350	1350	1350
Transactions (year 3): 120%	1800	1800	1800	1800
Total expense present process per year in Euro				
Order costs present (year 1)	132,003.00	132,003.00	132,003.00	132,003.00
Order costs present (year 2)	203,944.64	203,944.64	203,944.64	203,944.64
Order costs present (year 3)	271,926.18	271,926.18	271,926.18	271,926.18
Total expenses new process per year in Euro				
Order costs "new" (year 1)	132,003.00	74,403.00	56,403.00	44,397.00
Order costs "new" (year 2)	203,944.64	114,952.64	87,142.64	68,593.37
Order costs "new" (year 3)	271,926.18	153,270.18	116,190.18	91,457.82
Potential saving per year in Euro				
Saving (year 1)	–	−57,600	−75,600.00	−87,606.00
Saving (year 2)	–	−88,992	−116,802.00	−135,351.27
Saving (year 3)	–	−118,656	−155,736.00	−180,468.36
Saving over 36 months	–	−265,248.00	−348,138.00	−403,425.63

suppliers. A purely cost-oriented assessment of the systems would not provide a fair representation of the potential associated with the introduction of an electronic ordering process. Further positive aspects are described below using the process participants, who can be divided into the following groups:

- *Impact on consumer*: For the consumer, the introduction of an e-Procurement system is synonymous with higher service quality. On the one hand, processes are quicker, which means the consumer obtains the required products faster. At the same time, process transparency improves as the current stage of processing for an order process is visible at all times. Furthermore, online catalogues are considerably more convenient than traditional paper catalogues, thanks to more comprehensive and more up-to-date product data, search functions, or the saving of frequently required products.

– *Impact on Purchasing*: Purchasing can be considered as one of the players to benefit most from e-Procurement systems. The oft-quoted automation of routine tasks is not the only advantage here. Newly gained transparency is particularly beneficial, laying an important foundation for establishing efficient material group management. For example, low-value C-items can also be specifically bundled and efficiently procured. The greatest benefit to e-Procurement, however, only becomes apparent when the resources that have been freed up are correctly deployed. If Purchasing is given the necessary freedom to undertake strategic tasks, greater efficiency and considerable savings are possible.

– *Impact on accounting*: When it comes to profiteers, consideration also needs to be given to Accounting. Hidden costs incurred from creating and supporting creditor data can be reduced using e-Procurement solutions. A considerably greater impact is made when it comes to invoice verification and the frequency of errors. Any prices or payment conditions that need to be corrected here are generally negotiated beforehand using e-Procurement solutions and always kept up to date within the product catalogues.

– *Impact on the suppliers*: e-Procurement also has a positive effect on external suppliers, who receive orders electronically in standard format, which can then be directly connected to their own ERP system. Furthermore, the option to consolidate suppliers means several suppliers can be established as system suppliers.

Last but not least, e-Procurement facilitates adherence with compliance guidelines, as company guidelines can be created within the e-Procurement system using corresponding roles and approval value limits.

10.3.4 Critical Success Factors

As shown in the previous section, the cost savings and potential benefits brought about by using e-Procurement systems are big. In order to make the most of this potential success when introducing and using such a system, there are several factors to be considered, which can be derived from what is known as the productivity paradox of information technology. This describes the fact that, in reality, expected savings and greater efficiency can only be partially achieved following the introduction of an IT system.[7] It states that no general, empirically rich causal link could be found in the various scientific studies between IT investment and an increase in company productivity. It can be assumed here that the expected advantages of an IT system are influenced and inhibited by four

---

[7]Cf. Andreßen (2010, p. 295).

factors.[8] Turning this around, the following success factors can be determined, which are explained below.

10.3.4.1 Utilising Technological Potential

Finding and selecting the right system for the specific requirements of the company is crucial when introducing an e-Procurement solution. As shown in the previous analyses, selecting the right e-Procurement system is fraught with considerable difficulty depending on the database. The introduction of an unsuitable system not only reduces optimisation potential but also jeopardises acceptance of electronic procurement in all affected departments. In addition to a sound profitability analysis, a qualitative assessment of potential e-Procurement systems using technical, functional criteria is thus necessary.

10.3.4.2 Learning and Adjustment Effects

Through the introduction of an e-Procurement system, the field of responsibility for the Buyer shifts from operational routine activities to strategic and project-related tasks. These may be more complex, situation-related tasks that require a higher level of qualification and need to be supported through corresponding offers of further training. Furthermore, even simple and intuitively designed e-Procurement systems can take a little getting used to for those employees with less of an affinity for IT. Employee training must thus be provided before introducing the system, while a knowledge database in the form of a user manual or helpdesk is also recommended. Establishing a key user structure can also help create direct contacts in the respective departments and thus increase acceptance of the system.

10.3.4.3 Considering the Consequences of Delegation

With the introduction of an electronic catalogue procurement solution, employees are given more responsibility which can, initially, have a motivational effect. However, it must also be ensured that this newly delegated responsibility is not asking too much of them. In particular, a quick expansion of product ranges and the incorporation of new suppliers can put employees in a position where they must make decisions. Adding the high degree of system transparency, in which every action is documented, to the uncertainty that already exists, initial motivation can end in unnecessary and time-consuming product comparisons, with employees worrying about making mistakes. Therefore, when organising the product range, the consequences of delegation must be considered and the choice of alternatives restricted. The user must always feel confident enough to order products via the order platform at appropriate conditions and a high standard of quality.

---

[8]Cf. Andreßen (2010, p. 296 ff).

10.3.4.4 Using the Compound Effect and Network Effects

From a technical point of view, the aim should be to achieve the highest possible degree of integration for the e-Procurement solution in the existing system environment. Harmonised interfaces prevent e-Procurement from being viewed as an isolated solution unable to communicate with other systems.[9] Compatibility and connectivity should thus be taken into consideration when designing the system. This applies for one's own company, as well as for an integrative connection to external supplier systems. Compound effects can be achieved here through the use of standards.[10]

Network effects are based on the need to initially achieve a critical mass within a system, before user acceptance materialises. Once the critical mass is achieved, independent growth can be assumed. For the electronic ordering process, this means there must be a minimum quantity of products offered when launching the e-Procurement system in order to ensure comprehensive use by consumers. Furthermore, a strategy for developing the product range needs to be worked out and this communicated to users.

10.3.4.5 Further Recommendations

Supporting the selection, design, organisation, and introduction of an e-Procurement solution with professional project management is also recommended. With a broad spectrum of expertise required from the various company departments for implementing such a project, the project organisation concept illustrated in Fig. 10.11 is recommended when setting up the project teams. In addition to a Project Manager, both a Technical and a Commercial Project

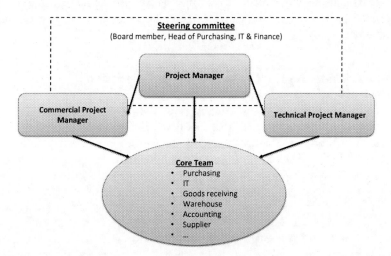

Fig. 10.11 Project organisation

---

[9]Cf. Stoll (2007, p. 68).

[10]Cf. Andreßen (2010, p. 303).

Manager will be required. A steering committee, comprising senior employees from IT, Purchasing, and Finance, will ensure that the project receives the necessary support within the organisation.

With the inclusion of various end users over the course of the project, sufficient consideration should be given to criteria such as simple operability, user friendliness, and adequate user training before the system is even selected. Furthermore, an early incorporation of employees forms the basis for an appropriate Change Management, which should run parallel to the system launch. Only when users are actively incorporated into the implementation process can long-term employee acceptance and the associated intensity of use be achieved.

References

Andreßen, T. (2010). Erfolgreiches strategisches Management des E-Procurement. In R. Bogaschewsky, M. Eßig, R. Lasch, & W. Stölzlte (Hrsg.) *Supply management research* (pp. 291–312). Wiesbaden: Springer Fachmedien.

Bundesverband Materialwirtschaft, Einkauf und Logistik e.V. (2014). *Elektronische Beschaffung 2014: Stand der Nutzung und Trends*. Würzburg: Bundesverband für Materialwirtschaft, Einkauf und Logistik

Kollmann, T. (2013). *E-Business, Grundlagen der elektronischen Geschäftsprozesse in der Net Economy*. Wiesbaden: Springer Fachmedien.

Meier, A., & Storner, H. (2012). *eBusiness & eCommerce – Management der digitalen Wertschöpfungskette*. Heidelberg: Springer.

Mercateo. (2014). *Presseinformation, Mercateo weiter auf Wachstumspfad*. München: Mercateo AG.

Simple System. (2013). *C-Artikel-Beschaffung – Einfach & Rundum Effizient*. München: Simple System GmbH Co. KG.

Stoll, P. (2007). *E-Procurement, Grundlagen, Standards und Situationen am Markt*. Wiesbaden: GWV Fachverlag.

Wöhe, G., & Döhring, U. (2008). *Einführung in die Allgemeine Betriebswirtschaftslehre*. München: Vahlen.